D1062835

BEST SERMONS

BOOKS BY G. PAUL BUTLER

EDITOR OF

Modern College Readings, 1936, co-editor
Best Sermons, 1943-44 (Vol. I)
Best Sermons, 1946 (Vol. II)
Best Sermons, 1947-48 (Vol. III)
Best Sermons, 1949-50 (Vol. IV)
Best Sermons, 1951-52 (Vol. V)
Best Sermons, 1955 (Vol. VI)
Best Sermons, 1959-60 (Vol. VII)
Best Sermons, 1962 (Vol. VIII)
(Protestant Edition)

CO-AUTHOR OF

Butlers' South America
Butlers' Mexico
Butlers' Caribbean, and Central America

BEST SERMONS

VOLUME IX

1964

PROTESTANT EDITION

EDITED BY G. PAUL BUTLER

D. VAN NOSTRAND COMPANY, INC.

PRINCETON, NEW JERSEY

TORONTO NEW YORK LONDON

D. VAN NOSTRAND COMPANY, INC.
120 Alexander St., Princeton, New Jersey (*Principal Office*)
24 West 40 Street, New York 18, New York

D. Van Nostrand Company, Ltd.
358, Kensington High Street, London, W.14, England

D. Van Nostrand Company (Canada), Ltd.
25 Hollinger Road, Toronto 16, Canada

Published simultaneously in Canada by
D. Van Nostrand Company (Canada), Ltd.

PRINTED IN THE UNITED STATES OF AMERICA

TO

Lawrence College

My

Alma Mater

and

especially to

the memory of

Dr. Samuel Plantz

Dr. Wilson S. Naylor

Dr. William E. McPheeters

Dr. Otho P. Fairfield

Professor F. W. Orr

INTRODUCTION

PREACHING: The Word of God

"This is the Word which is Preached," [1]

The great prophets have spoken through the centuries with the conviction that they were called of God to speak His words to man. Isaiah could say, ". . . the Lord spake thus to me, . . . the Lord hath spoken, . . . cry aloud, spare not, lift up thy voice like a trumpet." [2] In this confidence he preached to king and people. Likewise, Jeremiah could record, ". . . the Lord said unto me . . . thou shalt go to all that I shall send thee, and whatsoever I command thee thou shalt speak. Be not afraid . . . for I am with thee. . . . Then the Lord put forth his hand and touched my mouth. And . . . said unto me, Behold, I have put my words in thy mouth." [3] With this divine call Jeremiah stirred a nation.

Later, Peter and Paul and James and John could speak of the Living Christ and the Divine Presence to begin the conversion of the pagan world. Lacordaire, Luther, Calvin, Wesley and those who followed them in the pulpits of the world from Jerusalem to Athens and Rome all preached in this same divine tradition: "The Lord spake thus to me and I proclaimed His word." [4]

The Gospel is as alive today as it has ever been and in this spirit Karl Barth, Reinhold Niebuhr, Pius XII, Pope Paul, Ralph Sockman, Henry Van Dusen, Paul Tillich and thousands of others still bring God's message to human hearts in the great pulpits and in the smallest churches at country crossroads. The important matter is the call of God and a man committed to deliver the divine message.

The preaching ministry is the great means of information, evangelization, and inspiration for the church and Christian people everywhere. We need, therefore, to keep our ministry strong, well educated, well read, alive to the needs of the people. A shortage of well trained ministers is reported in

[1] PETER 1:25.

[2] ISAIAH 8:11a; 58:1, 14c.

[3] JEREMIAH 1:7b,c, 8, 9, 10.

[4] ISAIAH 8:11a.

many denominations and many ministers today do not take the careful training in homiletics which was once provided in our theological seminaries.

When Protestants go to church they expect a good sermon—and have a right to hear a sermon filled with spiritual values to increase their faith and Christian living. To this end the minister may well ask himself as he prepares his sermon each week: Will this sermon have a message for those who face temptations in business? Will it help parents to rear their families better? Will it help teen-agers not to be delinquents? Will it help young people to grow up sanely, sensibly? Will it help to solve the present racial problems that threaten our country? Will it put responsibilities on blacks and whites for the solution of community race conflicts? One important point needs emphasis in our current preaching: It is so easy for the minister to get used to talking about "you" when he criticizes evils—and to forget that he should say "we." I have noted that ministers easily slip into a critical attitude about their congregations. "Let us do this" is much easier for a congregation to take.

The problems of our day do not admit of complacency or self-satisfaction. Rather, the ministry has an opportunity for leadership which was never greater than in our own day. BUT the minister must keep himself prepared to meet the challenges of youth, adults, community. He must keep his reading up to date to prevent young college students from slipping away from church into agnosticism and atheism in their first contact with science or philosophy. How much misinformation has been given from some of our pulpits! Could this be the reason Radcliffe students recently sat facing stonily forward and did not bow their heads for the Lord's Prayer at Commencement? Are we ready to prepare our young people for the problems they will meet in college and in life?

The Sermons Which Have Been Preached

As Peter wrote nearly nineteen hundred years ago, "This is the Word which is Preached," so in Volume IX we present a new cross section of the best preaching in different denominations and in various schools of theological thought.

Dr. Sizoo, in one of the finest sermons of his whole career, says, "You may as well untwist moonbeams" as to think of a world without Christ. . . . Archbishop Coggan points out that "God had something to communicate to man" and shows man's place in carrying on the Church and the message. . . . Ralph Sockman, always one of the most inspiring preachers in the world, brings new insight to the interpretation of "the Reconciling Message," and says that men who "stand at the altar" to proclaim this message enjoy the "high privilege of the preacher." . . . Dr. Douglas M. Knight, for years President of Lawrence College and now the new President of Duke University, adds new stature to Baccalaureate sermons as he takes a passage from Milton's *Paradise Lost* and points to possible paradises ahead. . . . Clayton Williams again shows the power he had for more than a quarter of a century at the American Church in Paris as he discusses "The Face in the Mirror" and shows the evil of selfishness and the need for spiritual insight. . . . Bishop Kennedy stimulates his readers and hearers with his sermon on the plot and purpose of life and history, which have meaning through Christ.

"You Can't Go Home Again"

Dr. Cleland answers questions often asked and not always answered as he points out "The Marks of a Christian." And Dr. Arnold Lowe touches one of the sorest spots in human life, especially in family relations, as he discusses the unintended cruelty of "Thoughtlessness." Charles Trentham discusses the relationship of the Church and the Kingdom of God, then speaks words about loneliness which will be welcomed by many. . . . Foy Valentine uses Thomas Wolfe's *You Can't Go Home Again* to point out the way men can go with Christ in our world. . . . And Carlyle Marney, scholar and fine preacher of Charlotte, tells us how to recover our courage as Christians and as men and women.

Dean Cushman of Duke brings another Palm Sunday-Easter message which we are glad to have in BEST SERMONS. His discussion of the meaning of Good Friday and Easter is refreshing, challenging, rewarding. . . . Leslie Weatherhead shows the power which held his large congregations at City Temple as he presents "The Dynamic Personality of Christ." . . . Carl Henry gives us a "contrast of light and darkness" as he preaches "The Light that Shines Forever." . . . In Washington Dr. Pruden again demonstrates the reason for his long ministry in the famous First Presbyterian Church (where President Truman attended regularly): "Christianity and Freedom," he points out, are inseparable and many will be glad for his thinking. . . . But freedom must be "spiritually responsible" for "only as men accept a responsible freedom, and relate themselves to God . . . is freedom guaranteed."

The leading authority on Martin Luther, Dr. Roland Bainton, discusses Renan's, Bruce Barton's, and Bouck White's "Pictures of Jesus" . . . Dr.

Bainton's own concluding "picture" is the one most people will undoubtedly prefer. . . . Lee Bristol and Judge Youngdahl represent the laymen of America with their distinguished lay sermons, which could form the basis of many other fine sermons in pulpits across the country. . . . Ernest Gordon again gives us a sermon on the power of God and uses his graphic illustrations from prisoner-of-war camps when the Japanese were subjecting Allied prisoners to unspeakable miseries, yet love shines through Dean Gordon's sermon. . . . Robert Burns, one of the leading ministers in our country in preventing and solving marriage problems, asks, "What does it mean for the minister, as a man of God" . . . "to serve . . . in the full-time, church-supported ministry?"

Africa, Bread and Circuses and War

Africa comes into these sermons in Donald Harrington's visit for "Three Days with Albert Schweitzer at Lambarené." In this he talks of the accomplishments of Dr. Schweitzer and discusses the criticisms that have been made of the great doctor's work. . . . William Meyer of Immanuel Presbyterian Church, Los Angeles, analyzes the gradual encroachments of our federal government on the liberties of the individual, the states and the nation, the need for faith in liberty, and the road to keep faith in our nation and escape the curse of "bread and circuses" which destroyed ancient Rome. . . . Robert Moon, dynamic minister of Fresno, takes us into another far corner of life in his sermon on "Peace Making in our Time through Christ." Many may disagree with Dr. Meyer and Dr. Moon but both sermons bear careful reading and consideration. . . . Dr. Elliott shows the way of modern American pragmatic religion in his sermon on "Prayer and a Poultice." . . .

Dr. Peale again shows himself the master of the sermon which combines religion and psychiatry. There is no one else like him in the pulpit today; his story of Harlowe B. Andrews is one which might save many a man's sanity and courage in tight places. . . . Liston Pope combines insight, a fine sense of humor—almost satire—as he discusses religion and education in our day. The trouble is, so few college and university presidents and faculties will see it! . . . Dr. McCracken preaches courageously on racial problems and shows the joint responsibility of white and black men if the race problems of our day are to be solved. Rioting teen-age Negroes can destroy the goodwill that has taken years of work and patience to build. His quotation from Martin Luther King's *Strength to Love* will help the Negroes' cause. Walker Stockburger's sermon on science and religion in the space age speaks to young men and women of college age and can form the basis for sermons other ministers have to preach to teen-age and college-age young men and women who come in conflict with literalism and scientific discoveries. Only a faith that covers all life is big enough to keep men and women and young people steadfast when devastating problems threaten to destroy them.

Paul Tillich's discussion of "The Spiritual Presence" of Christ is worth reading a dozen times. Each reading brings new meaning and light. This great modern theologian has opened new windows in theology in our time. . . . And, to close this volume of BEST SERMONS, I saved Dr. Van Dusen's brilliant discussion of one of the most troublesome religious problems of the last nineteen hundred years of Christian thought: His handling of the problem of millenarianism, of recollection, anticipation, and affirmation will clear much fuzzy thinking—and his own presentation of the authentic Christian hope make this a sermon for careful study and repeated reading.

For Greater Preaching Tomorrow

In searching for sermons for this volume I have tried to find sermons by "Holy men . . . who . . . spake as they were moved." [1] It has required two years to read the mass of manuscripts received from 7,855 ministers who sent me their sermons for reading and consideration and I assure each that his sermon was read in the hope that it would be one of those of such excellence that it could be included in this volume. As the editor of nine volumes of BEST SERMONS I have now read more than 65,575 sermons in the twenty-two years I have searched for the finest preaching being done anywhere in the world. A total of 149,560 invitations have been sent to clergymen in a total of 65 different countries and the 65,575 sermons were received in response in 15 different languages from 55 countries.

Out of all this reading of sermons and conferences and correspondence with thousands of ministers has come a dream of a BEST SERMONS FOUNDATION to encourage more excellent preaching by providing scholarships or fellowships for young ministers for concentrated study of homiletics and several study or travel fellowships for men in the years of their mid-ministry to refresh and enrich their ministry. Ministers, church executives, bishops, seminary professors all over the country have expressed an interest in this and many have pledged their support. I would welcome further letters from other ministers or laymen.

In conclusion, let me say that I hope this volume will bring great spiritual

[1] II PETER 1:21.

insight and inspiration to all who read it. I am constantly amazed at the number of laymen—judges, lawyers, teachers, business men, financiers—who write me about the help BEST SERMONS is to them spiritually and in writing their speeches. I trust that the ideas and topics and illustrations in the 35 sermons included will afford hundreds of ideas for sermons by ministers everywhere. The index has been prepared to make it easy to find ideas or illustrations. Further, I hope the many theological seminaries which have adopted my volumes on publication will find this one full of surprises and useful material for sermon study and analysis for improving the standards of seminary training in homiletics. Let the word that is preached be fresh and vital to millions!

G. PAUL BUTLER, *Editor*

BOOKMERE
Little Silver Point Road
Little Silver, New Jersey
July 15, 1964

Appreciations and Acknowledgments

Once again it is a sincere pleasure to record my appreciation to the thousands of ministers and hundreds of laymen who have helped me to find the sermons included in this Ninth Volume of BEST SERMONS. Specifically, 7,855 ministers sent me their sermons for reading and consideration. This enormous number of sermons was equal to about 78,000 to 80,000 pages, averaging ten or twelve pages to each sermon (although some sermons were as long as 25 to 35 pages), or approximately 2,500,000 to 3,000,000 words, or the equivalent of about thirty volumes. All of this reading and selection required about two years.

Each man's sermon was read with care and each one included was chosen on the basis of its merits, not for the man's name, although it is true that great ministers almost always justify their greatness by preaching most excellent sermons. Always as I read I have the hope that each new sermon will be one of those with such a deep spiritual message that it can be one of those included. All sermons have been read once, some three or four times, a few as many as six or seven times.

Over the years it has been my privilege to know several thousand ministers, bishops and denominational church officers as my friends. Many have visited in my home and others have entertained me when I have gone to speak for women's clubs, churches, colleges, or other groups in communities from coast to coast. For their friendship and their help with this volume I would speak a special word of appreciation.

Further, I am grateful to the theological seminaries in many states and various denominations which have adopted BEST SERMONS as they were published as textbooks or for collateral reading and analysis of contemporary preaching. Many professors of homiletics have recommended their graduates and best students to me as men who should have a sermon considered for other volumes.

In preparing the next volumes I will welcome sermons from ministers of all denominations and hereby invite them to send me a sermon for consideration, but only one, please. Each man is requested to select the sermon he considers his best and to send it with his biographical background directly to me as the editor.

In all of my work with BEST SERMONS and preaching I am grateful to my own professor of homiletics, Dr. F. Watson Hannon of Drew Theological Seminary, who believed in preaching and taught it effectively, giving each man the benefit of his skilled homiletic guidance and criticisms. We need more great men to teach preaching in all of our seminaries today.

The index has again been prepared with great care to provide suggested topics for sermons, illustrations, and for ease in locating ideas or subjects.

While I did some of the work on the index, I would record my special appreciation to my wife, Erica, who helped in checking hundreds of details to make this the best index yet published in BEST SERMONS.

Finally, I am grateful to the editors and officers of the Van Nostrand Company for again producing another beautiful volume to carry BEST SERMONS to my readers.

It is a source of great satisfaction to me to have had the pleasure of having nearly all of the volumes of BEST SERMONS adopted by either or both The Religious Book Club and/or The Pulpit Book Club, both of which are among the fine book clubs of our time.

Grateful acknowledgment is made to the following publishers and individuals for permission to quote the selections indicated:

To Harper & Rowe, for permission to quote from Thomas Wolfe's *You Can't Go Home Again*, and from Karl Olsson's *Passion* in the sermon by Dr. Foy Valentine.

To Leslie Weatherhead for permission to quote from page 97 of *The Transforming Friendship*, in the sermon by Dr. Clayton Williams.

To Charles Scribner's Sons for permission to include the poem, "God Give Us Men," from *Poems*, by Josiah Gilbert Holland, in Dr. William Meyer's sermon.

To Mrs. Walter (Antoinette) Kilbourne Tuller for permission to quote from page 2 of *Freedom* by her late husband, Walter Tuller.

To Harper & Rowe for permission granted by Eugene Exman to Dr. Donald Szantho Harrington to quote from Norman Cousins' *Albert Schweitzer of Lambarené.*

To *The Pulpit* of Chicago, for information about and permission to quote in Dr. Clayton William's sermon the poem "Mixed" by Edward Sandford Martin from the volume originally published by Charles Scribner's in 1890 and reprinted in *The Pulpit* some years ago.

To Harper & Rowe for permission to quote from Martin Buber's *The Eclipse of God* in the sermon by Benjamin Garrison.

To Yale University Press for permission to quote from Eric Fromm's *Psychoanalysis and Religion* in the above sermon by Dr. Garrison.

To Harper & Rowe for permission to quote from pages 22-23 of Martin Luther King's *Strength to Love* in Dr. Robert McCracken's sermon.

The Studdert Kennedy quotation on page 306 is from his poem "Then Will He Come," published in *The Sorrows of God* by Doran in 1924. While the copyright has expired it is a pleasure to recognize this and give credit for its use in the sermon by Dr. Henry P. Van Dusen.

Special appreciation is also expressed to Abingdon Press for permission to include Dr. Leslie Weatherhead's sermon, "The Dynamic Personality of Christ," from *Key Next Door*.

G. PAUL BUTLER, *Editor*

CONTENTS

THE CHURCH

Sermon One

WHAT MANNER OF MAN IS THIS

Reverend Joseph R. Sizoo, D.D., Litt.D., S.T.D., LL.D.

A Minister of the Reformed Church and Professor of Religion and Director of the Chapel at George Washington University, Washington, D. C.

Dr. Sizoo, one of the great *preachers* of our country today, was born in the Netherlands, and was brought to the United States as a child. His first view of New York harbor made an impression he has never forgotten. He graduated from Hope College and took his ministerial training at New Brunswick Theological Seminary. In 1910-11 he was a missionary in South India, then returned to the United States and was successively minister of churches in Malden, New York, and Somerville, New Jersey. In 1923 he was summer minister of the American Church at the Hague.

He rose to prominence as minister of the historic New York Avenue Presbyterian Church in Washington, D. C., from 1924 to 1936, where he preached to several Presidents and many Senators and Congressmen. In 1936 St. Nicholas Collegiate Church in New York called him to be its minister.

Dr. Sizoo was President of the General Synod of the Reformed Church in America, Vice President of the National Council of Churches, and served a term as President of the Greater New York Federation of Churches. He was also President of New Brunswick Theological Seminary (1947-52) and in 1952 became Professor of Religion and Director of the Chapel at George Washington University.

His books have won him a secure place in religious literature: *The Kingdom Cometh, On Guard, Not Alone, The Way of Faith, Make Life Worth Living, Preaching Unashamed,* and *I Believe in the Bible.*

During the Second World War he traveled extensively to visit Army and Navy bases, addressing chaplains and enlisted men. Later he made a special tour of Korea to preach for the men on the fighting front. In 1953 he was voted one of the 12 Great American Preachers in a *Life Magazine* Poll. He was voted the "Clergy Churchman of the Year 1958" by Religious Heritage, Incorporated. His work has been recognized with the honorary doctorate by Hope College, Columbia University, Rutgers University, Lafayette College, and George Washington University.

In *What Manner of Man Is This* Dr. Sizoo speaks with conviction of the place of Christ in man's life today. It is one of the finest sermons Dr. Sizoo has given in his brilliant and distinguished career.

WHAT MANNER OF MAN IS THIS

The most distinguishing characteristic which separates Christianity from all other religions lies in the personality of its founder. Hinduism is loyalty to an idea; Confucianism is loyalty to a tradition; Shintoism is loyalty to a country; and, Islam is loyalty to a code. Christianity is loyalty to a person. You may conceive of Christianity without an organization; you may conceive of it without a ritual; you may conceive of it without a creed. But to think of it without Christ is as anomalous as it is impossible.

What is so disturbing, however, is that in the long years of its history the Christian Church has often lost sight of that fact. We have taken secondary things and made them primary; we have taken primary things and made them secondary. We have taken the things which lie in the center and pushed them beyond the circumference; we have taken the things that lie upon the circumference and put them in the center. We have lost sight of the gardener in His garden; we have forgotten the king in His kingdom.

We have become so engrossed and absorbed in institution building, in theological dialogue, and in liturgical technique; we spend so much time in the revolving door of peripheral activity that we have almost lost sight of the sustaining power of the Christian life. Can we keep our culture, if we lose sight of the figure who animates and inspires it? Albert Schweitzer wrote not long ago: "I wonder whether today we must not proclaim the uniqueness of Christ and His incomparable importance." This I believe. The greatest single contribution which the Christian Church can make in this year of grace is to recover or to rediscover Him, "Without whom all gain is loss, all labor vainly done, the solemn shadows of whose cross are better than the sun." The poignant cry of the Greeks is still our need, "Sir, we would see Jesus." For this I want to make a plea.

* * *

We know little about the details of His life. What Carlyle wrote is true of Him, "Great men have short biographies." He left no record. He wrote no book. He kept no diary. He left no order for anything to be written. All that we know about Him is crowded in a few pages at the opening of the New Testament. You can read it through in a few hours; try it sometime.

We do not have a biography of Jesus. There is not in existence a life of Christ, a detailed account chronologically arranged from His birth to His death. What we have are four gospels which are four testimonies, four interpretations, and four reflections by four men upon the Son of God. They do not give you a photograph of Jesus but a portrait of Him. Matthew presents Him as a teacher, Mark as a conqueror, Luke as a physician, and John as the light of the world. That is all we know about Him. Yet more books have been written about Him; more changes have come to pass through Him; more poems and plays have been produced concerning Him; more architecture has been fashioned for Him; and more cities and streets have been named after Him than that of any other man who has ever lived.

Such events as we have of His life are quickly told. The story opens with the birth of a babe in an obscure setting in a cave on a Judean hillside, "While shepherds kept watch over their flock by night." It is the ever-never old story of which childhood never grows weary and for which old age never loses its affection. It brings the wanderer home and cushions the blows of adversity. It is a story which affirms that there was a time when God broke through in history and walked this earth.

He grew up in a sheltered mountain village among the commonplace, the unwanted, and the forgotten. He had four brothers and two sisters. He attended a synagogue school. He was confirmed at the age of twelve. He grew up in a normal home, sharing normal duties. He knew how to fill lamps and to trim wicks. He knew what housecleaning involved. He knew how to build a fire. He could prepare a fish-fry. He learned the lesson of frugality. Years later when He fed the five thousand He said, "Gather up the broken fragments that nothing be lost." He learned the trade of a carpenter. He could tend sheep.

When Joseph died, Jesus, being the eldest, became the responsible head of the family. All the while a fire burned within Him. He was harnessed to an immediate task; yet He lived with a poignant awareness of a divine mission. Having fulfilled that responsibility, He walked out into the world. Then came His baptism, a historic fact told in poetic language to express an inner experience: His acceptance of the divine call and God's approval. There followed the temptations, a historic fact told in poetic language to express an inner experience: what that mission was and how it was to be accomplished. So at the age of thirty He walked into Gaililee preaching the gospel of God.

Every movement which has broken into history has had a watch-cry. No cause or crusade can succeed without a slogan. Men in Madison Avenue lie awake at night thinking up cliches and catch words. In the American Revolution it was "No taxation without representation!" In the French Revolution it was "Liberty, Equality, and Fraternity!" In the First World War it was "Make the world safe for democracy!" In the Civil War it was "With liberty and justice for all!" In Christianity it was "The Kingdom of God," the rule of God in the heart of the individual and the reign of God in society.

* * *

But what concerns us here is not what He said or what He did but who He was. How can you account for the impact of His life upon the world? What manner of man is He? Why is it that He has haunted history with ever increasing intensity for twenty long centuries? I would like to submit that there are four qualities about Him which have captured the imagination and the conscience of the world.

I

Mankind has been drawn to Jesus for His uniqueness. He never wrote a book. He never led an army. He never went to college. He never had a family of His own. He had no prophet to help Him, no newspaper to advertise Him, no army to fight for Him, no wealthy friend to support Him, and no political leaders to advance Him. He constructed nothing, and He destroyed nothing. Externally the world was the same at His death as it had been at His birth.

There was a uniqueness about His character. He was never petulant, never impatient, and never jealous. He never entertained suspicion. He was never in a hurry and never uncertain. He never vacillated. Jesus learned nothing from experience. He never faltered. He never compromised. He never accommodated Himself or His message. He was never proud, never overbearing, and never haughty. He never conjectured. He was never disturbed. He never forced Himself on people. All through history philosophers and thinkers have searched for the truth and speculated about it. Jeseus never did; He possessed the truth, He was the truth.

There is another element of uniqueness in Him. He lived with a God-consciousness never before known on this earth. He was completely God-possessed. He never debated or argued the existence of God with anybody, anywhere, at anytime. He took God for granted. God was to Him not a definition or a syllogism but a presence and an experience. In every crisis and in every circumstance He began His approach from God. We know more about the prayer life of Jesus than any other quality of His character. There were two things Jesus did not know how to do. He did not know how to hate and He did not know how to doubt. He was utterly unlike anyone before or since.

II

Mankind has been drawn to Him for his sinlessness. He is the only figure in history who can stand before the passing centuries and say, "Which of you convicteth me of sin?" He lived a blameless life. He was tempted in all things, like as we are, yet without sin. To the end Jesus was unrepentant. He never sought forgiveness or pardon for Himself; for there was never anything in Him that needed forgiveness or pardon. He knew nothing of guilt and remorse which are so poignantly and grimly real and haunt so many in this generation. Peter said, "Depart from me for I am a sinful man, oh God." The thief said, "We indeed, justly, but this man has done nothing worthy of death." Procula said to Pilate, "Have nothing to do with this just man." Judas cried out in anguish, "I have sinned, in that I have betrayed innocent blood."

III

Again, mankind has been drawn to Him for His gigantic claims. He claimed to be a perfect leader. He claimed to set a perfect example. He claimed to live a perfect life. He claimed to heal the sick. He claimed to raise the dead. He claimed to know all about God. He claimed to fulfill prophecy. He claimed to forgive sins. He claimed to rise again from the dead.

His self-assertiveness has no parallel in the history of mankind. He stood before His generation saying, "I am the light of the world"; "I am the door"; "I am the bread of life"; "I am the good shepherd"; "I am the resurrection"; "I am the Lord of the Sabbath"; "I am the way, the truth, and the life"; "Before Abraham was, I am"; and "Ye are from beneath, but I am from above."

He speaks with an omniscience that startles and astounds mankind. The adverbs which we use in our daily conversation are: "usually," "generally," "perhaps," and "maybe." Jesus always used "verily." And what is so striking and significant is that history has recognized the justice of His claims and accepted them. They are not out of place. Nobody denies them. He is entitled to them. When Napoleon and Hitler and Mussolini made some of these claims, the world laughed. Nobody laughs at Jesus Christ. If we deny Him these claims, we are through. His claims are pertinent and legitimate. He conceived a plan of which no one had ever dreamed: a new moral creation with a new moral order covering all lands and all languages and all ages.

IV

Then too, mankind has been drawn to Him for His compassion. The most memorable quality which the disciples carried with them about Him in later life was His deep concern. He always had time for people. He identified Himself with His generation. He became part of the ongoing life of His day. He was approachable. He did not show the world a clenched fist but an outstretched arm. He did not build walls but windows. He did not erect barriers but bridges. He did not separate people by the barbed wire entanglement of ecclesiastical, religious, social, economic, or political frontiers. He dragged the sorrows of His generation across His soul. At midnight it was a Hebrew scholar. At daybreak it was a foundering ship. At noonday it was a fallen girl by the well. In the afternoon it was a company of the hungry unemployed. Across the threshold of His home in Capernaum there fell the shadows of the limp and the lame, the halt and the blind, and he healed them, every one. He was the most compassionate person who has ever lived. He cared for people for whom nobody cared. He loved people whom nobody loved. And he saw a chance for people whom nobody gave a chance.

In the upper room of a widow's home in Jerusalem He broke bread and said, "Take, eat, this is my body broken for you." He poured wine and said, "This is my blood of the new covenant." As if to say, you can break my bones and drain my blood, but you can't stop me from loving you. "Having loved His own which were in the world, He loved them unto the end."

Such was His life: unique, self-assertive, sinless, and compassionate.

* * *

From the beginning there were certain reactions to Him. Little children ran at the music of His voice, the aged found comfort in His presence, and the sick found healing by merely touching the hem of His garment. He had His hours of popularity when the multitudes crowded about Him.

But there were also hours of adversity and unpopularity. It startles one to think that one so good should come to an end so cruel. Hardly had He begun when the unprincipled, unscrupulous, power-worshipping, expediency-serving religious and political leaders had Him checkmated. They turned the populace against Him. They laughed at Him, called Him a psychopath and determined to rid the world of Him at any cost. So after a mock trial at night, before an ecclesiastical and a civil court, he was condemned to death. Betrayed by those He trusted, abandoned by those He loved, and scourged by those He pitied, with a scarlet camp mantle flung contemptuously across His shoulders, crowned with a crown of thorns, He carried His cross to an outlaw's grave.

He who had been born in a borrowed manger, who rode to triumph on a borrowed beast, was laid away in a borrowed tomb. A heavy stone was rolled before His grave. Upon it was placed the imposing seal of Rome, with which no one would dare to tamper. They doubled the guard. Nobody believed He would rise again. They were sure that He was dead. The next morning women came. If they had believed He would rise again, they would have brought flowers and fruit. But they came to wrap his body in strips of freshly woven linen and to anoint it with aloes and myrrh for His permanent interment. Calvary was to His followers an irretrievable disaster. Golgotha scarred their souls. It was the end of everything.

Then the miracle begins. On the third day, out of the sepulchral gloom in the garden of the Aramethean, there came the voice, "He is not here. He is risen." He was alive. And what was so amazing, death had not changed Him. His compassion had not altered. His love had not vanished. Mary knew Him by His voice, the pilgrims to Emmaus knew Him by the way He broke bread, and the disciples knew Him by the nail print in His hand.

What was even more, not only that death had not changed Him but that death had not conquered Him. There was no grave deep enough, there was no stone heavy enough, there was no guard powerful enough, and there was no seal imposing enough to keep Him in His grave. Not Pilate but Jesus spoke the last word. On Good Friday the world said, "NO," on Easter morning He said, "YES."

And ever since, we have the assurance that issues in which He has a stake may be deferred and postponed but never ultimately defeated. So the disciples, fear-drenched at first, left the upper room of the widow's home, walked out into a world which hated them, unperturbed by cross-bearing and undistracted by pain. To hear them talk, you would think they slept on beds of rose petals, when as a matter of fact, they sang their hymns to Christ in the sewers and in the catacombs of Rome, because "Jesus Christ is alive."

* * *

So the Jesus of history becomes the Christ of experience. He who had been a figure in time becomes a timeless figure. His life begins and ends in a miracle. You cannot explain Him in human terms. We worship not a martyr but a saviour. He is man at His best and God in His fullest. We stand before a cradle that has no equal, before a cross that has no parallel, and before a grave that is empty. In His birth is our significance, in His life is our example, in His cross is our redemption, and in His Resurrection is our hope.

He is many things to many people. He is always beyond history but always contemporary. To Dante He was a redeemer. To Shelley He was a poet. To Blake He was the incarnation. To Ruskin He was the master of all things. To Sidney Lanier, the magnificent poet of the old South, He was the crystal Christ.

At His birth, men came from the east. At His death, men came from the west. And east and west meet in Him who said, "And I, when I be lifted up from the earth will draw all men unto me." He is a Latin in Rome. He is a Greek in Antioch. He is a Slav in Moscow. He is an Anglo-Saxon in London and New York. Titian paints Him like an Arab. Tinteretto gives Him the form of an Italian. Murillo makes you think of Him as a Spaniard. Rubens gives Him the physiognomy of a peasant in Flanders fields.

You may as well untwist moonbeams that hang over the hills all about you as to suppose you can untwist the name or the memory of the Son of Man from the hope and heart of the world. He stands the strong among the weak, the erect among the fallen, the pure among the unclean, and the confident among the confused.

He has changed the world. It has never been the same since He walked into it, no more than any human life can be the same when once it confronts Him. Loti was right: "When once you look into His face, nothing again will ever satisfy." Storms may break, winds may blow, pestilences may wreak havoc, civilizations may totter, atheism may rage, churches may fail, and communism may scream, but there is something about Him that is eternal. Christ is in the world to the end of time.

The Christian religion is not so much a philosophy or an ethics as a perfect life who having entered the world can never be expelled. What was written about Him is true, "All the armies that have ever marched, all the navies that have ever sailed, all the parliaments that have ever legislated, all the rulers who have ever ruled, and all the prophets who have ever preached have not affected or changed or challenged the life of man upon earth as this solitary figure."

St. Augustine, walking out of prodigality and shame to write "The Holy City"; St. Francis of Assissi, finding Him in poverty and in the song of birds; John Huss, praising His name above the crackling of the flames; John Calvin, discovering Him with his legal mind and logic; Wesley, emerging from cold ceremonialism; Martin Luther, finding no peace in penance; Spurgeon, Moody, John Bunyan, Phillips Brooks, Schweitzer—all these have looked into His face and affirmed with Thomas, "My Lord and My God."

Richard Watson Gilder wrote it this way:

If Jesus Christ is man
And only man, I say
Of all mankind I will follow Him
And follow Him all the way.

If Jesus Christ is God
The only God, I swear
I'll follow Him through heaven and hell
Through sea, and sky, and air.

The world is not done with Him, but the world is done without Him.

Sermon Two

DIVINE CONDESCENSION

His Grace, Frederick Donald Coggan, D.D.

Lord Archbishop of York, The Church of England, Bishopthorpe, York, England

Dr. Frederick Donald Coggan, the Lord Archbishop of York, is a noted Biblical scholar and theologian as well as a preacher of commanding stature. Born in 1909, Dr. Coggan was educated at Cambridge and Oxford, where his disciplined thought and dedicated purpose won him top honors in theology and Oriental languages. He was ordained in the Anglican Church in 1935, taught at the University of Manchester, then became curate at St. Mary's Church in Islington in London's East End, where he ministered to the temporal and spiritual needs of his impoverished parish.

Wycliffe College, Toronto, Canada, invited him to become Professor of New Testament, a chair he occupied until called to become principal of the London College of Divinity in 1944. In 1956 he became Bishop of Bradford and was called to the ancient See of York as Archbishop in 1961. Among his many writings are *A People's Heritage, The Ministry of the Word, The Glory of God,* and *Christian Priorities.*

His Grace pleads for the full-orbed preaching of the whole Gospel for the whole world. "The tragedy within the church today," he has said, "all too often, is that the Gospel that is preached is but a section, a fragment of the Gospel as it is given to us in the New Testament." . . . "One of the tasks of the Christian Church is to teach me how to die, as well as how to live; to teach me the bright hope of resurrection in Christ, both here and now, and there and then. And if one is emphasized or streessed to the neglect of the other, then to that degree a travesty of the Gospel is presented." His own sermons demonstrate his convictions. This sermon on *Divine Condescension* was preached for the Teachers of Merseyside in the magnificent new red stone Gothic Cathedral in Liverpool on October 6, 1963.

The Archbishop is also particularly interested in the wider publication and distribution of Christian literature in the languages of today. He serves as President of the United Bible Societies.

Laton H. Holmgren, General Secretary
The American Bible Society

DIVINE CONDESCENSION

> Jesus, knowing that . . . he was come from God and went to God . . . riseth from supper, and laid aside his garments; and took a towel, and girded himself. After that he poureth water into a basin and began to wash the disciples' feet.
>
> John 13:3-5

It is a high tribute to any teacher to say of him: "He was able to get down to the child's level without in any way appearing condescending." To see through the child's eyes: to view the particular problem as he views it; to stand alongside of him as he works his way through to a solution—this is to be a great teacher. And this is to earn the teacher's greatest reward, which is not a big salary or perfect working conditions (though we despise neither of these), but to see the look in the child's eye which says: "I didn't see that before. I've got it now."

I speak to you this morning as one who likes to think of himself as a teacher. Some twenty-two years of my life have been given to teaching work, though the students have been older than are most of yours: eighteen years and over. And whoever tries to *preach* should at the same time seek to teach; a sermon without teaching is not worth much.

But whether you are teaching little children or sixth-formers or University students or ordinands, or whether you are preaching to any kind of congregation, your problem is essentially the same: "How do I get alongside of my hearers? How best can I help them to see the particular aspect of truth with which I am concerned?"

It is not always the teacher who is most highly qualified who is most successful in solving this problem. Good degrees are much to be desired. But I suspect that it is the teacher who addresses himself, with real imagination and painstaking persistence, to the problem of what I have called the child's *level* who will meet with success in his demanding and thrilling task.

I have been deeply interested, in following the service so carefully drawn up by the Dean, to see how frequently the note of divine condescension occurs. I use the word without any unpleasant nuance—in the sense of getting down to our level. "Christ our Lord to earth descendeth," the choir sang. "Love divine . . . to earth come down," we sang together.

And the choir will shortly anticipate Christmas in singing "He came down to earth from heaven, Who is God and Lord of all." Now there has been much written lately about the use of spatial language when we are talking about God. Into that debate I shall not enter, except to say that I do not see how such language can be avoided while we are creatures of space and time; nor, perhaps, need we be over-nervous about using it (do we really believe that the Sixth-Form classroom is necessarily upstairs when we say "He will go up into the Sixth Form next term"?

When we speak of God coming down to earth, we mean (among much else) that He had something to communicate which was of the utmost importance. If that communication was to take place, He had to come down to our level, to see through our eyes, to stand alongside of us, to share with us in our deepest experiences. Only so could He teach us what was in the Mind of God. Only so could He *be* to us what God for ever is.

This is what the Gospels are all about. In pre-Christian days, the message of God came to men through prophets and priests and leaders. They *bore* the word of God to men. Jesus, so the Gospels insist, *was* the Word of God. And if you want to see what God is like, if you want to see the heart of God bared and the mind of God disclosed, you look at the manger: God disclosing His strength in the form of human weakness, "a little baby thing that made a woman cry." You look at the carpenter's bench where, amid tools and dust and dirt and, I doubt not, under-pay, the Word

> . . . wrought
> With human hands the creed of creeds
> In loveliness of perfect deeds,
> More strong than all poetic thought.

You look at the Baptism, where, at the lowest point on the earth's surface, Jesus went down into the waters and stood in with us sinners. You look at the Ministry—don't wax too poetic about the Galilean hills. Lovely they were, but they were peopled with folk in pain and fear and ignorance and sin; and Jesus spent those brief years wrestling with those very problems, healing sickness of mind and body and soul, liberating prisoners, letting the bruised go free. You look at the Foot-washing. Does St. John ever reach such heights in his Gospel as he does in the passage which I have chosen for my text? "Jesus knowing that . . . He was come from God and went to God . . . laid aside His garments, and took a towel, and girded himself, and poured water into a basin, and began to wash the disciples' feet, and to wipe them with the towel wherewith He was girded." Here is the divine condescension incarnate. Here is the Son Who is also the Servant, doing the dirty work and doing it with infinite grace and love. You look at the Cross where He bore the heaviest load of all and cried, as they drove the nails in, "Father, forgive them, for they know not what they do." You look at the empty tomb, symbol of victory, of battle hard fought and well won. You look at it all—the divine condescension, the standing in with us of the Son of Man Who is Son of God, and you say: "Jesus *is* what God has to say to men. Thanks be to God."

As you look at this tremendous coming down to our level, as you watch our Lord standing alongside of us, you begin to say—as the child in your class says when you have been teaching well—"I didn't see that before. I think I've got it now." And when that moment dawns, life takes on a new meaning; it begins again; you are a new creature. For, instead of being self-centered, you begin to move out in love and response and penitence to Him Who, "for us men and for our salvation, came down from heaven."

This is a *teachers'* service, and I have, naturally enough, had in mind so far those whose profession it is to teach boys and girls in school. I realise that what they *are* is even more important than what they *say* in class or outside it. If they themselves have thought their way through to a living faith, and if they are wrestling with the problem of communication in some such ways as I have suggested, then (I was going to say) there is no limit to what they can do for their young people. But it would not be true to say this. There is a limit to the teacher's work. And the limit is set by the *home*.

All too often the work done for the child in school, in the building of his character as well as in the training of his mind, is undone in the home. The discipline, the self-control, the lessons of service taught in school are denied by what he sees at home. There is a dichotomy set up in his mind between the two places where most of his time is spent. He cannot make sense of this. Sometimes, of course, the reverse is true. The lessons taught at home are denied by what he sees at school. The result is almost equally disastrous. The truth is that, if a child is to build his life on the surest foundation, he must have three things:

(i) A *home* where God is reverenced, His laws are obeyed, and the child is trained by the parents in the things of God;

(ii) A *school* where teachers, themselves possessed of a faith which works out in service, seek to build up a character which is strong and Christ-like;

(iii) A *Church*, to which parents and teachers do not *send* the child but to which they come with him—to which they do not delegate the teaching of the Christian faith and Christian principles, but with which they co-operate in this huge task.

Given these three things, we need not fear for the youngster's future. It is where one of these three (home, school or church) fails to play its part, or abrogates its responsibility, that the foundation of the child's life becomes insecure, and some of the baneful results ensue which afflict our national life today.

As I close, let me come back to my text. It was taken from the passage which tells of how Jesus, just before His crucifixion, washed the disciples' feet—did the menial job which one would have expected the youngest of the apostles to have done, if they had not been so busy arguing which of them was the greatest. Peter protested, but Jesus persisted. Then He said: "I have given you an example, that you should do as I have done to you."

This is His message to us in this Cathedral and far beyond, today, His message to us who *teach,* to do our work in the spirit of Him Who stooped to serve the least, stooped, and so conquered; His message to us who are *parents,* to serve our children, not indeed by giving them everything they *want* but by giving them what they *need,* of Christian example and Christain teaching and Christian co-operation; His message to those of us in positions of responsibility in the *Church,* to seek ever fresh ways of ensuring that collaboration with school and home which will give to our children a unity of Christian training.

Along these lines we shall fit them for their destiny in this life and train them for eternity.

Along these lines we shall find ourselves, in school, in home, in the Church, to be collaborators with God in His great plan for human lives.

Sermon Three

THE ROOTS OF THE RECONCILING MESSAGE

REVEREND RALPH W. SOCKMAN, PH.D., D.D., LITT.D., LL.D.

Minister Emeritus, Christ Church Methodist, New York City, and Harry Emerson Fosdick Visiting Professor, 1963-64, Union Theological Seminary, New York City

Ralph Sockman is one of the truly great preachers of our contemporary world and in this message, delivered at his induction as Harry Emerson Fosdick Visiting Professor at Union Theological Seminary, New York, he shows his thorough understanding of the problems of the minister of the Christian Church. His positive discussion will help many clergymen to find answers to their own personal and professional questions in a day when the church and the pulpit face new challenges on all sides. His emphasis upon the divine viewpoint and reconciling love and ministry may help to direct many young ministers to a greater pulpit ministry and power.

Born in Ohio, he is a graduate of Ohio Wesleyan University, did his theological work at Union Theological Seminary, New York, and took his Ph.D. at Columbia University. His doctoral dissertation was in the field of history, which he often calls upon to give perspective to his preaching. He preaches all over America every year, counsels and corresponds with thousands of people. His National Radio Pulpit congregation is numbered in millions and is probably the largest in the world.

In 1916, while still studying at Union and Columbia, Dr. Sockman became associate minister of Madison Avenue Methodist Episcopal Church; in 1917 he was invited to become the full-time minister and later built Christ Church at Park Avenue and 60th Street (a beautiful edifice combining ancient mosaics and glass with the best in Byzantine architecture), where he continued as minister for forty-four years. When he retired in 1961, he was immediately made Minister Emeritus.

Dr. Sockman is the author of many books, including *The Higher Happiness, The Unemployed Carpenter, The Paradoxes of Jesus, Date with Destiny, The*

Highway of God, How to Believe, and *Whom Christ Commended,* his latest. He has received more than twenty honorary degrees, including doctorates from Ohio Wesleyan, Wesleyan University, Lehigh University, Washington and Jefferson, Syracuse, Northwestern University, Miami University, Columbia University, and Duke University. In 1941 he gave the Lyman Beecher lectures at Yale, and during 1947-48, he was Visiting Professor of Homiletics at Yale Divinity School. He is President of the Church Peace Union, now the Council on Religion and International Affairs. He served as a member of the Harvard University Board of Preachers and is Chaplain of New York University. As Director of the Hall of Fame of Great Americans of New York University he has the chance to keep the goals of true American greatness dramatically before the people of our country. In his work at Union Seminary he has an opportunity to impress upon the preachers of tomorrow his ideals and methods in the pulpit. Whenever Ralph Sockman speaks, men listen; when he preaches, they are thrilled anew with the divine message.

THE ROOTS OF THE RECONCILING MESSAGE

Frequently we are told that we are living in the post-Christian era. Some connotations of this term are unclear to me. But there is one sense at least in which this expression seems justified.

Many, perhaps the majority, of our church members confess creeds and convictions which they have inherited but not experienced. They carry the label of Christian but their patterns of living are taken from the secular community rather than from Christ.

Also, those outside the church have inherited many cultural elements derived from Christ but they do not recognize or express any relationship to him. They live, as it were, in a world illumined by indirect lighting. Christ came as the Light of the World. He so radiated his influence that laws, institutions and social concepts became luminous with his spirit. In a land like ours multitudes enjoy this illuminated environment without looking for the source of the light.

Thus both inside and outside the church people are living in the afterglow of Christ without appreciating or appropriating the actuality of his presence.

The preacher, therefore, is caught in a dilemma. As leader of a church whose members are groping for Christ but not gripped by him, he lacks power. And he is trying to reach outsiders who have absorbed some Christian culture by osmosis and assume that they know what the pulpit's message would be. Hence for them the preacher lacks news appeal.

Dietrich Bonhoeffer passed through a period in his ministry when he longed to leave Europe and go to India, Pakistan, or some other region where the Christian message would be news.

Facing this predicament, the preacher is tempted to make up for the lack of power in his parish by multiplying its organizations. Thus he veers toward mere activism. And in his effort to reach the surfeited and sometimes pleasing pagans outside the church, the preacher is tempted to step up the news appeal of his sermons. Thus he veers toward sensationalism. If he yields to either temptation, he becomes dispirited by the futility of his efforts.

On every side we hear voices lamenting the waning power and appeal of the pulpit. The press recently carried the report of an American Cardinal urging the Ecumenical Council at Rome to bring about some solid reforms in Roman Catholic preaching. To a friend of mine Bishop Dibelius of Berlin expressed his alarm over the lack of able candidates for the ministry in Germany. And the shortage of ministers in American Protestantism is giving leaders grave concern. The Methodist Church needs fifteen hundred preachers to fill its pulpits. Last Sunday in a Southern Presbyterian church I was told that the shortage of clergy numbers eight hundred. And the Sunday before I was speaking at an inter-church Festival of Faith in the largest Lutheran Church of a leading mid-western state—a church of twenty-four hundred members. At the close of the service the pulpit committee of that church came to me asking if I could help them find a minister. I submit to you that when a Lutheran church asks a Methodist minister to help it find a preacher, the need must be pretty desperate! In our theological seminaries there is a marked trend toward forms of ministry other than that of preaching. The warning signals are up that this so-called post-Christian era could become a post-preaching era.

The hope of the pulpit lies in deepening its message to meet the real crises of life and not in shallowing its appeal to catch the interest of the casually curious. And now we confront a crisis so wide and deep that it could lead the pulpit to regain its latent power.

The population explosion, the revolution of rising racial and national expectations, the resulting turbulence and the sharpening tensions have brought the general public to a fever of anxiety even if not yet to their knees. Both those inside and outside the church, although they may not be interested in how to live with God, are becoming intensely concerned about how to live with one another. All thoughtful persons realize that it is reconciliation or ruin.

There is one saying of Jesus which even those outside the church would endorse as being relevant. It is this: "If you are offering your gift at the altar, and there remember that your brother has something against you, leave your gift there before the altar and go; first be reconciled to your brother, and then come and offer your gift." The critics of the church would admit the sound sense of that command. They may see no need of going to the altar, but they do recognize the imperative necessity of finding reconciliation with our fellow men.

Yet there is one word in this statement of Jesus which I have never heard stressed. Maybe it was not meant to be emphasized in the original text. But in the present world contest and mood, this word strikes me as of crucial import. Listen again: "If you are offering your gift at the altar and *there* remember that your brother has something against you . . . go . . . be reconciled to your brother." That little word "there" points to the roots of our reconciling work. The altar is the place of remembering. It is at the altar of God that we remember the persons to be reconciled and the resources for reconciling.

Consider first how the altar of God in Christ conditions us for the work of reconciliation.

For one thing, it brings to remembrance the divine source of reconciling love. When Paul confronted the tensions in Corinth, he pointed to the redemptive work done by Christ. He wrote: "All this is from God who through Christ reconciled us to himself and gave us the ministry of reconciliation." While in this particular sentence Paul was probably referring to the ministry of reconciling man with God, his letters make amply clear that to the apostle reconciliation with God involves reconciliation of man with man. Paul's thinking is in line with the Epistle of John: "We love because he first loved us." (1 John 4:19) Gratitude for God's redeeming love thaws the icicled springs of our minds and opens the streams of refreshing memories which flow out in all directions toward our fellow men. When we recall what God in Christ has done *for* us, we are lifted out of our bitter thoughts about what others are trying to do *to* us. As we stand before the altar trying to comprehend with all saints what is the breadth and length and height and depth of the love of Christ which surpasses knowledge, our love gains new dimensions and our reconciling thoughts take new directions. We remember persons and points of reconciling which would not occur to us on the street.

And at the altar we remember that God, the ground of being, is love. When we grasp this fact we realize that in our effort, at reconciliation we cannot be laughed out of countenance as feckless "do gooders" or chided as going against the grain of human nature. Cynics masquerading as realists are ever mouthing the old sayings that man is a fighting animal—always has been and always will be, therefore wars are inevitable. In the light of God's reconciling love we see that man is not primarily a fighting animal but a member of God's family; created for love but estranged by sin.

Furthermore, at the altar the remembrance of God's goodness to us begets humility as well as gratitude. We "pour contempt on all our pride." We cease to prate about the excessive taxes we pay for the support of others and realize that however much we pay we are "under obligation both to Greeks and to barbarians, both to the wise and the foolish." We are all "standing in the need of prayer." We all do pray for mercy and that same prayer doth teach us all to render the deeds of mercy. And when the sense of mercy seasons our sense of justice, we are mellowed into a mood of reconciliation.

Also at the altar we catch Christ's spirit of compassion. When in the press and on the screen we see the sadly puzzled look of little children peering at schools where they cannot study and at parks where they cannot play, when we see women knocked down by fire hose and police dogs, when we behold the small shoe held by a mother weeping over her little daughter bombed in a church, we are stirred to passion over man's inhumanity to man. But the cross on the altar does not arouse our anger against the crucifiers of Christ. The curses and cruelty of the mob are drowned out by the words of Christ from the cross, "Father, forgive them for they know not what they do." The Cross arouses our compassion rather than our passions; and it is compassion that we need for our work of reconciliation.

Thus at the altar we are moved to gratitude, humility and compassion, which condition us for our ministry of reconciliation.

Secondly, when we come before God's altar we get a deeper understanding of the human beings to be reconciled.

Hendrik Kroemer, a former holder of this professorship, writes: "The point constantly stressed in the Bible is that God alone knows man in his inner motives and being, and therefore the knowledge of self goes through the knowledge of God, and not the reverse."

In our work of reconciling we must begin with God and then with our own selves for a better understanding of ourselves. And if we recognize the need of knowing God in order to know ourselves, we delve more deeply than do the practicing psychiatrist and psychologist who ignore religion.

Also we must dig more deeply than some practitioners of the psychiatric art inside the church who talk much about religion but so superficially that, as Robert Fitch says, they try to "give the peace of God which bypasseth all understanding."

Further, when we go through the knowledge of God in order to understand ourselves we go below the attitude of those persons who see no need of either religion or psychiatry. Many a man on the street who thinks himself healthy and normal dismisses the discussion of religious counseling by saying that the only counsel we need is that given by Polonius to Laertes in Shakespeare's *Hamlet:* "To thine own self be true, and it must follow as the night the day, thou canst not then be false to any man." But suppose Polonius had given that advice to Hamlet rather than to Laertes. Would the distraught young Dane have known how to be true to himself? He was "beside himself." He did not comprehend his true self.

It was said of Christ that he knew what was in man. Christ not only bids us be true to ourselves but he also reveals our real selves to which we are to be true. This recognition that the Knowledge of self goes through the Knowledge of God is demonstrated by the induction today of my colleague, Dr. James Knight.[1]

Also it is at the altar of God that we get a better understanding of the other persons to be reconciled. A few years ago at a goodwill conference of Roman Catholics, Protestants and Jews, a woman came to me at the close and said, "Why do you speakers make so much ado over this matter of brotherhood? It is all very simple. Just practice the Golden Rule, 'Do unto others as you would that they should do unto you.'" "Yes," I replied, "but one trouble is that we do not use sufficient imagination to understand what we would want done to us if we were in the other person's place, with the result that we do to him what we think is good for him and that usually irritates him." The Golden Rule practiced without imagination is often just sheer irritation.

And it takes more than imagination to safeguard the Golden Rule as a reconciling principle. It requires divine perspective. A judge might look at a prisoner before the bar and say to himself, "If I were in his place, I should want to be let off. So I'll release him." But such action would be injurious to the prisoner and play havoc with justice. Human imagination must be illumined with divine light to insure justice, peace and reconciliation. Earthly rule doth then show likest God's when mercy seasons justice, but not when it supplants justice.

---

[1] Note: Both Dr. Sockman and Dr. Knight were inducted as members of the distinguished Union Seminary faculty in October, 1963.

Nor can we rest the reconciling process wholly on the much-praised formula, "reverence for personality." Important as this factor is, it is too flexible and subjective to stand up alone in the heat of racial strife or even of bodily passion.

Dwight Morrow is reported to have said that one of the most difficult barriers to international understanding is this: "We judge ourselves by our ideals and intentions but we judge others by their actions." Is not this trait pretty near the crux of the controversies between nations and races and even neighbors? For instance, we Americans know that we want no other nation's territory and would not be the first to start a war, but other governments judge us by our bomb piles, air bases and our Operation Big Lift. The Soviet Union asserts that she desires general disarmament but we judge her by her conduct in Cuba and at the Berlin wall.

How can we develop the insight and imagination to judge others as we would that they should judge us? This goes more deeply than the Golden Rule, for judging of others is deeper than doing to others.

Here is where our efforts at reconciliation need rootage in the reconciling love of God. When Paul wrote to the Corinthians that God through Christ reconciled us to himself and gave us the ministry of reconciliation, he put in the same paragraph these words: "From now on, therefore, we regard no one from a human point of view." When we go through God for our knowledge of men we regard them not according to their bodily color, their social position, their wealth or any other human status-making factors. We behold them as persons standing under God's judgment but so beloved of Him that he sent his Son to redeem them.

This viewing of men from a divine rather than from a human point of view helps us to judge others as we would they should judge us. It is necessary if we are to advance from civil rights to social civilities, from the removing of legal barriers to the curing of personal prejudice. And all this cannot be developed by congressional action or crowd demonstration. It has to be developed by cultivation. And in the atmosphere of God's reconciling love.

Suppose that a curtain were drawn across the nave of this chapel. I could not see you in the rear pews. But there is a way by which I could see you. If there were a mirror in the ceiling, I could look up into that mirror and it would enable me to look down into your places. That is a parable. The world is curtained off. We cannot see through on the sidewalk level. But when we go into our houses of worship and look up to God who is the Father of all men, it is like looking up into a mirror of compassionate love and thereby we can see into the places of those whose creed and culture and color may differ from ours. And if we do it sincerely enough and repeatedly enough we sensitize our judgments and imaginations into the likeness of him who said "Whosever hath done it unto one of the least of these has done it unto me."

Before my third and last point may I pause here parenthetically to ask for help. I have just used a figure of looking up to God. Now, before I read Bishop Robinson's "Honest to God," I knew that God is not "up there" or "out there." I endorse Paul Tillich's concept of God as "the ground of being." But in the pulpit we preachers almost impulsively and, I believe, rightly use gestures in communicating our message. When we direct our thoughts to the transcendence of God, we look up. When we speak of God's universality we are prone to stretch our arms outward. But when we talk of God as the "ground of being," where shall we point? We can hardly direct our gaze downward for God is not "down there," any more than "up there." Realizing that God is the "Beyond within" as Bishop Robinson says, the most appropriate gesture would seem to be to pound the chest or hug the diaphragm. And these are not very graceful. Hence I ask you theologians to help us in the department of homiletics.

Yet whatever gestures we use, when at the altar of God, we think of his reconciling love, we not only become conditioned for reconciliation and get a deeper understanding of the persons to be reconciled, but also we are moved by a deeper motivation in our reconciling efforts.

Our ministry of reconciliation must be deeper than enlightened self-interest, which is the only motive for winning Congressional support of foreign aid. Legislators must be made to see that grants to other countries mean better business there, better markets for us, and most of all better bulwarks against communism. All this is plausible, but grants made through self-interest, however enlightened, prove so often self-defeating. The recipients are no doubt grateful but they suspect that our American aid is given with an eye to ourselves and to the communists. And this suspicion lessens the gratitude and even tempts some foreign governments to play up the threat of communism in order to secure more millions from America.

The Christian missionaries whose motive was to share the blessings of Christ are being supplanted by government "missions" whose purpose is to build up the military and economic defenses of weaker nations against the threats of Russia and China. The Christian way of life is a bulwark against communist subversion, but the Christian gospel is a message of salvation and not of security.

Also, the motive of our reconciling work must be deeper than that of reform. Seventy years ago the Reverend Dr. Charles H. Parkhurst set out to clean up the vice conditions of New York City. He stirred a great campaign against gambling, prostitution and police graft. For a time his efforts gave promise of real reform. But eventually the crusade began to lose momentum and Dr. Parkhurst in a mood of discouragement is reported to have declared one trouble to be that "the good people got tired of being good before the bad people got tired being bad."

Why do so-called good people seem to get tired so quickly in their crusades of reform? It is because they are not rightly motivated. They start campaigns for law enforcement because they fear lawlessness and hate lawbreakers. They feel proud contempt for fallen women and seek to drive them out, but they have no real concern for their redemption. The motives of fear and pride and hate do grow wearisome. But love does not. "Love bears all things, believes all things, hopes all things, endures all things. Love never ends." And if good people would win against the forces of evil, they must seek to redeem and not merely to reform.

Albert Camus in "*The Fall*" says: "God is not needed to create guilt or to punish. Our fellow men suffice, aided by ourselves." But God is needed to create and keep creative the spirit of forgiveness and love essential to a ministry of reconciliation. Amid reform movements which spring up like mushrooms, the Christian minister stands at the altar of God's reconciling love to present Christ as the Redeemer.

When two hundred thousand Americans—and I was one of them—marched on Washington last August to further the cause of civil rights for all citizens, we witnessed a demonstration of human dignity which caused us to feel more sharply the indignities of the past and the need of laws to correct the injustices of the present. But when we come to the altar of God in Christ, our feelings go beyond the call for corrective laws to the cultivation of creative love. In crusades of reform we so often try to do by agitation what we fail to do by demonstration. Reconciliation between races would be speeded if there were more interracial conferences and cooperation dealing with common problems and fewer forums dealing with race problems.

To keep and enforce laws is wearying business, but to keep and cultivate love is a continuing adventure.

Furthermore, the motive of our reconciling ministry must go deep enough to avoid the dangers latent in Good Samaritanism. We rejoice in the purposes of the Peace Corps. We applaud the manifold well-intentioned relief activities which keep multiplying. But in the prevalent talk about the poor and underprivileged peoples of the world, there is the danger that pity may taint the attitudes of the rich and strong. Remember, pity spoils friendship. Compassion, yes. But not pity. We white Americans must recognize that the ministry of reconciliation does not flow between nations or races or persons like a stream from a higher to a lower level, but moves like the tides of the ocean on the level drawn by the attraction of a heavenly body.

And the power of attraction which draws the tide of reconciliation is the God "who was in Christ reconciling the world to himself." At the Last Supper after Judas had left the room, Jesus turned to his disciples and said, "A new commandment I give to you, that you love one another." In view of all that Jesus had said during his ministry about the necessity of loving our fellow men, why did he call this a new commandment? The secret is in the clause which he added: "Even as I have loved you, that you love one another."

Christ's love for us is utterly beyond enlightened self-interest, or the Golden Rule or Good Samaritanism. Christ's love is the one absolutely selfless love ever manifest on this planet. It is beyond our grasp but it lengthens our reach and what is heaven for?

Henry George, the American humanitarian and tax reformer, was once talking to Cardinal Manning, the English prelate, of their common interests. "I loved the people," said Henry George, "and that love brought me to Christ as their best friend and teacher." Manning replied, "And I loved Christ and so learned to love the people for whom he died."

This stand at the altar from which men go forth to a reconciling ministry and to which they return for the resources to keep going—that is the high privilege of the preacher.

Sermon Four

BACCALAUREATE SERMON

DOUGLAS MAITLAND KNIGHT, PH.D., LL.D., LITT.D.

President of Duke University and a member of The Congregational Christian Church, Durham, North Carolina

Baccalaureate sermons are a high water mark in the lives of young men and women as they graduate from college or university and in this Baccalaureate by Dr. Knight there is an excellent combination of poetic insight, educational wisdom and vision for minds and lives seeking Paradise.

Born in Cambridge, Massachusetts, June 8, 1921, Douglas Maitland Knight attended Yale, where he took his A.B., M.A., and Ph.D. degrees; he then taught English at Yale, 1946-53, was Visiting Professor of English at the University of California in Berkeley, in the summer of 1949, was a Morse Research Fellow, 1951-52, and was elected President of Lawrence College in 1954, where he served until Duke, seeking a dynamic new president, called him to head this great university in 1963.

Dr. Knight is a layman and a member of the Congregational Christian Church; in his administrative and teaching duties he meets all faiths on an open, friendly basis. He is the author of *Alexander Pope and the Heroic Tradition,* editor (and author of several chapters), *The Federal Government and Higher Education, Religious Implications in the Humanities* (the Hazen Foundation), author of more than a score of scholarly articles and is currently completing work on one section of a definitive edition of Pope's *Iliad* and *Odyssey* (translations).

In his distinguished career Dr. Knight has been an officer or member of many important educational committees, societies or foundations, including the Phi Beta Kappa Council, Board of Directors, Society for Religion in Higher Education, American Council on Education to the Committee on International Exchange of Persons, Board of Directors, Rockefeller Brothers Theological Fellowship Program; Board of Trustees, Woodrow Wilson National Fellowship Foundation, Board of Trustees, Edward W. Hazen Foundation; National Committee on Utilization of Scientific and Engineering Manpower; Board of Trustees, Education and World Affairs; Board of Directors, National Merit Scholarship Corporation; U. S. Delegate (one of three) to SEATO Conference of Asian University Presidents,

Karachi, Pakistan, 1961; former member Editorial Board, *Christian Scholar* magazine; Former Chairman, Wisconsin Rhodes Scholarship Committee; former member, State Selection Committee (Wis.) Fulbright Awards Program. His work has been recognized with the LL.D. by Ripon, Knox and Davidson colleges and with the Litt.D. by St. Norbert College.

In his teaching, Douglas Knight combines scholarship with humanity; in his emphasis upon religion in life he is soundly New Testament in viewpoint; in his views on education and religion he is modern, progressive, intelligent. *Baccalaureate* was delivered at Lawrence College, long distinguished for its personal contact with students and high academic standards.

BACCALAUREATE SERMON

. . . longer in this paradise to dwell
Permits not; to remove thee I am come,
And send thee from the Garden forth to till
The ground whence thou wast tak'n, fitter Soil.
He ended, they both descend the Hill;
Descended, *Adam* to the Bow'r where *Eve*
Lay sleeping ran before, but found her wak't;
In either hand the hast'ning Angel caught
Our ling'ring Parents, and to th' Eastern Gate
Led them direct, and down the Cliff as fast
To the subjected Plain; then disappear'd.
They looking back, all th' Eastern side beheld
Of Paradise, so late thir happy seat,
Wav'd over by that flaming Brand, the Gate
With dreadful Faces throng'd and fiery Arms:
Some natural tears they dropp'd, but wip'd them
soon;
The World was all before them, where to choose
Thir place of rest, and Providence thir guide:
They hand in hand with wand'ring steps and
slow,
Through *Eden* took thir solitary way.

From *Paradise Lost*, Books XI and XII

Whatever it may be for you, Commencement Day is always a very special privilege for me, as it is for all of us who have worked with you, taught you, learned from you, put up with you these last four years. At the same time there is a quality of heartache that goes with the very real triumphs of this day; it grows in part from our sense of all that might have been done, all that still remains to do; but it grows above all from the high value we put on what you are and what you can be. We hate to let you go. It is heartache without sentimentality, in short, an emotion which can justify itself in a harsh, uncertain and often terrifying time.

I do not really need to use phrases like the last ones when I talk to you. There is no need to load you further with the burdens of the world, as though it were some hideous disease which you must either defeat or succumb to. Diseased it often is, of course; but disease is not its nature any more than it is yours. If I am going to be of any use to you as you leave, I need to talk about the things that are truly and permanently at the heart of our world. Enough has been said about our nightmares; perhaps we need to look at our common life instead, asking ourselves what we are and also what we must do and be as educated people.

Right at this point, and whether we like it or not, we must meet our first parents, Adam and Eve. So hopelessly human that God himself could not change them, they do more than speak to our condition; they speak our language. They act out our hungers, our follies, our fond hopes. And they act out, too, the path we travel as we grow in wisdom—or at least as we grow toward the beginning of wisdom. As Milton sees them, they do more than interpret to us one of the great persistent myths of man's religious past; they focus and put in order the nature of the human self.

So does any major work of art, of course; it just happens that no other story can do as much as the story of the Fall, no other events insist so sharply on what we are and are not. The image of perfection, the destruction of that image, and the recovery from its collapse—these are the dreams that each one of us lives with over and over again. Look with a sharp eye at the great events of life: an education, a career, a marriage, a family. Each of them has implicit in its very existence the story of the Fall—and acted out not just once, but countless times.

What is it in us, then, that the myth dramatizes with such fearful symmetry? First of all, this: we are so much less than we wish we were. Eve watching herself mirrored in the pond; Adam explaining the mechanism of the stars; Eve again, in the incredible bondage of her naïveté, telling the serpent that reason is her law—at these and a hundred other points we hear the true accents of Paradise. Paradise is the place where you are until you know better; it is the place that you can only understand after you begin to lose it. It is more and other than Alice's garden seen from a dark hall; it is more than childhood remembered, or more than Freshman Year to a Senior (though it has a sense of dream about it, just as these other events do). When we say that Paradise is everything good, we have said only half; we can call it good only after we have learned what goodness is. And it is no part of life, for men at least, to possess the good without learning something of evil.

The Paradise in our private daily lives makes this point clear, I think.

It is often the place we describe with an *if*, and most of us have several gardens of this kind. *If* the faculty would stop these foolish expectations, you say in February, what a college this would be. *If* all the students were shipped to New Zealand, say the faculty in March, what a college this would be. *If* we get through Commencement, I say on June first, what a college this will be. In these and a thousand more serious cases, we set out to make our private Paradise by some radical change in the face of reality.

It is important to understand, however, that the meaning of the Garden of Eden does not stop with this kind of wish-fulfillment; it merely starts there. Adam and Eve think, of course, that there is nothing more involved, just as some of you may—at one time, and in the distant past—have thought that there was nothing more to life than playing a simple game by the right rules. It is the great purpose of myths like the garden myth to remind us that life even at its simplest is not this simple. But why isn't it? Eve, for instance, is sure that it *is;* she tells Satan so.

> Serpent, we might have spar'd our coming hither,
> Fruitless to mee, though Fruit be here to excess,
> The credit of whose virtue rest with thee,
> Wondrous indeed, if cause of such effects.
> But of this Tree we may not taste nor touch;
> God so commanded, and left that Command
> Sole Daughter of his voice; the rest, we live
> Law to ourselves, our Reason is our Law.
> *Paradise Lost*, IX, ll. 647-654

Eve is really saying that Reason is an all-sufficient guide for Adam and herself; while, as she proves just a few minutes later, she is animated by anything but reasonable and rational motives.

None of you had better scorn her for this, however, saying "how like a woman," unless you are willing to say "how like a man" as you watch Adam in turn fall for Eve's invitation. Each is pulled by his own desire, though called by the name of Reason; and each tries to rebuild the universe according to that personal desire. If only I had power over Adam, Eve says; I mustn't lose Eve, says Adam. It is not that these are simple-*minded* people; they are simple in their attitudes toward will and desire, not in their intellectual range or power.

And this is really, I suspect, why I talk to you about them this morning. Adam and Eve remind us of a good many things; but above all they remind us that it is not enough to be subtle and competent of mind; one must be equally sensitive to will, desire and purpose. There is an integrity, a coherence of spirit that has to bring order into the myriad kinds of knowledge and judgment which make up a person—or a college, for that matter. Without that integrity of spirit we are perpetually on the road to wisdom, and yet we can never arrive; we are looking for the answers, we say, but we want them always to be our private answers, and not the real ones.

The fabulous and yet earthy tree in the Garden exists to make clear this difference between egotistical conviction and true understanding. Adam and Eve are amply warned, in a sense; they realize that they are dealing with the tree of the knowledge of good and evil. What they do *not* realize, however (and, like us, they do not want to realize it), is that to know good and evil is to experience them—not just to learn about them, not just to learn the abstract pattern of what they are. Their comfortable and self-gratifying hope would turn knowledge into one more possession of theirs, and so they eat the fruit. Then they discover that knowledge is first and last an experience, that they are possessed by *it;* and in the shock of this discovery they lose their Paradise.

They lose it, not because God is vindictive, but because they cannot stay where they are and be what they are. Paradise is the place for the innocent, the unknowing; once Adam and Eve move beyond innocence, they must change their world. As creatures of experience, they are forced to be aware of the light and the dark in their lives.

But this, as I have suggested to you, is not merely their adventure; it is ours. It is the inevitable outcome of our nature. Any life worth living —any thoughtful, self-aware, purposeful life—is made up of losses and discoveries, of Paradise constantly cast away and yet recovered in another form. Without this alternation of events there would be nothing we could call education, nothing we could call growth, nothing indeed that we could call life itself.

We exist, perhaps, between two kinds of Paradise: one, the past that we shall never recapture as soon as we recognize that it is past—in short, a Paradise that we can understand only by losing it; and the other, the Paradise that we never fully take possession of—one that we recognize by its transcendence over everything we are. Our life at its best—our *educated* life at its best—is lived in this dual recognition of the things which were and cannot be, and the things which are not but might be.

But why should this recognition be your particular duty as educated people? Because it is your obligation truly to understand what you do. Others without your privileges can live uncritically, without self-awareness. You are no longer free to do this; you have many other kinds of freedom, but you no longer have the freedom to be naïve, no longer the freedom to accept standardized or unconsidered decisions. Whether you know it or not, whether you like it or not, you have, like Adam and Eve, left this dubious kind of Paradise behind you. Instead you must accept the second kind—the kind you will never fully possess, but the kind which represents your best vision of excellence not only for yourself but for us all.

As a result, if I had to pick just one kind of understanding as the most definitive among the many you have confronted here in college, it would be this: the ideas, the insights, the relationships which you do not yet fully possess are far more important than those which you have already acquired. A distinguished person of any kind is marked by this understanding; he must always continue, all his life long, to "justify" himself by what he reaches for. If this is the heart of faith, as Saint Paul defines it, it is also the heart of educated human experience.

And like all precious experiences, it is the easiest thing in the world to lose. If the naïve kind of Paradise is destroyed by experience, the sophisticated vision of the ideal can be destroyed by the very forces that brought it into being. The powers that bring maturity also bring weariness; with the repetition of experience comes a dulling of what it means. Family, friends, associations closely held and institutions long believed in —each of these essential kinds of experience has to be revisited and reinterpreted constantly, so that while it remains familiar it can also be new, unexpected, compelling.

When I say these things, you must realize that I am talking to you about times and kinds of events that do not yet fully exist for you. I am talking really about the struggle to stay intellectually and spiritually alive, which will be harder but also infinitely more important for you twenty years from now than it is today. I suggest to you, furthermore, that your years here have a tremendous amount to do with the possibility that you *can* be more alive than you are today. This, I suspect, is why teachers never know until too late whether they have been any use; the evidence of their work only shows up a generation later. But if we have succeeded, then you already know what it is to move from ignorance to experience; and you know, at least in part, what it means to dream of more than you can perform, and to believe in the importance of the dream. This will be your true Paradise in the years ahead. It will not be comfortable, it will not be measured by houses or money or newspaper copy; it will have no smell of fame, no varnish of popularity. But it is the persistent life behind each transitory pleasure that the world may chance to bring you.

I cannot guarantee you anything as you leave Lawrence except this; if you have caught the idea of what we are, then, like Adam and Eve, you will never be fully satisfied again. I suspect that many of you will do great things, and that some of you may be wealthy when you die; but I hope and pray that all of you will have the one essential thing—a Paradise within you, happier far than any outer reward or gratification could ever be. If so, if you have seized on the idea of the hungry, questing, curious and yet reverent spirit—then we have done something, then we are content. In that kind of life we wish you well; we wish you Godspeed now and in all the years ahead.

Sermon Five

LIFE IN THREE DIMENSIONS

Bishop Herbert Welch, D.D., LL.D., Litt.D.
Bishop of The Methodist Church, Retired, New York City

Bishop Herbert Welch, now more than a hundred years old, is one of the great men of the Christian Church in our day. Born in New York City on November 7, 1862, he took his A.B. from Wesleyan University in 1887, his B.D. at Drew Theological Seminary in 1890, and entered the Methodist ministry that same year. He held pastorates at Bedford Station, and St. Luke's in New York; Summerfield Church, Brooklyn; First Methodist Church, Middletown, Connecticut; Chester Hill Methodist Church, Mt. Vernon, New York.

In 1905 he was elected President of Ohio Wesleyan University, where he served with distinction until he was elected Bishop in 1916. For twelve years he administered the work of The Methodist Church in Japan and Korea, then was called home to become Bishop of Pittsburgh, 1928-32. He returned to the Orient as Bishop of the Shanghai Area, 1932-36. Although he retired in 1936, he was recalled to the active work of the bishopric and served as Resident Bishop of Boston, 1938-39.

A list of Bishop Welch's extra offices and memberships reads like the curriculum vitae of several men. He was Chairman of the Methodist Committee for Overseas Relief, 1940-48; was a member of the Board of Managers of the Missionary Society, 1895-1905; a trustee of Wesleyan, Ohio Wesleyan and Drew Universities; a member of the University Senate; State Committee of the YMCA of Ohio, 1913-16; President, Methodist Educational Association, 1914-15; Vice-President, National Christain Council of China, 1935-36; Trustee, old John Street Church (the historic Methodist church in New York). He has served with the American Bible Society; China Relief, 1941-46. He was chairman of the Nanking Theological Seminary Board, 1937-43.

He was decorated with the Third Order of the Sacred Treasure of Japan, 1928; received the Medal of Korea, 1952, and was made an honorary citizen of Korea in 1956. China awarded him an honorary citation in 1952.

He is the author of *The Christian College, That One Face, College Lectures* (in Korean), *Men of the Outposts, Selections from the Writings of John Wesley.*

On his one hundredth birthday his autobiography, *As I Recall My Past Century*, was published. He was always known as a fine minister, an educator, a good Bishop and an excellent preacher. *Life in Three Dimensions* shows the Bishop's strength of intellect and vital power in the pulpit. The editor of *Best Sermons* is proud to have his sermon in this volume.

LIFE IN THREE DIMENSIONS

Without forgetting the numberless public problems which stare us in the face in this tremendous day, I address myself this morning to a human and personal situation which is set forth with some fullness in the first three Gospels (Matthew 19:16-22; Mark 10:17-22; Luke 18:18-23).

Here, in a nutshell, is the story of a young man of parts who became a Bible character only because of a brief interview with Jesus Christ. Though young, he had already reached a position of some prominence, perhaps because of inherited wealth, and there was something loveable about him which especially attracted the Master. His cup might well have seemed to be full, with youth and wealth and status, but he himself was conscious of a vacuum and was looking for a more complete life, which he called "eternal." In answer to his questions, as to how to attain this, Jesus pointed first to five of the Ten Commandments, the five which were concerned not with worship and ritual, but with human relations; and when the young man stated that he had already mastered these elementary lessons and asked, "What next?" Jesus confronted him with the startling challenge of our morning lesson.

Jesus was drawn to this youth, I suspect, not so much for what he was as for what he might become. He saw in him possibilities which the man did not know he had—possibilities of courage, kindness, daring, self-sacrifice. Just as Jesus saw rocklike strength and endurance hidden in impulsive Peter; saw loyal discipleship lurking in office-seeking James and John; saw a possible Christian leader in Zaccheus, who had been no more than a fat official; saw promise of sainthood in Mary Magdalene; so here. This righteous young man seemed a potential disciple who would stop at nothing. Well, let us see. "One thing thou lackest . . . go . . . sell . . . distribute . . . come . . . follow." An opportunity for greatness was offered to him.

Mind you, Jesus was not proclaiming a general rule for the Christian use of property. He was testing a particular individual for an important post, not improbably within the small circle of "apostles," which would involve the surrender of other ties and responsibilities. Whatever limited the largest development of life must go: in this case, wealth.

Now, this man was no moral derelict who needed a radical clean-up. He believed in a moral order and undertook to play the game according to the rules. He was honest, truthful, chaste and just; and that is no little thing to say of a young man in that day or in any day. No doubt all around him were men of his own age and class who were not observing the Ten Commandments—men with whom some form of dishonor was a way of life—irreverent, profane, shifty, licentious, grasping; and it is never "as easy as rolling off a log" to be different, to be upright and downright, to venture to "wear the white flower of a blameless life." God bless those "righteous" men who keep the world from going foul, the men who fight their way up out of the clutching bog of mere passion and self-indulgence and take their stand upon the solid ground of duty! There is a touch of grandeur about the martyr who can, for his principles, endure opposition, ridicule and loss, and, having done all, still stand like a rock.

Duty, in its way, is magnificent—"stern Daughter of the Voice of God"! How glorious it would be if all the world should rise to the level of duty! But what a tragedy it would be if all the world should be let down to the plane of—duty! A landscape of nothing but rocks makes a dour world. Even the virtues of a righteous man may lack charm. Duty may become just a time-server, a clock-watcher; honesty may be hard, purity may be cold, justice itself may be cruel. Duty by itself would reduce life to a matter of prohibitions and regulations, and leave no room for spontaneity, for sweet impulse and inspiration, for creative imagination, for generosity and romance and adventure. It would take the color and fire from human annals, and leave but a drab page.

In fact, the individual who has no higher guide than the rules of propriety may be righteous rather mechanically, because he was trained that way, or from fear of the consequences of wrong-doing, or from a dread of public opinion. The result may be a self-righteous prig who will never be regarded as a "good guy"! I may keep all the Ten Commandments, and yet be only a dull fellow. "One thing thou lackest." Monuments are built and honors bestowed for those who go "above and beyond the call of duty." For greatness I must have a fire lit in my soul. The "one thing" which is lacking may make the difference between mediocrity and greatness.

Take the simplest examples from our common life. There is no greatness for an athlete, be he sprinter or pitcher or half-back, unless he gives all that he has and more than he thinks he has. There is no great coach who does not demand seeming impossibilities from his men. There is no great teacher whose heart is not wrapped up in his students, who does not spurn the conception of his occupation as that of a hireling, employed to give so many hours of instruction for so many dollars. As one has put it: "Though I speak with the tongues of scientific men and psychological angels, though I understand all mysteries and all knowledge, and have not love, I am nothing." "One thing thou lackest."

No artist is great who simply draws lines and applies colors according to the rules of some textbook; he must have those fascinating and tormenting visions of beauty, and an unquenchable longing to see his vision become visible on canvas or audible in an inspired orchestra. There is no great scientist without a passion for research; no great philosopher who is content with the history and criticism of his field, but fails to be a consecrated devotee of the truth. "One thing thou lackest."

To pass from occupational qualifications to the deeper questions of personality, there is no great man who has not found "some great Cause, God's new Messiah," offering him adventure and risk, but demanding all he is and all he hopes to be, calling for that quality which we sometimes name "faith" and sometimes "love" and sometimes "dedication." Without that "faith" it is impossible to please God or to realize to the full the possibilities of life. "Without shedding of blood there is no"—no what? No anything great! Only from the soil that in some real (though not literal) sense is soaked with blood, will the loveliest flowers and the ripest fruits come to their perfection. "He that loseth his life, he alone can really save it."

But hosts of men do not believe that. The cult of "success" finds many followers; the "go-getter" is apt to be the hero of the hour. Wealth, power, fame are the deities which allure many worshippers; and we have homes without love, business without brotherhood, learning without commitment; and those reckless saints who dare to be great, and who write in gold letters upon the pages of history, are awarded no higher title than "fool."

Look at the four Chaplains on the deck of the doomed troopship *Dorchester*, giving away their life-jackets to raw recruits and sinking to immortality in a sea of glory. The cynic may cry, "Folly supreme! Be reasonable. Are not your lives of more value than many GI's?" But another Voice cannot be hushed: "These are my beloved sons, in whom I am well pleased."

Here is Walter Scott, at the height of his popularity and prosperity, taking upon himself the burden of another's debt; giving up his baronial splendor to spend his last years in struggle and pain, toiling at a speed which ambition never reached, and all for dear honor's sake! You fool! Why not live in peace at Abbotsford and comfort yourself by mumbling: "Let him stew in his own juice! Am I my brother's keeper?"

Albert Schweitzer, you fool! Why did you give up the scholarly ease and dignity of your professor's chair for the hardships of primitive existence? Why did you turn your back upon Europe and your books and your organ and your Bach sonatas, abandon your ivory tower and go where ivory was not in towers but in tusks, just to cure the sores of a pack of savages? Once at least you called yourself a fool; but your humble helper Joe was wiser—he said, "They did not call you that in heaven." " 'Fanatic' termed, and 'fool,' yet well content—So he could be the nearer to God's heart."

What shall we say of the whole life program of the dozens or the thousands down through the story of the centuries who, defying all our maxims of worldly wisdom, have buried themselves in some obscure spot or lowly task to serve a brother's need and to find the life eternal? Jesus called them "the salt of the earth . . . the light of the world," as if it were those humble and merciful men who really justified the experiment of creation! "These all died in the faith . . . therefore God is not ashamed to be called their God." Men in high places and men in low places, men of ten talents and men of few—bigness did not enter into Jesus' estimate of a man. Even the man of one talent, if he also possessed the "one thing" which some so sadly lacked, could stand high on his honor list. The important thing, as taught by the Master of life, who knew what was in man, was not size but motive, not success but sincerity. The smallest task is worthy of the biggest man, and a cup of water with love may weigh more in the divine scales than a nugget of gold tossed from a careless hand. Greatness inheres not in the gift but in the giver, not in the enterprise but in the enterpriser.

Well, the universe is what it is, and sooner or later, we must come to terms with it. We cannot "remold it nearer to the heart's desire"; therefore we must make our own adjustments to it. Many influences play upon us to help us find the way. One of the most puzzling problems is how to bring them all into harmony, so that life shall become like the seamless robe of Jesus, woven of one piece from top to bottom, and the inner discord shall be stilled.

This adjustment is not solely or even primarily intellectual. "The canine appetite for knowledge," of which Emerson speaks, is not the keenest hunger of the human soul. John Wesley sought above all else two things: truth and love; but, scholar though he was, he concurred with that other earlier scholar, Paul of Tarsus, that "the greatest of these is love."

Life in the large is finally to be measured not simply by what I have learned, but by the sum of my relationships. It has well been pointed out that no man is complete in himself; his friends, for example, are a vital part of him. "A single man," says Poor Richard, "is an incomplete animal. He resembles the odd half of a pair of scissors." The family, the school, the church, the larger community must share in socializing him, fitting him to live in fellowship with other souls. But his adjustment to the three-fold life is not rounded out unless it also includes a "correspondence fixed wi' heaven."

Our chief trouble, after all, is not ignorance or stupidity, but a power vacuum. Without some lifting force, man is like an eagle creeping along the ground instead of soaring into the blue. He denies his own spiritual nature who does not live life in three dimensions; and in the end, anything less will prove "flat, stale and unprofitable." We might almost say that religion is to life what color is to nature—with well-nigh infinite room for variation, but no place for neutrality.

The Gospel is the good news that God is love, with whom man may enter into fellowship, and that God and man together may create the new humanity for which the whole creation waits. We cannot do this alone; true. The fire which can burn without consuming must be kindled by a flash from heaven.

Christianity is a religion not of water, but of fire. The question which weighs on me is not, "What do you possess?" but "What possesses you?" Have you any sense of destiny? Have you something which grips you and holds you, so that you begin to say, "I am not my own; I have been bought at a price." Then, like Gilder's poet, you "give your soul away, Magnificently free"; and you chant with the blind preacher, "Make me a captive, Lord, And then I shall be free." Commitment transfers guidance to a wiser Head and a stronger Hand. If one would befriend me, let him challenge me with an opening where I can make my life count for something, by ministering to the safety, the comfort, the happiness, the intelligence and the moral and spiritual progress of the human race. Let me ask:

> "Is there some desert or some pathless sea
> Where Thou, Good God of angels, wilt send me?"

Jesus promises few earthly rewards. He does better! Instead of "I will give you," He says, "I will make you." He speaks like Churchill addressing Britain, promising "blood, sweat and tears"; or like Garibaldi to his troops: "You shall have long marches and hunger and fatigue and wounds and perhaps death; and then you shall have a free Italy."

Let us sum it all up:

To talk about *culture* and *civilization* and ignore their spiritual values is to leave the mainspring out of the watch. To talk about *spiritual values* in general terms and ignore their concrete expression in religious institutions like the Church is to live in a balloon rather than a castle. To talk about *religion* and ignore *Jesus Christ* is to lose all historical perspective and more than to leave Hamlet out of the play which bears his name. Even paganism dates its doings from the birth of the only-begotten Son of God! The mystery of the universe finds its answer in God; and the mystery of God finds its answer in Jesus Christ. "Jesus, good Paragon, thou crystal Christ!"

"He spake as never man spake," so that "all the people hung upon His words." He lived as never man lived, "in Him was found no fault at all." He loved as never man loved, and died to prove it. He died as never man died, with words of mercy and of triumph upon His lips.

Revealer of God, Lord of Life, Prince of peace, Molder of history, Hope of mankind, He stands supreme. And to eager seekers after truth, to men everywhere craving something which will make life worth the living, He challenges again, "Follow Me and I will make you."

Sermon Six

THE FACE IN THE MIRROR

REVEREND CLAYTON E. WILLIAMS, D.D., LL.D.

Minister Emeritus of The American Church in Paris, a Minister of The Presbyterian Church, and now minister pro-tem of Portalhurst Presbyterian Church, San Francisco, California

Clayton Williams has had a dramatic career as the minister of the American Church in Paris, which he served for thirty-two years. His work with the United States Air Force in providing recreation and billets for servicemen at the church was only one of the many valuable contributions he made in association with this great church.

A native of Illinois, Dr. Williams attended Butler College and the University of Pittsburgh, then when World War I began, he spent the last half of 1917 and early 1918 in France as a Y.M.C.A. secretary with the Second Division. In mid-1918 he joined the United States Air Service as an officer. Later he studied at the University of Paris and served with Herbert Hoover's Food Administration. During 1920-21 he did social work at Chateau Thierry. When he returned to the United States he joined the staff of First Presbyterian Church in Indianapolis, and then entered Western Theological Seminary, Pittsburgh, graduating with his theological degree in 1925. On being graduated he was called as assistant pastor of First Presbyterian Church, Poughkeepsie.

In 1926 he was invited to return to Paris as assistant pastor under Dr. Joseph Wilson Cochran of the famous American Church, where he directed the Students' Atelier Reunions for American students. On the resignation of Dr. Cochran in 1933, Dr. Williams was asked to become the minister. During World War II he was active in aiding refugees and, after taking his family to safety in the United States, returned to France, bringing quantities of relief supplies. Urged to return to the United States because the Nazis were suspicious of him, he went to Cincinnati where he was pastor of the Seventh Presbyterian Church from Pearl Harbor Day until VE Day. He then returned again to Paris to rebuild the congregation of the American Church.

Dr. Williams' work has been recognized by the French government with the Legion of Honor in which he holds the rank of Commander. He is the author of *The Dark Road to Triumph*, a book of Holy Week sermons, which was a Religious Book of the Month Selection in 1960. During the summer of 1959 he was preaching chaplain at Lake Chautauqua and spoke in leading pulpits across America. There is a vitality about his preaching which people immediately sense. He is scholarly without being narrow, evangelical without being dogmatic. *The Face in the Mirror* is refreshingly new and stimulating. This is the sixth volume of *Best Sermons* in which he has been chosen to represent the great preaching of our day. This sermon was preached in Paris and in San Francisco.

THE FACE IN THE MIRROR

> If one is a hearer of the Word and not a doer, he is like a man who beholdeth his face in a mirror, and goeth his way, and straightway forgetteth what manner of man he is.
>
> James 1:23

Some years ago there appeared a play by Jean Anouilh, called *Le Voyageur Sans Bagage* (The Traveller Without Baggage). It portrayed the predicament of a returned soldier suffering from amnesia and trying to find out who he was. He was a man without a past, bereft of any intellectual or emotional baggage, seeking to penetrate life and to discover some clue to his identity and the world to which he belonged.

In his case it was particularly difficult since his post-war experience had made him over into a different kind of person from that which he had been before, creating in him a fund of compassion and sympathy which had been entirely foreign to his pre-war personality; so that when he finally discovered who he was and the kind of a person he had been, he was disgusted and revolted. Fortunately he repented and repudiated his past and began life anew in different surroundings.

The play, for the most part, deals with his search to find out who he really is.

Now in a sense, that is what we are all trying to do. Most of us are a mystery to ourselves. We know well enough the self which we have created to get along with but we have suspicions that we may be really quite different, or at least that there is more in us than we have been willing to admit. Indeed, modern depth psychology tells us that deep down in our hearts there lies hidden a part of us that we do not really know, and that you and I are not in fact the persons that we think we are. Not only do we hide ourselves from others but we hide ourselves from our own selves.

Shakespeare has made one of his characters say, "To thine own self be true and it must follow as the night the day thou canst not then be false to any man;" which is good as far as it goes. But the question remains to what self shall we be true? Even considered superficially we have many selves.

There is the self we think we are, which is often only a pale distorted reflection of our real hopes and feelings. And there is the self that others see in us, which depends upon their perception—love sees us better than we are, hatred sees us worse. Then there is the self that we present to the world, which is often an artificial self, colored and clothed by our pride and concern for appearances, a self which many see through despite our devices. And then there is also that seemingly malicious self, whom we all know, who interferes like a gremlin to defeat our best efforts so that we say, "I don't know what has gotten into me today; I do everything wrong."

And finally there is our real self, that God alone sees and knows, a strange mixture of good and evil, hopes and fears, loves and animosities, prejudices and compulsions masquerading as convictions, and suppressed desires and hidden motives, really a better and worse self than we think we are.

Our souls are haunted houses peopled with saints or near-saints and devils. As Edward Sandford Martin says,

> Within my earthly temple there's a crowd,
> There's one of us that's humble, one that's proud;
> There's one who's broken-hearted o'er his sins,
> There's one who unrepentant sits and grins;
> There's one who loves his neighbor as himself,
> There's one who cares for naught but fame and pelf.
> From much corroding care I would be free
> If once I could determine which is me.

That is our problem. But it is complicated by the fact that we don't want to resolve the dichotomy of our innermost selves. We are afraid to see ourselves for what we really are and so we have complicated our lives and our world so that we can't possibly do it.

We have created for ourselves a picture of a self with which we can come to terms, but the real fact is that we are strange, puzzled, ambiguous beings who live in a strange, confused, contradiction-ridden world which we, in our extremity, have made.

We scurry and scramble and struggle in our search for security, and then when we have it we don't know what to do with it. We strive and fight for liberty, and then we don't know how to use it. We work hard to acquire leisure, and then we fill it with meaningless things, like cocktail parties and club luncheons and bridge parties and dull or exciting movies and trashy television shows and business conventions and celebrations of one sort or another; and we pay for them all with stomach ulcers and nervous breakdowns and alcoholism and hardened arteries.

We are a mixture of honest desire to be something and a passionate compulsion to escape being anything, and the result is inner frustration and humiliation which we strive desperately to hide under pre-occupation.

That's the kind of a world we have made and that is the way most of us live.

Then one day, perhaps out of the blue, or after some personal crisis or revealing experience, there comes to us—if we are at all spiritually sensitive—A Moment of Insight into Reality when, as it were (as James says) a mirror is held up before us and we catch a true glimpse of ourselves, when the artificialities of life are swept aside, and the fog on the mirror clears, and we have a penetrating moment of insight and see ourselves in God's Mirror as we really are.

Have you never known such a moment of insight, when some situation, some thought or act, suddenly unveiled to you depths of your being which surprised and shocked you? Have you never had such a fleeting vision of yourself so startlingly real that afterward it seemed unreal, when the evil within you was too frightening, or when the goodness in which you had put store, was revealed as utterly inferior in the presence of God's Goodness?

Sometimes the reflection which we see in the mirror is a picture of the essential selfishness which has a hold on us, the deep-set drive of self-will which uses all our conventional acts and ways of doing things for its own selfish purposes under a multitude of guises, which for a moment are taken away so that we see ourselves with our souls stripped bare. Our self-righteousness, our pride in success or standing, our complacency with what we are and are doing are pushed aside for a moment and we get a glimpse of our true selves.

Sometimes it is a fleeting vision of the goodness which we might have, of a goodness which is quite different from our goodness which we have thought of as acceptable, a brief reflection of a goodness which we feel we ought to have, a strong, generous, love-possessed goodness which is at once humble and sincere and confident because its source is God, a vision which lures us to repentance.

Indeed, we may actually repent for a moment, but the tragedy is, as James says, that we turn from it and straightway forget it.

If it could be our salvation, why do we forget it? Why do we turn from it?

One reason, I think, is because it seems unreal, so out of character with the world we have to live in. We can't take it seriously; it's too far from the reality we live in. It isn't reasonable; it's like a vision from another world—which it may be! We can't adjust to it, so we turn from it and forget it.

And another reason, I think, is because it is too personal. It shows us what WE are, not what someone else is, not the man down the street, or the man who sits next to us in church, or the man in the newspaper, or the man in Russia or China, but WE, you and I personally: Not Man in general about whom theology speaks but you yourself. And because it is personal we don't like the reflection we see.

When the picture *La Dolce Vita* was shown on the screen in Italy it caused a storm of protest from the people in Rome. You see, they didn't want the mirror held up for them to see themselves. And we are all like that. We Americans didn't like *The Grapes of Wrath* and I was warned not to use this illustration when I preached in California. Men don't like to see themselves, either as they are or as they should be; and the Mirror makes them do that. That's why so many men hated Jesus and that's why they crucified Him. He held God's Mirror before them and made them see themselves and they couldn't stand that. And that is why the Grand Inquisitor, in Dostoievsky's novel, wanted Jesus banished.

Man is always trying to forget what manner of man he is and what manner of world he has made.

And I think another reason is because when he sees himself as a possible son of God, it overwhelms him. It is impossible. It is too high for him and he becomes afraid of such goodness. It seems to him, as it did to the Grand Inquisitor, unrealistic, unattainable, impracticable. It can't be. Far better be "realistic," unhaunted by dreams of such goodness! Far better a normal goodness adapted to this world, that can make out in this world and survive! And so he pushes it out of his mind and turns back to "real" life again, the life he belongs in as he is, with a goodness which is not too good as Christ's kind of goodness is. And consequently he turns away from the Sermon on the Mount and the 13th Chapter of First Corinthians and the 12th Chapter of Romans, which he may read but quickly forgets as beautiful but impractical and unreal for this world we are in; and he repudiates the life of love, and with it, the God of Love whom he transforms into a "realistic" God of Wrath and Judgment, like himself and fit for our world.

Psychologists tell us that we tend to forget what is too painful to remember. A modern writer has portrayed a scene in which one of Pilate's friends, in the course of a conversation with him in Rome, asks Pilate about this man, Jesus of Nazareth, who was said to have been crucified while Pilate was ruling Palestine. But Pilate cannot remember that he has ever known of such a person.

So Man forgets the reflection of the evil that is in him. He forgets it because it is too painful to his pride, too suggestive of impending judgment. He can't stand the ugly reality of his sin-beset nature. When he sees it it frightens him and to protect himself he rationalizes it so he can be rid of it. He says that he is not really a sinner. He is the victim of circumstances, of social determinism. He is not as bad as he seems. He's as good as the next man. After all it isn't healthy to remember one's evil, to feel guilty about it. And so he uses a host of extenuating circumstances to blur out the vision of the evil that lurks within him and has control of him, and he seeks to drown it in the pool of forgetfulness and to find refuge in life as it really is, neither too bad nor too good. He denies that God's mirror has any validity, that, indeed, it IS God's mirror. And in the end he forgets God himself and says that there is no God. He may keep the word on his lips but he has stripped it of all reality and seriousness.

But he is fooling himself, for we cannot get rid of our evil either by forgetting it or denying it. Our forgetting, as the psychiatrist says, is only pushing it down into the depths of our hearts and clamping down the lid on it where it remains a damning reality against the day when we shall find it out or it shall find us out.

The tragedy of forgetfulness is that it blots out all possibility of repentance until it is too late, for the day may come when we cannot see ourselves in the mirror anymore, as it was with the characters in Jean Paul Sartre's powerful play, *No Exit.*

In that play hell, which is a tolerably comfortable, if confining, nineteenth-century drawing-room, has no mirrors in it. There is no place where the victims can see themselves except as their selfishness is reflected, or rejected, back from their equally selfish companions in hell. Little by little the evil which has become entrenched in their dominant desires eclipses the goodness which once was there but which was repudiated.

The desire for peace of Garcin, the pacifist, has become the cowardice which has overlaid any goodness he had. Estelle's love of men has become the cruel, heartless, ruthless self-love that had haunted it. And Inez' affection for her women friends has become the victim of a passion which has wiped out all true friendship and has turned to sensual Lesbianism. Their goodness has turned to ashes and there is nothing left of it for the mirror to reflect. That's why they are in hell; there is nothing left that is appropriate for heaven. A mirror would no longer have a function. It is too late.

Selfishness does not want to repent, and repudiates hope. It says, "Let me alone. I don't want to be changed and I don't believe in goodness." And so deep down in their souls, behind the forgetfulness which for them has become complete, selfishness and cynicism have entrenched themselves against the judgment of God and now, at last, they have taken over and have made their unhappy victims impervious to grace.

You see, we cannot stand the judgment of God if we will not see ourselves as we are and accept the mercy and compassion of God. If we are to be saved from evil we must see both the "misery and grandeur of man" and the mercy and compassion of God. That is what the mirror is for. It is the mercy of God which holds it before us. It is his point of contact with our souls, warning and luring us to save us.

These fleeting moments when we catch a glimpse of ourselves in God's mirror are both crucial and precious, crucial, because it is fatal to look upon the reality which we see in the mirror and forget it and slip back again into the petty round of conventional goodness and corroding evil which will mean our damnation; precious, because it is the love of God behind the mirror that is startling us to save us. Behind the moment of insight is the Word of God in Christ. Indeed, if we have eyes to see it, we shall see that it is Christ who is holding God's mirror before us, Christ who is convicting us of our evil and wooing us toward sonship.

As He holds it he is looking at us. He sees us as we are reflected in the mirror, with all our yearning for goodness and our insidious evil. He sees us as we are reflected in the mirror but he is not shocked at what he sees as we are shocked by what we see. He, who knows both our flesh and God's mercy, accepts in us what we cannot accept.

And in that moment of revelation he is speaking to us and if we have ears to hear, we can hear him say, "What you see in the mirror is what you are but not what you are meant to be. Look at me. I am what God means you to be. The vision in the mirror may be your salvation for it has been given you not to condemn you but to save you. God accepts you as you are as I accept you, and he offers you free and full forgiveness both for what you have done and what you are. Don't be afraid for he wants you to see yourself as you are in order that you may repent and become like me through discipleship."

This moment of insight is our potential moment of salvation. But if we would be saved from ourselves and from the death that is in our world, we must act, as the text says, when we are confronted by this word of Christ. This does not mean that we must act to do something to justify or change ourselves. It means that we must act by accepting this word we hear, for when we grasp this Word in Christ and realize that forgiving, out-pouring, creative Love is the final reality in which we live, the Love which accepts us, unacceptable though we are, and asks us to accept him and share his spirit, then there is no need for us to forget, for the sting will have been drawn from our remembering and we shall be reconciled to the world, to ourselves, to our fellows and above all to God.

It is this act of accepting that is crucial. There is nothing more that we can do for we are reconciled not by our disgust of ourselves or by our attempts at righteousness but by our accepting of this Love in Christ as the revelation of the ultimate reality of existence, in which we live and by which we live. So Christ becomes our Saviour and our Lord, for we are saved not by anything we can do but alone by committing ourselves unconditionally to the Love that we see revealed in him and humbly asking for grace to follow him in the way that he will open to us.

Let me close with the story of one man's Moment of Insight as recounted by Leslie Weatherhead:

Here is the picture: "A crowd of people listening to Jesus at Capernaum. On the outskirts of the crowd is a man past middle age, whose face we can tenderly read.

"You notice the lines under his eyes. You notice that he drops his eyes if anyone looks keenly at him. You notice that the corners of his mouth run down and that there are heavy lines there too. You notice his stooping figure and shuffling gate as he walks homeward as the crowd breaks up. You catch the gleam of tears in his eyes. His heart is heavy. He is a despised tax-gatherer. His name is Matthew, a despicable name.

"But when he listened to Jesus something that was still splendid and not quite dead fluttered within his breast. And as he is going home he is saying to himself, 'Ah, It is very beautiful and I should like to be like that, but I am not. The tracks of habit are too deep. And how should I get my living and what would people say?' "

You see, he has seen the face in the mirror.

"He has caught a glimpse of the world that Christ offers but rather sadly he is shutting the gates, not passing through them, letting the vision fade. And heavily he turns back to his books, slipping into the groove which was becoming a grave, a grave for a soul.

"But the gospel says that 'as Jesus passed by He saw Matthew sitting at the receipt of custom.' A shadow fell across Matthew's ledger onto a page on which but recently the tears of a man growing old made the ink run. And Matthew looked up into those eyes that are the homes of all men's dreams; and looking into the face of Jesus he realized in a flash, two things, that Jesus believed in him, and that Jesus knew what was holding him back." Knowing his worst Jesus believed in his best.

"The finger of the Great Physician went unerringly to the spot. The eyes of Jesus were saying, 'This is what is stopping you.' And then a voice that drove out all his fears, fears of the past, fears of the present, fears of the future, a voice that took responsibility for all the consequences, said to him, 'Matthew, Follow Me!' And Matthew went through the gates into the new world that Christ offered, the world of love, joy, peace and power."

And in the same way in our moment of insight he calls to us.

Sermon Seven

DISCIPLES SECRETLY

REVEREND ROY M. PEARSON, D.D.

A Minister of the Congregational Church and Dean of Andover Newton Theological School, Newton Center, Massachusetts

Roy M. Pearson is chiefly interested in the preaching and pastoral aspects of the Christian ministry.

Born in Somerville, Massachusetts, in 1914, he graduated from Harvard, 1935, and from Andover Newton Theological School in 1938, in both cases with honors. He entered the ministry of the Congregational Church and held pastorates at Southville, Swanzey, and Amherst, in Massachusetts. During his residence in Amherst he was given a leave of absence to serve as a Chaplain in the United States Army. In 1947 he was called to the Hancock Congregational Church in Lexington, and he became Dean of Andover Newton Theological School and President of Andover Theological Seminary in 1954. At the present time he is engaged in building a new library, new classroom buildings, a chapel, and a new women's dormitory. The Hill is a busy place under his leadership.

Among his published works are *Here's a Faith for You, This Do—and Live, The Hard Commands of Jesus, Seeking and Finding God, The Ministry of Preaching, Hear Our Prayer, The Preacher: His Purpose and Practice* (1963), *The Believer's Unbelief* (1963). In 1948 he won The Churchman's Award for the "Sermon of the Year," which was dramatized on a nationwide program with Frederic March, Florence Eldridge, Ralph Bellamy and Arthur Kennedy in the character roles. His sermon "On the Anvil of the Desert" was chosen for inclusion in *Best Sermons, 1955 Edition.* In 1957 he was awarded the honorary Doctor of Divinity degree by Amherst College. He has conducted retreats at the United States Military Retreat Center in Berchtesgaden, Germany, and has preached by invitation in Britain, France, Switzerland, and Holland. He is one of the dynamic leaders of the Protestant Church today.

DISCIPLES SECRETLY

> After this, Joseph of Arimathea, who was a disciple of Jesus, but secretly, for fear of the Jews, asked Pilate that he might take away the body of Jesus, and Pilate gave him leave. So he came and took away his body.
>
> John 19:38-42

One feels a sense of mingled admiration and regret as he reads those words about Joseph of Arimathea. Like Peter the fisherman on that terrible night in the courtyard, Joseph followed Jesus "at a distance." But at least he followed him. Like Nicodemus the ruler of the Jews, Joseph came to Jesus "by night." But at least he came to him. Those were not easy days for men who believed in this despised Galilean, and any reservations which we may have about the cowardice of men like Joseph must always be tempered with praise that they showed what courage they did. Better to follow Jesus at a distance than not to follow him at all. Better to come to him by night than to stay away completely. Better to be disciples secretly than not to be disciples.

Yet our admiration for what Joseph did is inescapably tinged with regret that he did not do more. Joseph is the patron saint of all the helpless mourners who kneel in remorse at the biers of their dead. If only they had been more kind to this man while he was still alive in their midst! If only they had told him how much they loved him! If only they had gone to see him more frequently, listened to him more sympathetically, shared his burdens more gladly! But by the time Joseph had beaten down his fears, the only service he could render Jesus was one that Jesus never knew was being rendered. All he could do was to bury Jesus' dead body, and the joy of doing *something* must have turned to bitterness in the grief of being able to do *so little*. Better to have been a disciple secretly than never to have been a disciple, but how much better still to have been a disciple openly!

I

Disciples secretly. Is not this one of the principal marks of Christianity today? We are disciples all right, we members of the church. We are disciples in the sense that we are learners; for through parents, through teachers and through our own independent study we have become more or less familiar with the life and the teaching of Jesus. We are also disciples in the sense that we are believers; for we see no ultimate salvation for the world outside the way of Christ, and when we think about ourselves, we know that however bad we may be now, we should have been much worse had we never been touched by Jesus' influence. So we are disciples all right, we members of the church; but we are—so many of us—disciples secretly.

Think about our life at home, for example. In his autobiography Harry Emerson Fosdick recalls that in the home of his boyhood, religion was "a force and not a form," but in how many of our Christian homes today is religion even a form? In how many is grace said before meals? In how many is there any regular family devotional service? In how many is religion ever discussed in any other context than the dogmatic pronouncement: "Now, Bobby! We won't talk about it any more. You're going to Sunday School, and that is that!"?

In many of our homes it is almost as if we had entered a conspiracy of silence about the Christian faith. It is almost as if we were living in a communist state where every house was wired with microphones and death was the penalty of anyone found to be Christian. It is as if we had quietly agreed to keep religion in the same category with certain other matters which are better left unmentioned—like the night Daddy spent in jail after getting a bit "tight" at the office party, or the day Grandmother brought disgrace to the home by voting for a Democratic President. Many Christian families have much more to say about the relationship of a child to his knife and his fork than about his relationship to his God and his Christ, and the strangeness of our conduct becomes even stranger when we give serious thought to our deepest desire for the child. We should be horrified if he turned out to be an atheist or a communist, a Buddhist or a Mohammedan. We really want him to be a Christian.

Or consider our life in the church itself, and imagine Jesus suddenly set down in one of our churches at any time other than the hour of worship on Sunday. Would he know where he was? He might find himself at a church supper, and there is nothing wrong about good church suppers; but neither is there usually anything distinctively Christian about them. He might find himself at a dance, and there is nothing wrong in decent dancing; but neither is there usually anything distinctively Christain about it. He might find himself at a workshop on flower arrangements, at a lecture on foreign policy, at a travelogue about the West Indies or at a game of military whist; and there is nothing wrong about any of these events. Indeed, all of them can be thoroughly enjoyable, and some of them can be helpfully instructive. But what would there be in them to proclaim to this suddenly injected Jesus that these people were the successors to the apostles, that these were the lineal descendants of Peter and James and John, that these were the contemporary disciples?

Or turn to our life outside both the home and the church. We count ourselves to be a Christian nation, and we take great pride in our stewardship of faith and righteousness. Buy a bar of candy, and when you place your dime in the hand of the storekeeper, you let him know that "in God we trust." Salute the flag, and you assure the world that what this nation does, it does "under God." But have you never been disquieted about your own discipleship outside the home and the church?

When we dropped the bomb on Hiroshima, were you satisfied that what we did was a truly Christian act performed by a truly Christian nation, and when we notify the Russians that we are ready to drop an even bigger missile on Moscow, are you quite sure that we have thus proved ourselves to be even better Christians? It is the common thought that the principal purpose of a business is to make money, but sitting at your office desk or selling a can of beans in your store or driving down the road with your cases of samples, have you never found yourself a little uncomfortable as you tried to reconcile this common thought with responsibilities like seeking God's kingdom first or loving your neighbor as yourself or being your brother's keeper? Racial discrimination, juvenile delinquency, the acceptance of alcohol as the beverage of distinction, the tolerance of dishonesty in high places, the prevalence of gambling, the ridicule of purity in the sexual relationship—most of us are sufficiently Christian to regard these corruptions of our common life as offensive. "Have we not been good disciples?" we say to God. "Have we not looked with disdain on these sins of our fellows? Have we not kept ourselves pure and undefiled by the wicked world in which we live?" But has it never entered your mind that God may not accept the implication of our question and that he may be answering one inquiry by making another? "You claim that you are disciples," I seem to hear him say. "Are you disciples openly or secretly? And if you are disciples secretly, what have you accomplished openly?"

II

Disciples secretly. There is no doubt about it: this is one of the principal marks of Christianity today, and being one of its principal marks, it is also one of its major tragedies.

Think again about our homes, for instance. For the most part, our homes are decent and honorable institutions, but is it not true that built upon life, many of them have become places of death?

The fact is inescapable that the Christian belief about people is utterly incredible apart from the Christian belief about God. If God does not exist or if God is not Christlike, why should I seek God's kingdom first? Why should I love my neighbor as myself? Why should I take up a cross, or deny myself, or do good to those who hate me? Our fathers in the faith lived as they lived because they believed what they believed. The most that can often be said about us is that we live as we live because our fathers believed what they believed. And what then is to be said about our children? Will they live as we have lived for no other reasons than those of admiration or habit, or finding no cosmic warrant for the seemingly senseless sacrifices of Christian commitment, will they discard the *life* as so many of us have discarded the *faith?*

When a flower is cut, it may still be lovely, but already it has started to wither and fade. When the oil truck stops calling at your house, your furnace may continue to operate because your storage tank is full, but already—at least symbolically—the cold has begun to creep through your windows and doors. Parasites upon the Christian past, many of our decent and honorable homes can do nothing but die with the death of that on which they feed, and if our children are no more than parasites on dying parasites, how greatly does it matter that we have fed them vitamins or taught them to wash behind their ears?

Or consider again the church itself. That its members should be disciples secretly is no more sensible than that an orchestra play its music silently or an army fight its wars peacefully or a painter paint his pictures invisibly. It is of the very essence of the church that its members be disciples openly. They are to preach the gospel. They are to proclaim the glad tidings. They are to let their light so shine before men that others may see their good works and glorify their father in heaven. And a church composed of secret disciples is like a perfume bottle filled with odorless perfume.

It is strangely true that the names of God and Christ are heard more frequently in many a bar room than in many a church, and if the church is the body of Christ, the silence and the inactivity of so many of its members with respect to so many of Christ's greatest concerns can be nothing less than the misappropriation of his body. It is the gagging of his mouth, the binding of his hands, the hobbling of his feet. Providing no discernible evidence of being *for* Christ, the church takes its place with those who are *against* him. Being silent among his friends, it gives consent to the attacks of his enemies. And in the midst of the terrible needs of the times, the church must often seem to those outside it like a carpenter who, holding a hammer in his hand, cries out that he cannot do his work unless someone gives him a hammer.

Or turn again to the world outside both the home and the church, and see what happens there when Christ's disciples insist on secrecy in their discipleship. Eighty-one percent of the national budget is allocated to military purposes, and few people seem to be aware that if God would regret the further extension of communism, he probably regrets no less our own preoccupation with the death of human beings for whose abundant life he gave the world his Son. In one part of the earth men starve for lack of food to eat; in another part of the earth food rots for lack of men to eat it; and few people seem to understand that if this represents an unsolved problem in distribution, it also represent an inexcusable persistence in sin. Cultured and capable Negroes are denied the right to buy a house in a gracious community because it is said that their presence would lower the values of its real estate, and few people seem to be willing to ask when it was that real estate values, in this sense, became one of the proper standards for the judgment of right and wrong. Literature, art and science; newspapers, moving pictures and television; the politics of local government, the economics of the labor rackets and the sociology of sub-standard housing—what weakness we often find in these areas of our common life! What cruelty! What greed! And—what a prevalence of silence on the part of Christ's followers!

"You claim that you are disciples," I seem to hear God say again. "Are you disciples openly or secretly? And if you are disciples secretly, what have you accomplished openly?"

III

Disciples secretly. There is no doubt about it: if this is one of the principal marks of Christianity today, it is also one of its major tragedies. Yet consider what could happen if Christ's disciples secretly became his disciples openly, if the modern Christians sent up a few scouts from their catacombs, discovered how much of their own Nero's brutality was based on weakness rather than strength and then surged out of their caves to take over the city of Rome.

There is no dodging the fact that the first results would almost certainly be humiliating. It is one thing to sit in the stands and call down the wrath of the pigskin gods on the incompetent quarterback who is choosing the plays for the old school team, but it is quite another thing to have those same gods lift you bodily out of the stands, thrust you into a uniform and tell you to call the plays yourself. It is one thing to be the leader of Her Majesty's Loyal Opposition, scurrying around the edges of the party in power—objecting and protesting, harrying and sniping, but it is quite another thing to be the Prime Minister yourself, with all of the honors and privileges of your office but also with all of the terrible responsibility for making the actual decisions which govern your people's future. If Christians often do possess the harmlessness of doves, they frequently do not possess the equally necessary wisdom of serpents, and suddenly given the chance to shape their community according to their own desires, they would quickly discover that good intentions are not the only qualifications needed for effectiveness in Christian leadership.

But suppose that large numbers of Christians were willing carefully to prepare themselves for particular phases of community service. Suppose that they were wise enough and good enough to bridge the gaps between the various sectarian groups and to bind those groups in a singleness of purpose which neither perpetuated the old denominational quarrels nor diluted the special offerings which each of the parts could bring to the whole. Suppose that they assumed again the ancient obligations, that each of them counted himself to be one of the church's ministers and that loving God with all of their being and loving their neighbors as themselves, they actually, soberly, literally sought God's kingdom first in everything they thought and said and did. Have the forces of evil become so mighty that trembling once before twelve lowly apostles, they would now stand undismayed before the united assault of the millions of men and women who have become the apostles' successors?

When Charles Eliot became engaged to Ellen Peabody, Miss Peabody's family received a congratulatory letter saying of Eliot: "He is a regular cedar-post, firm, sound, and always in the same place." And how much it would mean in the home, in the church and in the nation if more of Christ's disciples secretly became his disciples openly at least in this sense of neither parading their faith in vanity nor concealing their faith in fear! At the Republican Convention in 1956 a Notre Dame football coach told the delegates that "when the going gets tough, the tough get going." And how much it would mean in the home, in the church and in the nation if more of Christ's disciples secretly became his disciples openly at least in the sense that hardship and opposition are considered reasons not for surrender but for battle! Not long ago, a man who had just returned from the deep South was talking about the attitude of intelligent Negroes in that area today, and he said that this attitude was best described in two words: "No more." No more sitting in the back seats of busses. No more segregated drinking fountains. No more separate schools and hospitals. No more refusals to admit Negroes to the better restaurants and hotels. And how much it would mean in the home, in the church and in the nation if more of Christ's disciples secretly became his disciples openly at least in this sense that—across the whole sweep of our social concerns—they dig in their heels, put a halt to their steady retreat and call for a counter-attack!

I am not talking about idealism now. I am not talking about the saintliness which is available only to hypocrites. I am not talking about the priggish prattle which vows that it would gladly do if it could what everybody knows that it can't but refuses to do when it can what everyone knows that it could. I am talking about Christians sober enough to understand that if this is really God's world, the only realism lies in doing God's will. I am talking about Christians saintly enough to know that they are sinners and that their only hope of forgiveness lies in the dedication of their imperfections to the service of him whose strength is made perfect in weakness. I am talking about Christians who mean what they say and say what they mean and daily doing the good that daily lies before them, leave the impossible in the hands of him with whom all things are possible. If these are they who love the Lord, these, too, are they whom the love of the Lord sustains; for if God desires faithfulness, will he then desert the faithful?

In the only sermon of James which the Bible preserves there is a short sentence which combines a command with a promise: "Resist the devil and he will flee from you." Are not these both the commission and the assurance of the Christian? Disciples secretly, we are called to be disciples openly: we are summoned to resist the demonic in the name of the holy. And standing on the rock that Christ provides, we are not to be afraid; for the gates of hell—or the powers of death—shall not prevail against it.

Sermon Eight

IN SEARCH OF A PLOT

Bishop Gerald Kennedy, Ph.D., D.D., LL.D., Litt.D., L.H.D., H.H.D.

Resident Bishop of the Los Angeles Area, The Methodist Church, Los Angeles, California, and President of the Board of Bishops of The Methodist Church

Bishop Kennedy's dramatic and dynamic preaching has earned him a place in the ranks of the world's great contemporary preachers. In this sermon he challenges the intellectual and spiritual in man, defines the issue between religion and atheism, points to the meaning of history and life, and shows the place of faith in attaining meaning for each man's life.

The Bishop has preached in many parts of the world and has traveled for the Methodist Church, visiting world wide mission fields. He has given the Beecher Lectures on Preaching at Yale and the Auburn Lectures at Union. He tries to make administration second to his preaching, yet he is an able executive. He has established a new theological seminary in Los Angeles and has directed his ministers in the building of many new churches.

Born in Michigan in 1907, Gerald Kennedy studied at the College of the Pacific and the Pacific School of Religion, then took his Ph.D. at Hartford Theological Seminary in 1934. He was ordained a Methodist minister in 1932 and began his ministry as pastor of First Congregational Church, Collinsville, Connecticut, 1932-36. He was appointed to Calvary Methodist Church, San Jose, California, in 1936, and to First Methodist Church, Palo Alto, in 1940. He was Acting Professor of Religion at the Pacific School of Religion from 1936 to 1940.

His talent for public leadership was first evident when he became pastor of St. Paul Methodist Church in 1942. There his preaching, influence in university circles, and participation in community work made him one of the important men in the city and state. In 1948 he was elected a Bishop of the Methodist Church and was Bishop of the Portland Area until in 1952 he became Bishop of the Los Angeles Area. This area includes Southern California, Arizona and the Hawaiian Islands. He has been President of the Board of Bishops of the Methodist Church since 1958.

He is a director of the Rockefeller Brothers Theological Fellowship Program and a trustee of the Pacific School of Religion, Southern California School of Theology, the College of the Pacific, and California Western University. His books include: *His Word Through Preaching, The Lion and the Lamb, Go Inquire of the Lord, God's Good News, I Believe, The Methodist Way of Life, The Reader's Notebook, The Second Reader's Notebook, The Christian and His America, I Believe.*

Bishop Kennedy has received ten honorary doctorates, including the D.D. from Pacific School of Religion, Redlands University, and Bucknell University, the LL.D. from the College of Puget Sound; the Litt.D. from Nebraska Wesleyan University, and the H.H.D., from Bradley University.

IN SEARCH OF A PLOT

> So teach us to number our days that we may get us a heart of wisdom.
>
> Psalm 90:12

There came to my desk, sometime ago, a literary magazine with a very curious announcement about a novel by Marc Saporta, a French experimentalist—whatever that is. The title is *Composition #1*. The book is unbound and comes in an envelope with its pages unnumbered. The reader shuffles the pages as he would a deck of cards and according to this chance arrangement, the story will take shape.

It came to me that here we have a literary device which reflects the spirit of the time. We assume that life has no real meaning and the sequence of its events is in no way ordered or significant. Life is not a story written in a book with covers and numbered pages, but according to the contemporary viewpoint, it can best be expressed through random sheets of paper with neither numbers nor binding. Such an attitude suggests that it matters very little, if at all, what is first or what is last since none of it is of much importance.

Underneath external signs of our contemporary spiritual and moral sickness, there is the widespread loss of meaning. This is the root of the illogical outbursts of teen age violence. Here is the mad hunger to belong to something, even a hate-group, and seek some satisfaction in suicidal destruction. We doubt that life has a plot, or a purpose, or a point. The fear that haunts us springs out of a suspicion that nothing matters beyond the moment. Or to put it in the framework of our thought, we search in vain for a plot for our allotted days. The psalmist in spite of terrifying questions and a fearful sense of the briefness of his life can still pray for grace to number his days that his heart may find wisdom. There is still in his mind the hope for understanding, but for so many of us there is neither faith nor hope. We can never find our way nor can we serve this age until we acknowledge and confront this condition.

I

We should begin with the recognition that here is the issue between religion and atheism. No one has ever found a definition of religion that is entirely satisfactory, and perhaps no one ever will. There are always exceptions to the general description and every man says that the definition does not get to the heart of what he knows religion to be. This is because defining is primarily a matter of comparing and when you face something unique, there is no basis for comparison. It is not like anything else and so we grope for words, or analogies, or figures of speech to help us say the unsayable. It is thus with religion.

With no idea of giving any final definition, but in the hopes of a gesture in the right direction, let me suggest that the religious man believes on the basis of his experience, that life has a plot, while the irreligious man denies it. This rising atheistic tide of meaninglessness has overwhelmed many and threatens to destroy civilization. The crisis is spiritual and the healing must be religious.

There are reasons for the acuteness of the crisis at this particular time. We are at the end of a long process of "ensmalling" human life. The almost complete capture of our imaginations by science has turned us into idolators of gods and closed our minds to God. We have put scientism in place of life and bowed before the arrogance of claims which have denied the reality of the unseen. We have assumed, often unconsciously, that the clue to human nature is to be sought in animals. Human behavior has been explained by way of rats in a maze or dogs being conditioned, or apes following their instincts in the jungle.

We are the victims of two world wars followed by a morale-destroying depression, followed by a long and discouraging cold war. The sheer size and immensity of things overwhelms us. Who can visualize a billion dollars, to say nothing of a country that can produce five hundred billion dollars in a year? The poor fellow who is worrying about paying back his household loan to the finance company, feels that he does not count in the world. There was a time when the world seemed a large place and a trip around the world was a considerable undertaking. Today the small boy who is told his father is going around the world is likely to ask: "How many times?"

This is the space age and distance is measured in light years. Who can possibly imagine the distance of a light year? Light travels at 286,000 miles a second. Now multiply the number of seconds in a year by 286,000 and you get a figure that is beyond most of our minds to grasp even dimly. Then think of 100 light years distance and see what it does to you. And all of this is space in which our earth is a speck.

When the Bible assumes that God and man are engaged in a continuing dialogue, the man of our time shakes his head in bewilderment. How can it be that a creature on this minute planet would dare to assume that he might engage the great God of outer space? If he hears a Christian talk about "the plan of salvation," he turns away in pity that anyone should think that God is concerned with man in any way at all. So we tend to become like the playwright pouring over the New York City telephone book. "No plot," he said, "but what a cast!" There was Pirandello's play with the title: "Six Characters in Search of an Author." Only with us it is millions of men who doubt that there is any author to be in search of.

Now facing this situation, Christianity makes three affirmations.

II

The first proposition of our Christian Faith is: Man is something special. This is said too simply, no doubt, but it is the heart of it. The religious man would not deny that man is a part of nature, but he would say with the old Scotch theologian that nature "is not as natural as it looks."

The long warfare between science and religion has much to be decried from both sides. There was often arrogancy instead of humility and too often there was fear in place of faith. The battle was fought often on the wrong fields and for the wrong objectives. But from religion's side there was a sense of doing battle for the meaning of human life and recognition of a duty to attack anything which made man merely a part of the natural world. Sometimes unexpressed or expressed in wrong terms, religion is always trying to defend man's dignity against definitions and attitudes which would destroy it.

The debate over evolution is something more than just a struggle between obscurantism and enlightenment. It involves more than a literal interpretation of the Scriptures as against a critical point of view. The issue often unexpressed and indeed unrecognized, has been the place of man in the order of things. For it has always been easy to assume that if man merely evolved, he was no more than the beasts. If he began humbly and naturally, can we speak of his glory or his divine destiny?

Loren Eisley's *The Immense Journey* is a naturalist's story of the world and the development of life. The title is itself significant for a journey assumes a purpose. One of the main points of the book is that man's appearance and growth came like a sudden explosion, so far as geological time is concerned. Eisley speaks of the miracle that man was achieved and lists four impossible conditions to be fulfilled.

1. His brain had almost to treble in size.
2. This had to be effected, not in the womb, but rapidly, after birth.
3. Childhood had to be lengthened to allow this brain, divested of most of its precise instinctive responses, to receive, store, and learn to utilize what it received from others.
4. The family bonds had to survive seasonal mating and become permanent, if this odd new creature was to be prepared for his adult role.

Nobody knows, says this writer, what touched it off centuries ago. One feels that he is about ready to say that natural processes cannot explain it and man means God. It is almost as if this is the only thing left to say but he controls himself because he is a naturalist and must keep the respect of his colleagues.

For the religious man, however, no such restraint is necessary. The Psalmist says:

> The heavens are telling the glory of God; and the firmament proclaims his handiwork. (Psalm 19:1)

And what about man in such a world?

> Yet thou hast made him a little less than God, and dost crown him with glory and honor.
>
> Thou hast given him dominion over the works of thy hands; thou hast put all things under his feet . . . (Psalm 8:5-6)

It is man's potential and the hidden power within him that impresses the Psalmist.

What is a man worth? Jesus speaks of a lost sheep sought by the shepherd after the ninety-nine are safe in the fold. He tells of a lost son for whom the father waits patiently and forgivingly. It was Jesus Christ who showed what man is and what man is to be. Says the author of *Hebrews* after quoting the 8th Psalm celebrating man's dominion over all creatures: "As it is, we do not yet see everything in subjection to him. But we see Jesus . . ." (2:8-9) And that is the climax of the whole promise and the basis for the Christian faith in man.

There is a small lake in Minnesota called Itasca. A visitor noticed a small overflow at one end and said to a fisherman: "The lake is leaking." The man replied, "Mister, that ain't no leak. That's the Mississippi River." So to those who would ensmall man, the Bible speaks of the mighty flow and the majestic wonder of a creature made by the hand of God and in His image. Man's book of life is something special indeed for the pages are numbered and it has a plot.

III

Christianity's second affirmation is that history means something. We who have grown up in the Christian tradition, simply assume this, but actually it is an unusual belief. Some religions find history an embarrassment and they either ignore it or deny it. To such religions, history is but an appearance which can teach us nothing, or a conglomeration from which we must extricate ourselves as soon as possible. They believe that man's spirit is contaminated by the blood and sweat of his earthy struggle and their promise is release from the whole sorry mess. History, they would say, has no meaning and man has nothing better to do than escape from it.

That history has meaning is denied by a number of historians and philosophers. The French proverb that the more it changes the more it is the same thing, expressed this viewpoint. To these scholars, history is like a child lost in the woods who wanders for hours. Suddenly he recognizes familiar objects and knows that he has gone in a circle and is back where he started. The idea of a beginning or an ending is denied. Indeed, the whole philosophy of progress is interpreted by these people as an illusion of man's pride.

The professional historian is very wary of admitting anything like a pattern or a meaning in history. He takes a dim view of Arnold Toynbee who dares to draw lessons from the rise and fall of civilizations. Obviously there are reasons for this attitude and they are good ones. But if man is something special then his story must be more than a series of unrelated happenings. At least that is what the Bible assumes.

History according to our Faith is the story of God's dealing with men. It has a plan with a purpose and in the events of human experience, God reveals His nature and His will. There is revealed in history no "Unmoved

Mover" but One who is not a gentleman but so involved in the human story that He is down in the muck and grime of the struggle. And, in some strange way, we are all involved in these happenings. So when the Jew speaks of the Egyptian slavery, he does not refer to something that happened to his ancestors but he says, "I was a slave in Egypt."

The life of Israel becomes a microcosm of all history. Without any fear of the scandal of particularity, the Bible tells the story of a particular people as if it had universal significance. For all men are offered the covenant with God and all men know slavery, freedom, exile, sin and hope. Here is the old, old story which is ever new. Here is the essential record of God at work.

But the main clue to history's meaning is the birth, the life, the death, and the resurrection of Jesus Christ. Here is revealed the nature of God who is our Father and the nature of the Kingdom which is love. The universe is not just brute force or meaningless activity. There is a more than human power making for righteousness and the world operates within the framework of moral law. It is in the historical appearance of Jesus, born at a certain time in a certain place and crucified under a certain Roman official, that God reveals himself completely. Jesus is the assurance that human history has meaning.

A friend of J. P. Morgan the Elder is supposed to have asked him what the stock market was going to do, thinking, no doubt, that he might get a valuable tip for an investment. Mr. Morgan merely replied: "It is going to fluctuate." But when the Christian wants to know something about history, he gets a better word than that it is going to fluctuate. He looks to Jesus Christ and he learns that history has spiritual and moral meaning because God is in it and God has something on His mind.

IV

The third affirmation a Christian makes is the result of the two we have been discussing. He proclaims that each man's life has meaning. An individual life is not a series of unnumbered pages in an envelope, but a book with a plot. That is why my favorite reading is biography or autobiography. No matter how poorly such books may be written, they are never dull. If a man will talk about his own experiences naturally and give his own ideas briefly, he will hold my attention. There is just nothing in the world as interesting as a man's life and we are driven to the conclusion that there is nothing more important. So our religion stands on the fundamental assumption that each man's life is of ultimate worth.

The crucial issue of our time is whether this faith shall prevail over the atheistic denial of it. A man told me one day that Methodism must not allow a pacifist position because it is communistic. I asked him if he had ever been to Russia, or knew what happens to conscientious objectors in that country. I asked if he thought the communist conquests had been accomplished without military activity. Of course he is simply a fellow who calls everything communistic he disapproves. But the real issue in the present struggle is the worth of the individual. Communism says he can be sacrificed for the good of the whole. A million farmers can be killed in the name of some future ideal. But the Christian denies that philosophy and proclaims the ultimate dignity of every man who must never be regarded as a means to an end.

I would have liked to hear the opponents of the nuclear test-ban treaty face the issue of deformed children as a result of the continuing contamination of the atmosphere by atomic fall-out. It was never mentioned and if it had been faced, the argument would have been about the percentage who might be affected. Woe to a people who think of percentages instead of individuals. One child deformed, if it is your child or mine, is enough to condemn the whole horrid procedure.

We are restored to sanity only when we respect every man and regard each child as a final trust. Dr. Albert Schweitzer put it very well when he urged a reverence for all life. We cannot prosper when men doubt their own importance and thus our future is dependent upon our faith in the potential greatness of each man. If we turn life into pages to be shuffled at will, we deny our heritage and we destroy our future.

One of the best known American epitaphs was written by Benjamin Franklin for himself and appeared in a 1771 almanac. Here it is:

The Body of Benjamin Franklin,
Printer,
Like the Covering of an old Book,
Its Contents torn out,
And stript of its Lettering and Gilding,
Lies here, Food for Worms;
But the Work shall not be lost,
It will (as he believed) appear once more,
In a new and more beautiful Edition,
Corrected and amended
By the Author.

On this note let us close. For man's life not only has a plot, but the wonderful assurance of our Lord is that it is an eternal one.

Sermon Nine

THE RECOVERY OF COURAGE

REVEREND CARLYLE MARNEY, TH.D., LITT.D.
Minister, Myers Park Baptist Church, Charlotte, North Carolina

A native of Tennessee, Carlyle Marney was born at Harriman, July 8, 1916, and attended Carson-Newman College and Southern Baptist Theological Seminary, where he received his Th.D. Wake Forest College conferred the honorary Litt.D. in recognition of his work.

He served for ten years at First Baptist Church, Austin, Texas, and was at the same time Professor of Christian Ethics at Austin Presbyterian Seminary. He became Senior Minister of Myers Park Church in 1958.

He has beeen Peyton Lecturer at Southern Methodist University (1962); Wells Lecturer at Texas Christian University (1961); Cunningham Lecturer at Austin College (1962); Willson Lecturer at Texas Technological College and Trinity University (1957, 1961); Meredith Lecturer (1957); Convocation Lecturer for the Summer Institute, Princeton Theological Seminary (1960, 1962) and at Union Theological Seminary (1961). He has also been occasional preacher at Harvard Memorial, Battell Chapel (Yale), Rockefeller Chapel (Chicago), Duke Chapel, Colgate-Rochester, Andover-Newton, and more than fifty other colleges and universities. He has traveled extensively in South America, Alaska and the Yukon Territory, Korea, and Japan. He has preached at many army and air force bases and was a missioner to the Far East Air Forces.

Dr. Marney is the author of several books: *Faith in Conflict, Beggars in Velvet, Structures of Prejudice, The Recovery of the Person,* and *He Became Like Us.* He has contributed articles to various theological journals and his sermons have appeared in several published collections.

He has served on the Study Committees of the World Council of Churches, the Theological Commission of the Baptist World Alliance, is a trustee for the *Christian Century,* Mars Hill College, and a member of the Editorial Council of *Theology Today.*

THE RECOVERY OF COURAGE

At least a half dozen times in recent months some older resident has asked, "Where is your church anyhow?" This is an immoral thing that the church should be so hard to find. And men should not have to depend on newspaper advertising to learn its street address. For the church that has not lost its courage will never have to advertise its location. There is something immoral in buying a certain size and number of ads to make up in attention gotten for what we fail to be and do.

When Paul came to Athens they said, "Let us hear what this 'seed-picker' has to say." I would not mind being classed as a "seed-picker," one who lives on market-place litter, if it meant that the courage of the church were such that a man could preach his gospel without reserve. But who would ever expect to hear anything *new* at church? You don't go to church for this. You go to have your flag waved, your religious hair curled, and to sing *old* songs—meaning those written fifty years ago for use under canvas, not in church!

Not many people truly look to the churches to say the things that need to be said in the front of the life of our time. And *the most awful social fact of our time is that there is in all the Western world no single social evil, no corporate evil, that alert, committed, courageous, free-churches could not have conquered.*

The man who taught me to read Ephesians also told me what the church is when it is Church. The church is God's creation and channel for his own achievement of his own purpose in human and universal history. The church is Christ's necessary completing counterpart, embodying his divine personality as the redeeming and consummating agency of God's love for a sinful world. The church, and all the saints, are dependent upon the spirit of God to unite, sanctify, empower for their function as the saving enlightening factor in history. The church is controlled by enunciated principles of God's purposive action in history and is situated in juxtaposition with, counter to, and occupied with this present human environment.

Months ago John DeFoore wrote from Edinburgh to say the same thing in easier words:

Today I stood in Rainey Hall amidst its traditional, stately, quiet, stern beauty. I have never seen as many colors, nationalities and races, nor heard as many different tongues and dialects. No light, except a dimness that filtered through smokey stained glass windows. And then tall gray-haired Watts stood up and called all the way to heaven—as if he were Moses and all the nations waited on his prayer. He prayed for . . . *the redemption* of the whole world! Something in my soul stirred that had never moved before—

John was just in Church, that's all. It ought to happen to you. It does happen to you when the church gets its courage back and is the Church. And this you do not have to advertise in newspapers. Not when the church is Church.

A deadly timidity characterizes the American church as a whole and all congregations in particular. We bring up our big guns for horse racing in San Antonio, or a prison rodeo on Sunday, or a new beer permit, or a county dry-election, but the timidity of approaching death characterizes the churches on anything of major importance. We find it grossly uncomfortable to run the risks of being out in front in anything; to go counter to our cultural patterns; to cut across established class lines. Consequently we are always being run over from the rear by that other kind of church which is at "the left hand of God."

I once saw a huge, ungainly cow, bawling and galloping down a narrow-gauge track just ahead of a chuffing little mountain engine and its train of timber cars. She was not leading a parade; she was being chased! The church has lost heart for the task. And because we have lost our fight, we have lost rank, position, station, and stature. No one outside really expects the modern churchman to have anything to say worth hearing. A friend of mine on the philosophy faculty of a good university mentioned to a colleague in his department that he frequently slipped in to hear me preach. "Why on earth would you go down there?" he asked, as if it were an idiotic waste of time. He knew the church had lost its confidence in its mission, its sense of being sent to redeem the whole world, and that it had therefore lost its heart for contact with its enemies.

I am reminded of a man who came out for football in my college days. The first day he turned out for practice he was the finest physical specimen I had ever seen! Six-feet-four, 234 pounds, not an ounce of fat on him, and with shoulder pads he looked like a General Sherman tank. But we discovered the first day of scrimmage that on the line you could open him like a gate, an unlatched gate. He had no heart for contact. In fact, he wasn't there for the rough work inside the twenty yard line. He was there to kick the extra points after someone else had scored!

After someone else scores! The Church, by and large, speaks *grandiozo* on very minor themes. We speak *sotto voce*, with a little voice, if at all, on major matters. And in areas crying for action, we delay interminably, then appoint a committee.

A current question reads, "Is there a revival of religion in America?" This is one of the most ridiculous questions of the last one hundred years. It is foolish to debate it. If there were a revival going on some of the homes splitting at the seams would know it. The first fresh fires of a new fidelity, and a new integrity would have begun to purge and heal. Some of the peace, joy, and confidence would be restoring that most fragile of relationships, the home. We will not have to debate its existence when revival comes. But too many things are not right in Christian churches.

We have a reputation for provincial backwardness. Who could expect a church to be open-minded. We have a record of barrenness in worship. It is such a vicious thing that not many would look for beauty in church, and some are shocked to find beauty here. Our reputation for social lethargy is such that no one would expect any church to act ahead of a university, or a big league ball club, or a theater, or a school board. Our record on the erection of social structures denies our word about freedom. We will let any man have his freedom for a while, but his ears will be pinched eventually, I think. And the church has such a reputation for fuzzy thinking that no one would expect any real clarity from its pulpits.

When these things are true, people say, "Where is your church anyhow?" And those of us up close to hear it say, "We just need to do more advertising." I submit that so long as a man has to ask where it is, it doesn't matter much where or whether it is. And when he does know where it is, truly, this is not geographical information. This is spiritual knowledge which results from his exposure to something he considers to be important and fresh, new, thrilling, even compelling. Then, he says, "Come, hear a man and a people who feel like Church!"

The church which fears a new position, the church which lurks timidly in the crowd, loses itself in the rush of the city. The church that will not speak like a cross-roads church is shunted to a side-street, because it has no word truly for our current needs, our social ills, our contemporary sins. For the church, without its courage, has no new word to utter, because it has received no fresh word from God, and expects none. Therefore, such a church seldom has a relevant word. Any relevance it has is accidental for it has lost its Lord, and therefore, its road, and therefore it loses its language, its power, and its hearing. Because it lost earlier its courage, it now settles down in the culture that gives it its life and its heresy. Without its courage it is no church.

II

Now what is wanted, to get us our courage back? What is desired, if we would take our city's heart? What must we gain if we would be the church? Where is this deeper quality of zest for living to be found? Must we seek a different spirit and a better source?

A year ago, late on an afternoon, as I turned in our drive, to my horror, my surprised chagrin, there, big as life, leaning up against the receptacles of garbage waiting for the city truck, was the beautiful walnut head-board of the first piece of furniture we had owned. It had been sawed-off and thrown away! That precious old relic we had bought to start life with—sawn asunder and thrown away! I entered with fear and trembling. I wondered what other old relic might have to go! It was a new day. I anticipated with bated breath the new zest, other changes, a different spirit. And it was all there. My wife had gotten up her courage to throw some old things away! And out of this, came, as always, that clean and courageous feeling of something fine accomplished. The church, too, has some things to throw away!

About a month before old enmities were thrown away and the Austin Association admitted Negro Churches to its fellowship, a great debate was on in the Minister's Council. Eventually, one of the older, more conservative brethren got the floor, and I shall never forget it. He told of his grandfather, how he had loved him, how great a soldier of the Confederacy he had been, and how as a little boy he had hung on the old man's words, had adored him, had followed him to the grave, brokenhearted, and how that sometime he would see him again. But that for now, he, in his sixties, a preacher of the Gospel for forty years, did publicly, once for all, renounce the social framework and the content of his grandfather's thinking, and that no matter how he loved, he would not be bound by the chains of his grandfather's thinking. And with tears, he took his stand with us, muttering as he did so that if the old man were alive he would have changed too! This is a *different* spirit, the one Paul prays might strengthen us with might.

And during Christmas I sat with Blake Smith in a coffee house and his tears spattered on the hard table top as he told me how it feels, after fifteen years, when your congregation rises up and takes an *action* which means you don't ever have to preach on that any more ever again. The people have done it! Wouldn't that be something! To know a congregation so close to Christ that on stewardship, and ethics, even racial matters, it would *do* the will of the Father?

III

What is wanted? Religion will never regain its old power, its old thrill, its old place until it can face change in the same spirit that science faces change. Professor Whitehead pointed out that the principles of faith are eternal, but the expression of those principles, the vehicle, the carriage, the bucket, the cup, the glass, the container for the expressions of faith, and the action resulting from faith—these must change, develop, seek new forms. Without this willingness to remodel the wagon, to overhaul the chassis, without the protestant principle of critical re-evaluation of our institutional bases, religion dies. Young men and women walk away from its sagging structures in droves. The death of religion comes with the death of any high hope of adventure. The moment your youngsters feel that nothing truly adventurous or daring or truly sacrificial will happen in this place they go looking for the place where such can be expected. Even a movie house may then offer better religious fare!

The recovery of our courage waits on the birth of a different spirit. Because what we seek is a *quality* of life it waits on a different spirit: a new *raison d'être*. Because a new spirit is required, the whole matter of recovery waits on our discovery of the great Source we have well-nigh abandoned. There must come now a new commitment to our Eternal Source.

As Markus Barth put it in a lecture at Chicago a year ago: "All true authority, be it of Jesus Christ, of an apostle, of father and mother, of the Word, . . . is derived from God . . . " Jesus and Paul and the devil and the Roman, Pilate, know this. All authority, even political power, is from God. The commitment, call, and claim on us in our time do not come from the Communist party, or the state of North Carolina, or the Supreme Court of the United States of America, or the Constitution, or the NAACP, or any one of the one thousand and three hundred fifty chartered do-good orders in America. Our charter, claim, and call come from Jesus as the Christ.

We must recover *this* source of our authority. We speak for God in Jesus Christ. If a man or a church become convinced in any culture that we must speak for Christ—we foreswear social acceptance, for we will speak of things that are not socially acceptable—we forego any insurance of tranquility, for we will be dealing with matters that are turbulent. We foredoom ourselves to isolation, we forsake the established, we foreshorten our peace when we speak for Christ.

This is how the United Brethren preacher, Kermit Eby, who was a professor of sociology at Chicago, got those scars on his soul: He was an original organizer of C.I.O. in Detroit, when the labor markets of this world were worse than white slave dens. This is how John Wesley, who never weighed more than eight stone in his life got those scars on his high bald forehead—scars he was still wearing at seventy-nine when he preached to four thousand miners on a smoky four o'clock in the morning.

When a church undergoes this commitment it foreswears, foregoes, foredooms, and forsakes, in the name of its commitment to its Eternal Lord, but it assures the recovery of its courage. And when courage comes back, nearly everything else comes back with it. And, most wonderful, joy! A church escapes that deadliest drip on the face of the earth: a hired clergyman, in the name of a petrified priesthood, slithering here and there among his erring people, culture, and church, exhaling a long and semi-agonized "Tut-Tut!"

Out in a Western state last summer an old man handed me a yellowed and ancient hand-written letter signed by a man whose name we know. It was dated:

Charlotte, North Carolina
April 23, 1865

and read:

Gallant Comrades: You have fought your fight; it is over. During four years struggle for liberty you have shown courage, fortitude, and devotion. You are the victors of more than 200 sternly contested fields; you have participated in more than a thousand passages of arms; you are heroes! The bones of your comrades lie in Kentucky, Tennessee, Virginia, North Carolina, South Carolina, Alabama, and Mississippi. You have done all that human exertion can accomplish. I bid you adieu.

I desire to give you my thanks for: your gallantry in battle; your fortitude under suffering; and your devotion to the holy cause you have maintained.

I . . . invoke upon you the blessings of our Heavenly Father to whom you must always look for support in this hour of distress.

Brethren, in the cause of freedom, comrades in arms, I bid you adieu.

Joe Wheeler, Major General
C.S.A.

The address to his command
at their surrender
Charlotte, April 23, 1865

I could not yet read this over myself, or over you, if the fight were done and we had been whipped, or had won! We are more or less like Longstreet's forces the first day at Gettysburg; we are not yet committed to battle. Indeed, we are not yet sure it is our fight. It's comfortable here in the trees. But out in front of us goes the long thin crawling line that will be mentioned five hundred years from now; like Picketts' twelve thousand; the line of those men and women of no church, on God's left hand, who do God's will and work in the name of social justice, if not the name of Jehovah.

The Churches will linger in the woods, without that new spirit and new source which must precede the recovery of our courage. And this war we are in, against principalities and powers—this is every man's warfare.

Sermon Ten

TWO MARKS OF A CHRISTIAN

REVEREND JAMES T. CLELAND, TH.D., D.D.

Dean of the Chapel and James B. Duke Professor of Preaching, Duke University Divinity School, Durham, North Carolina, and a Minister of the Presbyterian Church

Dr. Cleland has a vitality and a glow in his preaching that captures the imagination and the heart. As a preacher to university students his sermons have an intellectual content which makes them stimulating. And in his preaching for important churches everywhere he preaches a religion that sings. In his teaching of preaching at Duke he emphasizes the importance of preaching in the Christian Church.

Born in Glasgow, Scotland, in 1903, he attended school there, graduated from Glasgow University in 1924 and served as assistant in three parishes of the Church of Scotland during his theological training. He graduated from Glasgow University Divinity Hall in 1927, with distinction in the study of ecclesiastical history. Shortly after this he came to America and was appointed to the Jarvie Fellowship at Union Theological Seminary in New York, then returned to Scotland on the Black Fellowship at Divinity Hall, Glasgow University. From 1929 until 1931 he was Faulds Teaching Fellow at the University; in 1931 Amherst College called him to its Department of Religion.

In 1938 he was ordained a minister of the Presbyterian Church, U.S.A.; he spent 1938 and 1939 on leave of absence in Europe and the Near East. In 1944-45 he did graduate work at Union, and in 1945 was appointed Preacher to the University and Professor of Preaching in the Divinity School of Duke. In the summers of 1948 and 1955 he was guest Professor of Homiletics at Union Seminary. In 1954 he received the Th.D. from Union. In 1953 he delivered the Frederic Rogers Kellogg Lectures at the Episcopal Theological School, Cambridge, Massachusetts; these were published as *The True and Lively Word.* He has also given the Hoyt Lectures, the Wells Lectures, and the Perkins Lectures. He gave the Warrack Lectures at the Scottish Universities in 1964. He has contributed three expositions to *The Expositor's Bible* and writes a bimonthly article for *The Chaplain* under the heading, "Preacher's Clinic." *Wherefore Art Thou Come* was published in 1961.

Dr. Cleland, widely sought as a preacher, is on the regular list of guest or visiting preachers at Riverside Church, New York, and at many other churches, colleges, universities, and preparatory schools. At Amherst and again at Duke his love of soccer led him to coach the soccer teams with success. His preaching in the ideal setting of the Chapel of Duke University with its magnificent stained glass and wonderful organ is very popular with faculty and students.

TWO MARKS OF A CHRISTIAN

One of the questions which all of us have heard, and some of us have asked, over and over again, is: "What are the distinguishing marks of a Christian?" This may be answered in various ways. But, almost without exception, Jesus of Nazareth, who was called the Christ, finds a place in the reply. Today we shall look together at an answer suggested in the morning lesson (Acts 1:15-16) and try to find its relevance for us.

This passage describes the first official meeting of the early church. There was but one item of business on the agenda (most lucky meeting!): namely, the appointment of a successor to Judas Iscariot, that complex figure who had separated himself from them. Peter, who presided, laid down the qualifications necessary, in verses 21 and 22:

> So one of the men who have accompanied us during all the time that the Lord Jesus went in and out among us, beginning from the baptism of John until the day when he was taken up from us—one of these men must become with us a witness to his resurrection (R.S.V.).

Two names were put forward. One—Matthias—was chosen by lot, after prayer. The two emphases stated by Peter are still two of the essential marks of a Christian.

I

The first mark is an intimate knowledge of the earthly life of Jesus, of his walk and conversation in the days of his flesh. Matthias was chosen because he was one of those who had been with Jesus throughout his active ministry. He knew "the facts" about Jesus. What are some of these facts? Jesus had been brought up in Nazareth with four brothers and, at least, two sisters. He had been educated in the local synagogue. He was at home with nature. He enjoyed the ordinary person in the market place. He had come under the influence of John the Baptist, and had identified himself with that movement. In the temptation experience he had faced the problems of the content and of the possible reception of his message. The Galilean mission had moved along successfully. People swarmed to hear both what he said and how he said it. But he had so aroused the hostility of Church and State, the Pharisees and the Herodians, that he was forced to leave the country for his own personal safety. Then followed the strange days at Caesarea Philippi. There he accepted the title Messiah, but interpreted it in so unusual a way that not one of the twelve had understood its meaning. He walked gallantly into that last week in Jerusalem, which opened with shouts of "Hosanna" and ended with cries of "Crucify him."

There was more than that to it. He was a teacher, and his teaching had centered on God, on God thought of as a "Father": one who creates, sustains, comforts, disciplines, and redeems. Man is supposed to behave as a son of that kind of father. If he does, he will be blessed, that is, happy away deep down inside of him. If, on the other hand, he refuses, then judgment will result. There are goats as well as sheep. Jesus was a stern man with humbugs. No one can accuse him of being either naive or mealy-mouthed.

The Crucifixion was followed by the almost unbelievable fact of the Resurrection and by the dramatic event of the Ascension. That is a too brief sketch of what a candidate for Judas' place among the apostles had to know.

Well, you say, such knowledge may have been possible for those who were with Jesus those three years of his public ministry, but is it still a distinguishing feature in the later history of the Church? It is. Look at one example which suggests that a knowledge of the earthly life of Jesus is one mark of the Christian.

Many people are surprised that there are so few references to the historic Jesus in the letters of Paul. They are few. Yet, let me read with you one of the best known Pauline passages. Here are four verses from the so-called "Hymn of Love" (I Corinthians 13:4-7), as translated in the Revised Standard Version:

> Love is patient and kind; Love is not jealous or boastful; it is not arrogant or rude. Love does not insist on its own way; it is not irritable or resentful; it does not rejoice at wrong, but rejoices in the right. Love bears all things, believes all things, hopes all things, endures all things.

Let us change one repeated word in that passage and also the tense of the verbs. Now, how does it read?

Jesus was patient and kind; Jesus was not jealous or boastful; Jesus was not arrogant or rude. Jesus did not insist on his own way; Jesus was not irritable or resentful; Jesus did not rejoice at wrong, but rejoiced in the right. Jesus bore all things, believed all things, hoped all things, endured all things.

Love was *the* quality of Jesus' earthly life. More than that, love was the *essence* of his being. Paul must have learned that from those who had companied with Jesus in Galilee. These verses in I Corinthians seem to be his veiled portrait, in miniature, of Jesus. Paul had steeped and soaked himself in the earthly life of the one whom he called Lord. Isn't this equally true of person after person, in century after century: Francis and Erasmus; Calvin and Luther; Wesley and Rauschenbusch?

We are being told today that it is impossible for us to recapture a true biography of Jesus of Nazareth; that there is really no point in setting out on a quest for the historic Jesus. The facts are just not there. Now, there is a measure of truth in this assertion. No evangelist tried to pen a paragraph of data about Jesus to be incorporated in a first century *Who's Who*. They told us what he meant to them. Moreover, each man wrote with his own particular bias. To Matthew, Jesus was the expounder of the New Law given on the Mount of the Sermon. The Fourth Gospel is an old man's reflections on Jesus as the Word of God incarnate. Modern attempts at biography are also the understandable outcome of predilection and conditioning. I think of three authors who have influenced me, despite, or because of, their bias. Klausner is a Jew who feels that Jesus misunderstood Judaism. Simkhovitch is an economic historian who depicts Jesus as attempting the solution of Jewish-Roman relations. Case is a historical pathologist who does an interesting post-mortem on Jesus, with almost a cold detachment.

Yet, there is a swing back to a new quest of the historic Jesus. Robert Aron, a Jew, has just produced a readable volume on *The Hidden Years*, an attempt to picture the kind of influences on Jesus in the thirty years before his baptism. Bornkamm in Europe and Robinson in America are seeking to find how the early church thought of Jesus, so as to discover the first interpretations of the man whom they called Lord. This new quest is a legitimate one, one in which we should join. Therefore, it is back to the Gospels for us, not read as a succession of verses to be divided into groups of ten for bed-time devotions. But back to the Gospels, on a desk, with commentaries, to be studied so that we may know, at least, more about what was said of him who is, under God, the founder of our faith. And there is no harm to supplementing the Gospels with modern studies, even attempts at biography.

For the first mark of a Christian, according to Peter, is that he has kept company with Jesus in his earthly ministry.

II

But, you say, isn't that the only mark of a Christian according to Peter? Yes and no. Peter extracted one item, one event, out of Jesus' life, and put the emphasis on it. The successor to Judas was chosen because he could do one thing: he could, and must, bear witness to the Resurrection.

The Resurrection was the utterly new fact about Jesus. The grave had not held him. He was raised from the dead, and he was seen. The man to take Judas' place must be a witness to the Resurrection. Now, the physical raising of Jesus from the dead, the resuscitation of his earthly body, is not the important fact for the New Testament writers. When they try to describe what actually happened on that first Easter Sunday, they are in both confusion and disagreement. Ask them three questions: Where was Jesus first seen after the Resurrection? To whom did he first appear? What kind of a body did he have? Listen to the discrepancies in the answers. The Gospels are in harmony on the fact of the Resurrection. They are not in unison on the details. Nevertheless, it is because of the Resurrection that Christianity is a religion independent of Judaism. Listen to Paul: "If Christ did not rise, then our preaching has gone for nothing, and your faith has gone for nothing too" (I Corinthians 15:14. Moffatt). If there had been no Resurrection, the followers of Jesus might well have become another sect within Judaism: the Nazarenes, like the Essenes and the Pharisees and the Sadducees. But the early church was so convinced that Jesus was not holden of death, that Matthias was chosen because he was able to witness to the Resurrection, and to continue witnessing.

In the long history of the Church, the Cross, rather than the Resurrection, has usurped for many people the central place in the faith. This is symbolized in the fact that "The Old Rugged Cross" is usually in first place in the popular vote for the favorite hymn. What would some of us prefer? Wouldn't it be another hymn of the Cross: "When I Survey the Wondrous Cross"? The Cross is important, meaningful, inescapable. Perhaps no one can really experience the joy of Easter unless he has sat in sorrow and in shame and in despair through the Three Hours Service on Good Friday. Three o'clock in the afternoon of the first Good Friday must have seemed to the followers of Jesus to be the ringing down of the curtain on a most unsatisfactory drama.

If the Cross were central, we should worship on Friday, on each Friday of each week. But we don't. We worship on Sunday. No, not really. We worship on the Lord's Day. The first day of every week is a little Easter. There was an English minister who, late in his ministry, discovered that Easter should be his focus rather than the Crucifixion. To symbolize his discovery, he had an Easter hymn sung at the morning service each Lord's Day. To acknowledge and ratify his discovery, we sang a hymn of the Resurrection today. We witness to the fact that ours is a Resurrection faith.

But it is impossible for us to be eye-witnesses of the Resurrection as Matthias was. We are chronologically defeated. May we be eye-witnesses as Paul was? In I Corinthians 15:1-9, Paul records the accepted list of Resurrection appearances, as he had received them. Then he adds: "Last of all, as to one untimely born, he [Christ] appeared also to me." Paul does not hesitate to equate the appearance of Jesus the Christ to him on the road to Damascus with the appearance to the other disciples in the forty days following the first Easter. Yet several years must have elapsed, because Paul was not a follower of Jesus during his earthly ministry. For Paul, the Resurrection is not primarily posited on the testimony of the early disciples, but on the living, working presence of the Spirit of Jesus the Christ to—and, finally, in—the believer. As Paul himself put it: "It is no longer I who live, but Christ who lives in me" (Galatians 2:20). He was not an *eye* witness *of* the Resurrection, as Matthias was. He was a witness *to* the Resurrection, i.e., *to* the living, working presence of the Christ within him. The earthly life of Jesus had revealed the *love* of God; the resurrection of Jesus had disclosed the *power* of God. That love and power were united for Paul in the spirit of the Christ which had captured his spirit, daily expressed in a love made potent by his confidence that this love was backed by the power of God. That is why he wrote: "love never ends . . . ; the greatest of these is love . . . ; make love your aim."

Where do we *today* find the fact of the Resurrection? Is it not in a person who evidences the power of love in action? The proof of the living Christ is in the daily expressions of good will. The author of the First Epistle of John knew that: "If we love one another, God abides in us, and his love is perfected in us" (4:12). Such a person, living lovingly, may not know that God is, who God is; but God, his Father, knows him. Love is the essence of God; love was the gospel of Jesus the Christ; love is the hallmark of a child of God, even of one who thinks he is a spiritual orphan. He who loves is born of God and kin to Jesus and a contemporary witness to the Resurrection.

Let me share with you an analogy which may help us to understand this experience. The Professor of Moral Philosophy at Glasgow University in my day was A. E. Bowman, who had come to Glasgow from Princeton. The impact of his teaching and his person was tremendous. He died very suddenly, and one of his students, reflecting on the matter, said something like this: "Bowman is dead. This is the end. No, Bowman is not dead. He was never more alive than he is today. As long as I live, and as long as hundreds of other students live, Bowman will continue to live. Because I live, yet not I, Bowman liveth in me." This is but an analogy. Yet it gives an insight into the domination of the life of the believer by the indwelling Christ.

For the second mark, the primary mark, of a Christian, according to Peter, is that he bear personal witness to the Resurrection.

III

In 1910, Albert Schweitzer, whom *Time* magazine has described as "the great man's great man," wrote a most significant book: *The Quest of the Historical Jesus*. It was a critical history of the efforts to recover the historic Jesus by setting him free from the graveclothes of theological dogma. Painstakingly, with Germanic thoroughness, Schweitzer worked his way down from 1778 to 1901. His conclusions disturbed the theological halls of Europe and of America. This suggests that we, too, may be in for surprises, if we seek to walk with Jesus from the baptism to the garden tomb, and the days thereafter. But Schweitzer's conclusions are not nearly as exciting as his commitment. Here is a sentence from the second last page of that long quest: "But the truth is, it is not Jesus as historically known, but Jesus as spiritually arisen within man, who is significantly for our time and can help it" (p. 399). You know the last paragraph of that book, probably the most quoted statement from all Schweitzer's writings. It is worth hearing over and over again: "He came to us as One unknown, without a name, as of old, by the lakeside, He came to those men who knew Him not. He speaks to us the same word: 'Follow thou me!' and set us to the tasks which He has to fulfil for our time. He commands. And to those who obey Him, whether they be wise or simple,

He will reveal Himself in the toils, the conflicts, the sufferings which they shall pass through in His fellowship, and, as an ineffable mystery, they shall learn in their own experience Who He is" (p. 401).

Knowledge, yes, but also, experience of Jesus—teaching, crucified, risen, indwelling—are still two of the marks of a Christian. Yet, the power of Christianity lies in the Resurrection. We do not know Christ until we have experienced the Resurrection in us. At the heart of our faith is one who lived in Palestine and one who is ready to live in us. It is to this that a Christian bears witness.

Sermon Eleven

MAN IN ORBIT: CHRIST IN HEAVEN

REVEREND DAVID HAXTON CARSWELL READ, D.D.

Minister, Madison Avenue Presbyterian Church, New York, New York

Year by year Dr. Read becomes more popular and more influential as a preacher at the famous Madison Avenue Presbyterian Church in New York. Born on January 2, 1910, at Cupar, Fife, Scotland, he attended Daniel Stewart's College in Edinburgh, and studied at the University of Edinburgh from 1928 to 1932, then at Montpellier, Strasbourg, and Paris (in 1932 and 1933), and at Marburg in 1934. He took his theological degree at New College, Edinburgh, and was ordained and installed at Coldstream West, Church of Scotland, in 1936. From 1939 to 1945 he was chaplain to the Forces of the British Army, and was a prisoner of war from June, 1940, to April, 1945.

From 1939 to 1949 he was minister of Greenbank Church, Edinburgh. He was the first chaplain to the University of Edinburgh, in 1949, and was appointed chaplain to Her Majesty the Queen in Scotland in 1952. When Madison Avenue Presbyterian Church in New York City sought a minister to succeed Dr. George Buttrick, Dr. Read was called, in January, 1956. He received the honorary D.D. from Edinburgh University in July, 1956.

He was Warrack Lecturer on Preaching at the University of Glasgow in 1950-51, Old Saint Andrew's Memorial Lecturer on Worship in Toronto in 1954, and George Shepard Lecturer on Preaching at Bangor Theological Seminary in 1959; he has led University Christian Missions in Scotland, Australia, Canada, and the United States. He has also had much experience in the field of radio and television.

Dr. Read has written *The Spirit of Life, Prisoners' Quest* (a collection of lectures given in prisoner of war camp), *Call It a Day, The Communication of the Gospel, The Christian Faith, I Am Persuaded* and *Sons of Anak.* He has also published articles in *The Scottish Journal of Theology, The Atlantic Monthly, The Expository Times,* and many other religious and secular journals.

His sermons for special occasions, such as his Christmas sermon-fantasy preached several years ago, *Star Out of Orbit* (included in Volume VIII of *Best Sermons*), and this Ascension Day message, attract wide and increasing attention.

MAN IN ORBIT: CHRIST IN HEAVEN

> Now that he ascended, what is it but that he also descended first into the lower parts of the earth? He that descended is the same also that ascended up far above all heavens, that he might fill all things.
>
> Ephesians 4:9, 10

Last Wednesday another brave man was projected into space and circled the earth twenty-two times while you and I went about our ordinary business. Astronaut Gordon Cooper now belongs to the small, historic group of trail-blazers into space who symbolize the new era that is dawning for mankind. The research, the scientific genius, the technological skills, the masterpiece of coordination that lie behind this enterprise are so astounding that we are left wondering what kind of world we are now living in, and where humanity is heading. As John Donne said in the sixteenth century, when scientific discovery, mental and moral revolution, and the exploration of what was called the "New World" were combining to excite and bewilder the minds of men: "This new philosophy calls all in doubt."

Next Thursday the Christian Church has called Ascension Day as a reminder of the tradition that forty days after Easter Christ ascended into heaven, and—continuing the words of the Creed—"sitteth on the right hand of God." I want to ask this morning if there is any possible connection between these two recorded events—the report in our newspapers of a man in orbit round the earth, and the report in the Bible and the Church of a man who ascended into heaven.

For some the answer is easy. The unbeliever simply says that while the record of the man in orbit is plain reporting of what happened last week, and can be verified by anyone who takes the trouble, the record of the man who ascended into heaven comes from an ancient document of a pre-scientific era that has been preserved by a Church that has an interest in fostering such myths. There is therefore no connection between the two whatever. The story of Gordon Cooper belongs to the future. It is a signal of events to come. The story of Jesus Christ belongs to the past. It is a fantasy from the childhood of the human race.

There are those who count themselves Christian believers who also see no connection between these two stories. I suppose there must be a lot of Church people who seldom feel any need to relate the doctrines they profess to the world picture of modern science and its spectacular achievements. There is a popular schizophrenia whereby religious ideas are tucked away in a special department of the mind, safely isolated from contact with the accepted facts of the secular world we live in. They are not denied, or even seriously questioned. They are simply kept from mixing with the assumptions of modern life. In recent years there has been a strong tendency to regard religion as a strictly private area where a man may indulge any kind of odd, or even ludicrous beliefs, without their affecting in any way his judgment as a scientist, historian, a statesman, or just a man of practical commonsense. And so the statements of the creeds and confessions of the Church are kept in a little black bag marked "For Sundays Only," and for one of them—say, the ascension of Jesus Christ—to pop out on a Wednesday morning as an astronaut was being blasted into space would be considered improper, alarming or absurd.

Yet there are a growing number of thoughtful Christians—many, I am sure, in this church today—who are not prepared either to throw overboard their religious convictions or to isolate them from the facts of life in 1963. Religion for them is not a private indulgence unrelated to the implications of the age of space, or the decisions imposed by our turbulent era. Doctrines for them are not ancient symbols to be acknowledged in church and ignored in Wall Street, Washington, or Cape Canaveral. When they profess a belief in Jesus Christ they believe that he is *the* way, *the* truth, and *the* life—not just a religious way, a religious truth, and a religious life. So they are ready to examine any traditional dogma in the light of the discoveries and events of our day, and they expect to find that the Gospel of Jesus Christ will offer guidance and illumination in every area of human life, no matter how far our horizons are extended.

When I speak about a connection between a modern probe into outer space and the doctrine of the Ascension of Jesus Christ I have to clear up one possible misunderstanding right away. We are not talking about two different methods of doing the same thing—that is, soaring off from this earth into the skies above. I hardly need to say that to an instructed Christian congregation, yet lots of people still think that this is what we do mean by Ascension, and I suppose all of us have some lingering picture from our childhood of Jesus disappearing into the clouds and eventually arriving at a place called heaven. We can not begin to understand the real meaning of the Ascension till we rid our minds of any notion that this was a kind of first-century space-flight. The belief that Jesus Christ "ascended into heaven" is not a statement about a physical movement of a body in space, but a proclamation of the ultimate power and authority in the universe of this Man who was crucified "under Pontius Pilate." Heaven is the actual presence of God, the invisible dimension where his will is infallibly done. It is the ultimate reality that lies behind all that we see and know and experience every day. And when we say that Christ is *there* we mean that his ministry did not close when he was no longer seen on earth but that he is alive and active for ever, identical with the God from whom he came. This is the real miracle with which we are confronted—that Jesus Christ now reigns as Lord, that the love and truth we find in him are at the very center of all that is, the guiding and creative power we give the name of God. That is hard enough for us to believe, but we should not be distracted from it by an effort to conceive of a literal projection of Christ's body upward to some location in outer space.

It is often alleged that this is a modern reinterpretation of what the Bible says, a way of wriggling out of literal statements that we can no longer accept. It is true that Scripture writers operated with a picture of the universe startlingly different from ours, but it has been too easily assumed that they all had a simple literal picture of heaven, earth and hell—the "three-story universe" our demythologizers are for ever talking about. What does St. Paul actually say in our text? "He that descended is the same also that ascended up far above all heavens, *that he might fill all things*." The New English Bible translates "so that he might fill the universe." Does that sound as though St. Paul thought that Christ was actually located somewhere in space? A word like this gives us a flash of insight into the thinking of the apostle and the early Church. When they spoke of Christ's ascent into heaven they no more thought of a journey to a point so many miles away than when they spoke of his heavenly position they imagined, like the little boy in the story, that God couldn't move his right hand because Jesus was sitting on it. We must give Bible writers the credit for having at least as much imagination and common sense as we have. To express a mystery like that of Jesus Christ "filling the universe" we have to use some metaphor, some picture-language. St. Paul likes to use a phrase like "ascended up far above all heavens." For some reason this worries the modern mind. If he had said "penetrated to the inner depth of being" somehow that would have made it all perfectly respectable.

But what, someone may want to ask, is the historic fact on which this doctrine is built—if it is not sheer myth? The answer can be simply stated. The Gospels tell us that the disciples saw Jesus alive after his crucifixion.

These were fleeting glimpses, enough to convince them that he was really there, the same Lord now resurrected. Then the glimpses ceased. As St. Luke put it: "he was parted from them." That raised a problem. Where was he? The Ascension is the answer that was given them. It was the assurance that this same Jesus was now the Lord who filled the universe, the cosmic Christ, united with his Father in heaven and His Spirit on earth—One God for ever.

The passage from the Epistle to the Ephesians we read this morning is often used in a church like ours to encourage and instruct us to be a real family of Christ, "keeping the unity of the Spirit in the bond of peace." It brings before us both the unity of our fellowship and the diversity of our gifts. And often, I must confess, when reading it I have been tempted to skip the words of our text, which our Bibles have bracketed off. All this about "ascending and descending" seems to interrupt the flow of the argument. Yet in a sense this is the mightiest parenthesis in all literature. For the apostle is telling us that the life of the Church, the gifts of each individual Christian, our growth into the stature of Christ, all depend on the fact that Jesus Christ not only came from God to reach down to the very lowest hell where man could be found, but has returned to God to be the ruler of all nature and human nature. To believe in the Ascension then is not to be committed to some strange tale about a flight into space, but to live in the assurance that, in spite of all human confusion and wickedness, in spite of all demonic forces that seek man's destruction, Christ reigns—and he is the ultimate reality with whom we have to do.

Now let's return to the astronaut. What is the real significance of this probe into space? Surely it is not just the temporary excitement of a brave modern explorer making his "Columbus circle" around the earth. Nor is it just the demonstration of the astonishing perfection of the instruments involved. It surely lies in the new direction being given to human history, the new horizons that are opening for the human spirit, the infinite new possibilities for good and for evil that are opening for the human race. It is too soon to be certain that humanity is indeed committed to the adventure into space. It could prove to be a cul-de-sac—from which we return a little wiser and much sadder. But all the indications are that we have entered a new era. The man in orbit is the precursor of the next stage in human development. His achievement raises all kinds of fascinating speculations about further discoveries among the planets, the colonization of the moon, the use of space for all kinds of control over the earth (sinister or beneficial), and a revolutionary extension of automation in the affairs of men.

At such a time, what is the duty of the Church? Some would suppose that her chief duty is to cry: "Stop! Come down!" like an anxious mother to the small boy climbing the back-yard tree, or to run flapping about like a hen watching her brood of ducklings making for the water. Others would have us capitulate to the materialist philosophy and find our god in the triumph of technology, abandoning any talk about the world of spirit, the supernatural, or a personal God. Surely what is needed above all is neither alarm, nor surrender, but a cool understanding of the central problem, and an expansion of our faith to meet it. That central problem remains man himself. There is a parable in the very fact of a man in orbit. It is argued that everything necessary can be done by automation, every adjustment made, every photograph taken, every piece of information collected. Yet we send a man up there, and already others are training for the landing on the moon.

The man in orbit reminds us that it is the mind of man that has penetrated the mysteries, that has devised the machines, that evaluates the results. The man in orbit reminds us that it is the will of man that decides to make this exploration, and the will of man that will decide how it is to be used. And the man in orbit reminds us that no technical skills, no spectacular controls, no revolutionary discoveries can ever rid us of the ultimate questions as to who we are, why we are here, and how we should behave. We take with us into any new era that awaits the life-and-death questions that have been with mankind from the beginning. Automation will not solve them. They will travel with a round-trip ticket to the moon. The quest of the soul for meaning, the hunger of the heart for love, the struggle of the mind for ultimate truth—these are still the priorities for the human spirit. The man in orbit carries with him the anxieties of us all as we watch here on earth the ancestral passions of hatred, suspicion, greed, fear and despair set man against man, race against race, and nations against nations.

This, then, is the Word the Church has to declare—and believe and live. Christ in heaven. Jesus Christ, the man of purity, goodness, faith, and suffering love, at the very center of creation. It is not enough to say that he once upon a time taught us how to live. The most empty cliché of the modern sermon is the remark that if only everyone would live by the Sermon on the Mount there would be no more troubles. The vital point is that the Sermon on the Mount was incarnate in Christ himself, and is alive with him for ever in the most real world of all. To say that he has ascended into heaven means nothing less than this: that the God who sustains this universe, the God who is its ultimate meaning, the God with whom we all will have to do, bears within himself the humanity of Christ. The love, the goodness, the aspirations, the hopes that seem so weak and powerless, so continually crucified in the world we know, are really enthroned at the heart of all things. Christ is in heaven. His death-struggle with the powers of evil has been won, and he offers the victory-gifts to men and women of faith. "When he ascended up on high, he led captivity captive, and gave gifts unto men."

It is in this faith that we can tackle the intensely human problems that await us on our doorstep as well as in the brooding space above. It is in this confidence that the apostle says: "If ye then be risen with Christ, seek those things which are above, where Christ sitteth on the right hand of God." And it is in this sense that he reminds us that through all the joys and sorrows, the strife and passion, the achievement and the failure of our mortal days, our life "is hid with Christ in God."

Sermon Twelve

FROM SECURITY TO MATURITY

REVEREND R. BENJAMIN GARRISON, D.D.

Minister, Wesley Methodist Church, and Director of the Wesley Foundation at the University of Illinois, Urbana, Illinois

In his dual role of Minister of Wesley Methodist Church and of the Wesley Foundation at the University of Illinois, Dr. Garrison ministers and preaches to faculty, students, and people of the town,—a man of Town and Gown.

Born in Indiana, the son, grandson, and nephew of Methodist ministers, he studied at DePauw University and Drew Theological Seminary and received the honorary D.D. from MacMurray College.

He has published articles and book reviews for the religious and scholarly press, including *The American Jewish Post and Opinion, The Indiana Catholic, The Indiana Magazine of History, The Hymn, The Christian Advocate, The Pastor, The Pulpit, Christianity Today, Religion in Life;* also *Collier's Encyclopedia* article on "Hymnody" with Ralph T. Daniel. In 1964 he published *Portrait of the Church—Warts and All.* He is a member of the Association of College and University Ministers of the Methodist Church, a member of the Inter-Conference Commission on Student Work, a member of the Board of Trustees and Visitors of MacMurray College and of Onarga Military Academy. During World War II he was in the 51st Signal Operations Battalion.

He has held pastorates at the Bishop Janes Methodist Church, Basking Ridge, New Jersey, 1951-1957, Associate Pastor, First Methodist Church, Bloomington, Indiana, 1957-1958, and became Senior Minister of the same church in 1958; in September, 1961, he was appointed Senior Minister of Wesley Church, Urbana, and Director of the Wesley Foundation at the University of Illinois. He has been college preacher at DePauw University, Evansville College, Hanover College, Otterbein College, MacMurray College, Manchester College, the University of Richmond, South Dakota State College, Wesley College, and guest lecturer at Drew University, Indiana University and the Chicago Sunday Evening Club. This sermon on the insecurities of our time was preached at the Chicago Sunday Evening Club on February 4, 1962.

FROM SECURITY TO MATURITY

Ours is an age of vast and deep-reaching insecurity. It has been called, variously, the aspirin age, the atomic age, and the age of anxiety. It has been cussed at, defended, worshipped, and feared. It has been the object of reform and the subject of prayer. But beneath all of this, as a dark and constant common denominator, is the unbudgable fact of insecurity.

The aspirins only betoken this. And the atoms. And the anxieties. Whether we are cursing our culture or defending it, whether we are worshipping our nation or fearing another; whether we are trying to quit drinking or to start believing, ours is an age of insecurity: national and international, personal and interpersonal. I would guess that if we levied a tax on every use of the word security, we could pay our national debt in short order. The very frequency with which we use the word—the very carelessness and wistfulness of it—is evidence that we do not know what it means or where to find it. Insecurity pursues us like a shadow on a summer day.

Consider, as samples, such statements as these, any one of which could have been heard or read since you got up this morning, every one of which is evidence that someone's world is threatened: "Why they ever made *him* executive vice president is more than I will ever understand." (If I were speaking to my usual congregation at the University of Illinois, I should have said, "Why they made *him* an associate professor is more than I will ever understand") . . . "Will I get a raise?" . . . "Will there be a strike?" . . . "Does she love me?" . . . "Because I said so, that's why" . . . "Nikita Khrushchev announced in Russia today" . . . "Dear President Kennedy: on the subject of fall-out shelters" . . . "Dear President Kennedy: on the further subject of fall-out shelters" . . . "Will God forgive me?" These concerns, all of them real and some of them right, eat and cheat and wound because our times, and we with them, have been dipped in the acids of insecurity.

Though it admittedly gives small comfort, it *is* worth noting that insecurity was not born yesterday, or yesteryear. Consider, as samples, these ancient paraphrases of our plight: "Good teacher, what must I do to inherit eternal life?" . . . "And they said to him, 'Grant us to sit, one at your right and one at your left, in your glory' " . . . "And he said, 'I will pull down my barns and build larger ones; and there will I store all my grain and my goods' " . . . "Yea, Lord, thou knowest that I love thee" . . . "But the Egyptians pursued after them, all the horses and chariots of Pharaoh, and his horsemen, and his army, and overtook them" . . . "God be merciful to me, a sinner" . . . The aspirin had not yet been invented, the atom had not yet been split. But the anxiety? the insecurity? There all right, even then.

The reason is that insecurity is given with our eye color and our heart beat and does not cease until they do. Mr. Justice Holmes observed that "complete security can be found only in the graveyard." Insecurity is as human as hunger, and as recurrent, and as inescapable.

Nor is this all bad. Like fear, insecurity may act alternately as a spur or as a brake. It causes us to save our money, to husband our health, to seek out one another in love. It can produce wars, but it can also weld a United Nations Organization. It can cause us to flail the waters helplessly, but it can also motivate us to learn to swim. It can lead to hypochondria or to health insurance. It can drive a man to suicide but it may lead him to faith.

Still if some measure of insecurity is an inescapable part of life, some measure of security is an equally imperative part of the full life. If we are forever bailing out the boat, we may never learn to sail. A harbor, either as a genuine memory or as a live hope, is essential to the voyage. Battle fatigue is almost as dangerous as enemy bullets. A boy who has never had a dollar to his name is difficult to teach how to spend one. If we are to learn, with Paul, in whatever state we are to be content, it must be because somewhere we have known real contentment.

What is wrong, then, is not security but the worship of it. For to worship it is to destroy it. "Whosoever seeks his life shall lose it" said the most secure and mature Man who ever lived. Security is a launching pad, not a garage. It is a doorway, not a fortress. To spend it is to gain it; to hoard it is to lose it; to worship it is to destroy it.

Perhaps nothing so clearly demonstrates the abuse of security in our time as the cult of adjustment. Everything and everybody is subject to its cultic magic: the osteopath adjusts your back; the government adjusts your taxes; the tailor adjusts your clothing; the organization adjusts your salary; the psychiatrist adjusts your neuroses; the church sometimes attempts to adjust your god; and the culture adjusts your values. But Erich Fromm, the psychiatrist, has wisely warned us: "the vast majority of people in our culture," he says, "are well adjusted because they have given up the battle for independence sooner and more radically than the neurotic person." [1] That judgment makes me uncomfortable. It means, I take it, that there is a type of insecure individual whose very neurosis is a sign of health; it means at least he has not quit; it means that beneath the insecurity is a real, live human being, however twisted and stunted and mixed up he may be.

Nevertheless, in the fullest sense, *security* is penultimate, semi-final, secondary, incomplete. So, for the Christian at least, *to give it up is to nail it down*. Like freedom, the only way to have a chance of keeping it is to be willing to risk it. One thinks, politically, of those thirteen little scared and quarreling colonies who finally decided to brew tea in Boston Harbor. One thinks, philosophically, of an impoverished lens-grinder named Spinoza, invited to a comfortable stipend if he would dedicate but one volume to Louis XIV. But Spinoza was not overly fond of the French monarch, so he kept at his little lenses and at his great thoughts. One thinks, religiously, of Jesus placing the chips of his life on the table of death and risking them all in one great redemptive toss, proving to those who had the eyes and the ears and the stomach for it that loss was gain and tragedy triumph. And one sees in them all—in the colonists, in the philosopher, and in the Prince of Peace—the purpose, the pattern and the price of security: you nail it down only when you give it up.

II

I find now, as I face it, that the task of defining maturity is by no means easy. Its Latin root means ripe or seasonable (though parenthetically we might note the warning that when something grows too mellow it becomes soft if not rotten. That, I think, is about equally true of apples and of churches). *To become mature is to become, in growth, in development, and in fact, what was intended but only potential in the beginning*. The classic statement of *Christian* maturity is Paul's prayer that "we all come . . . unto the measure of the stature of the fullness of Christ: That we . . . may *grow up* into him in all things." That does not define it. It does describe it.

Mature people do not need to pretend about themselves. Their weaknesses and failures are accepted and faced. Their strengths and virtues are received with grace and used with humility. When someone compliments them, they are not always saying, "Oh, you shouldn't say that,"

---

[1] Erich Fromm, *Psychoanalysis and Religion*, Yale University Press, New Haven, 1958, p. 83.

which, being interpreted, means, "I'm mighty glad you did." They are able to distinguish between flattery and praise or between honest criticism and petty jealousy. They engage in neither self-deprecation nor in self-adulation. They do not have to, for they are mature.

By the same token the mature person feels no need to *lean* upon others. Notice I said *lean* not depend. Some of the most immature persons in the world are those forever declaring that they are self-made men. (Somehow we suspected as much, from the outcome.) The mature man recognizes that life is interlaced with life. But he sees too that they are separate lives and must be. I would even suggest that the love between a man and a woman is still immature if it comes to rest in the "I need you; don't ever leave me" stage. Love based upon mutual need easily drops into self love or else ceases when the need does. Maturity may not stand alone. But it does stand erect.

Full maturity, however, depends ultimately upon what I might call cosmic security. Dr. Tillich has placed our generation in his debt by defining faith as ultimate concern. But this is not really quite enough. It must also prove out that what I am utterly concerned about can bear the weight of my concern and will not let it down. If earth holds no place in the heart of heaven; if heaven itself is an icicle which melts when men's hopes breathe upon it; if what I am living for and groping after and dying by is finally unreal—if, in short there is nothing securely in the Heart of the Eternal to match and mold the securities and hungers of my heart, then human life is a frail raft cast precariously upon an imaginary sea. If there is no cosmic security, there is no security.

III

Strangely enough the Biblical focus of security and maturity, seems, at first glance, to be the utter denial of it. Listen: "The man who tries to save his life shall lose it; and it is the man who loses his life for my sake that will secure it." This is not an exhortation but a description. Our Lord is not saying, "Come now, fellows, you really ought to be a little more sacrificial, you know. Besides, what you sacrifice our dear heavenly Father will give back to you in the end. So now, how about it?" That, I'm afraid, is the way it has often been presented and interpreted. No, he is being as coldly factual as a traffic cop. He's saying: This road on which you travel simply is not going to get you where you think. There are laws you know, and one of them—indeed the primal one—is this: he who tries to save his life shall lose it; or, translated into the terms with which we have to do this evening: if you hang onto security your hands will be too full to grasp maturity.

Again, listen to this, which follows: "How is a man the better for it, if he gains the whole world at the cost of losing his own soul? For a man's soul, what price can be high enough?" Or, as we might paraphrase it, What profit if he gains but *pays himself as a fine?* This, you see, is what happens when we are hell-bent for security: we use ourselves as currency; we post ourselves as bond. Notice again how Jesus' question is not a question; it is a verdict. As we survey the things in which we think to find security—wealth, health, education, good deeds, good intentions, what have you—as we notice how they yield their bounty only in exchange for ourselves, we know the verdict is right: he who gains, loses.

Is this not true individually? Think now of the utter absurdity of many of our job interviews. Think what has happened within the soul of a man when he is more interested in the pension on which he will retire than in the purpose for which he will work. Besides you miss so much of life this way, so much plain and cleansing joy. Somewhere I read of a young couple who had assiduously applied themselves to the counsels of their psychiatrist in order to "adjust" to their marriage. After considerable time and some success, the wife said, refreshingly, "Honey, now that we're so well adjusted, couldn't we just have a little fun." To seek is to lose.

And, though it is a harder lesson to learn, I would suggest that the same is true nationally. I think even the most partisan of us will admit that Dag Hammerskjold was neither a war-monger nor a dreamer, although he fought his quota of battles and dreamed his share of dreams. Yet it was he who reminded us of the meaning of national maturity when he said, "It is when we all play safe that we create a world of utmost insecurity." The mature nation will neither brandish its swords nor trade them for tinker toys. The mature people will recognize that there are some things worse than death—servitude, for instance. They will also know that peace requires risk, that risk demands maturity. They will rest their hopes neither in fall-out shelters nor in the absence of them. This way is dangerous; this way is insecure; but down this road alone, I suggest, lies national maturity.

There too lies spiritual maturity. The Church cannot expect to gain her life, save as a sunken-eyed skeleton of what she was meant to be, by hoarding it. Perhaps the time has come to make membership in the church of Christ harder, not easier.

One day I was walking down the street of a little village in New Jersey where I was serving my first church. On the opposite side of the street was a youngster who was president of our high school fellowship, a very attractive and very undumb blond. I whistled at her in a manner difficult to describe but easy to imagine. When she turned her head I chided her by saying, "So, Carol, that's all the boys have to do is whistle." Her answer was devastating. "Oh, Mr. Garrison," she said, "I knew it was you—and you're harmless!" A man would rather be called just about anything except harmless!

Now in utmost seriousness let me suggest that the church has engaged in far too much of what I shall call, for want of a better term, flirtation evangelism. The world turns its attractive head because she knows we do not mean it, or at least are not prepared to do anything about it. Then she walks on. She concludes that the church is harmless. Anybody can afford to flirt with the church, because it is safe. She can go right on with her real loves while at the same time enjoying a mild case of ecclesiastical puppy love with the mild and safe puppy known as the church. I would far and away rather have the church accused of being narrow-minded than have it said it is not serious-minded. No church can afford to be considered safe. That is just a shorter word for irrelevant.

That is why I say that the time has come to make membership in the church harder. And by God's grace a few men have been raised up within the Church willing to say, "Our church is stronger this year: eighteen people declined to join us because the demands were too high. We do not propose to make our church exclusive; but we do insist upon making it relevant. If that means reduced income or statistical panic or loss of prestige, we are sorry, naturally, but we are also committed. We think maybe we have been losing our church's life by seeking it. And that we refuse any longer to do."

I am saying that real *maturity is born from* the womb of *creative insecurity*. Martin Buber, the great Jewish philosopher, has reminded us that this is the genius of any religion that dares to call itself biblical. He says:

> The prophets of Israel have never announced a God upon whom their hearer's striving for security reckoned. They have always aimed to shatter all security and to proclaim in the opened abyss of the final insecurity the unwished-for-God . . . And confounds all who imagine that the temple of God is in their midst.[2]

That is what I mean by a creative insecurity: not the debilitating kind of insecurity that is unable to make up its mind even to make up its mind;

---

[2] Martin Buber, *The Eclipse of God,* Harper & Row, New York, 1952, p. 73.

but the insecurity that recognizes the partial nature of all our goals, the fragmented nature of all our achievements, the pride which insinuates itself into our faith; but then the creativity which casts us forth in the midst of all this insecurity, to grope and grow, to trust and obey, to give and receive, to live with questions on our lips and to die with some of them unanswered; but to know, within it and beyond it, a verdict and a promise: "If any man has a mind to come my way, let him renounce himself, and take up his cross, and follow me."

This creative insecurity, this real maturity, involves and requires a kind of divine nonchalance. It sees change and decay and admits it; it experiences suffering and defeat and accepts it. But such a man is able to take a God-may-care attitude toward it all, knowing that beneath the change is constancy, that within the suffering is joy; confident that, because God *does* care, what today calls defeat tomorrow claims as victory. He humbly accepts such small securities as this life offers, but if necessary tosses even them aside in the name and for the sake of a higher security, a realer maturity, sought and secured in "God the Father Almighty, maker of heaven and earth, and in Jesus Christ his only Son our Lord."

Sermon Thirteen

THE PERILS OF THOUGHTLESSNESS

REVEREND ARNOLD H. LOWE, D.D., LITT.D., LL.D
Minister, Westminster Presbyterian Church, Minneapolis, Minnesota

Dr. Arnold Lowe preaches to one of the great congregations of America, where he has a cross section of the people of the mid-west Sunday after Sunday—owners and directors of the great corporations, railroad presidents, store owners, doctors, nurses, and men and women from all walks of life. Even a group of several hundred Chinese, still living in Minneapolis from the days of the railroad building to the west, attend his church with their families. Each year he plans his sermons for twelve months ahead, then issues a printed folder giving the main topics of each sermon each two months so that his congregations know what his topics will be and holds himself to the subjects he feels his people need.

His books show the range of his interests: *Adventuring with Christ, The Importance of Being Ourselves, Start Where You Are, When God Moves In, Power for Life's Living, My Guide for Spiritual Discipline, The Marks of a Christian, Guidelines to Courageous Living.* He served in the early days of his career as a missionary in West Africa, 1912-15, then became assistant minister of First Presbyterian, Wilkinsburg, Pennsylvania, Professor of Philosophy and Biblical Literature in Missouri Valley College and minister of Odell Avenue Presbyterian Church in Marshall, Missouri. From 1927 to 1941 he was minister of Kings Highway Presbyterian Church, St. Louis, and was called to Westminster Church in 1941. One of the highlights of his ministry here is running Abbott Hospital, where the touch of the Christian Gospel is brought to suffering men and women. Westminster Church finances the hospital. Although there are thirty-six hundred members in Westminster Church, Dr. Lowe knows practically all of them by name, serves them in many ways, yet is scrupulous in taking time early in every week for his study; his sermons reflect many facets of life; this sermon on thoughtlessness discusses a subject men and women and young people of our day need; it is a sermon to be recalled many times after reading or hearing it. It was preached as one of his regular Sunday morning sermons on October 13, 1963.

He attended the College of Wooster, Western Theological Seminary, then did graduate work at New York University and in Germany and Switzerland in history. The honorary D.D. was conferred upon him by Missouri Valley College, the College of Wooster, and Westminster College, the Litt.D. by Huron College, and the LL.D. by Macalester College. He is a member of many church boards, including the Board of Christian Education of the Presbyterian Church in U.S.A., Advisory Council, National Presbyterian Church, Washington, D. C., World Alliance of Reformed Churches, a delegate to the World Council of Churches in Amsterdam, a director or trustee of Westminster College, Lindenwood College, Western Theological Seminary, McCormick Theological Seminary. He is chairman of the board of trustees of Macalester College in St. Paul, Minnesota.

THE PERILS OF THOUGHTLESSNESS

Father, forgive them; for they know not what they do.

Luke 23:24

Let me begin with a question. As we consider the sequence of events in history, what has been the source of greatest injury and misfortune: outright evil intention or sheer thoughtlessness? Moving from the broad scene of history to a narrow compass, what has caused the greatest annoyance and concern in your business: unscrupulous competition or thoughtlessness? Let us hone the question to a fine edge and apply it to ourselves. What has brought the greatest sorrow to our lives and to the lives of those who are close to us: maliciousness, vindictiveness, deliberate cruelty, or sheer thoughtlessness? It should not take long to find the answer. We know that from Nero to Hitler there has always been evil intent in the world. There has always been maliciousness. But few of us have been the victims of such deliberate wrong, and few of us have been guilty of such wrong. In our lives and in the lives of those about us, the greatest injuries and the deepest wounds have been inflicted by thoughtlessness. What is so tragic about it all is the fact that while there is some defense against evil intention there is no defense against thoughtlessness. We can neither anticipate it nor prevent it.

All of us live amidst the perils of thoughtlessness. We find ourselves in unhappy or unfortunate situations, not because we plan to be there and not because we wilfully invite dark circumstances, but because we are thoughtless. We drift into them. We allow the tide to carry us along. At the end of it all we have nothing but lame words, "I did not think. I did not realize. I never dreamed of what would come of it. I did not mean any harm."

We think back upon that confusing scene in the courtyard of Pilate's palace. It must have been as close to bedlam as anything can come. Some shouted, "Barabbas," others screamed, "Crucify him." Rising above it all, the shrill voice of the high priest cried, "He is not Caesar's friend." At last Pilate, cornered like an animal, committed the prisoner into the hands of those who would soon nail Him to the cross. "I am innocent of the blood of this man," he pleaded, "see ye to it," as though he meant to say, "I myself mean him no ill." But in the end sheer thoughtlessness bore fruits as bitter as the cruelest intention could have borne. Perhaps now we understand that merciful prayer of Jesus, "Father, forgive them; for they know not what they do."

Such soul-searing tragedies are rarely ours, but there is much thoughtlessness which turns our nights into nights of tears and our days into empty hours. Here, for example, is ingratitude. What is ingratitude except thoughtlessness? It is not evil. There are in it no malicious purposes. It is not a cardinal sin which merits punishment and penance. There is no deliberate desire to bring hurt or injury to people who have been gracious and generous toward us. It is thoughtlessness. At times it is intolerable, inexcusable indifference. It is selfishness. It is living in a little narrow world which never allows a man to get beyond himself. It is living in a room of mirrors, where one never sees anything but oneself, where the whole world is composed of oneself.

Perhaps in our easy acceptance of our English language we have forgotten, or never knew, that the words *thank* and *think* come from the same Anglo-Saxon root. He who thinks thanks, and he who is thankless is so because he is thoughtless. Here a little knowledge of words reveals so many of the mysteries in the heart. One is reminded of the ten who were healed by Jesus. One returned; nine went their way. All were healed. Was there no gratitude in those who never came back to Jesus? I am sure there was. Did they not feel some warmth of appreciation? I think they did. Had they been confronted with their negligence, they probably would have said, "We never meant to hurt him. Of course, we are grateful. We were thoughtless." But the injury is the same and the hurt lasts just as long.

How many times you must have said, "Why does he not write?" or "It would have been good had he spoken to me." No one is ever so busy, no one is ever so occupied, that he cannot let his heart reach out or leave a touch of gratitude. I wonder how it is with us and God. In an hour which was flooded with passion, Jesus said, "If thou hadst known, . . . in this thy day, the things which belong unto thy peace!" "If you had only thought for a moment. If you had only for a few moments torn yourself from the things which you say are so important!" Is someone else's heart not important? Do our sacrifices count for nothing? Are our silent prayers for others only sighs of weariness in the night? Is what God has given us and done for us not important?

The tragedy of thoughtlessness is often the tragedy of the familiar. Whenever we return from abroad and drive through our own city, I remind myself that we take so much at home for granted—the sky, the green lawns, the woods, the soft lakes, the sprightly sailboats. How much truth this holds for our lives. There is so much to which we never give a second thought. At times we barely give it any thought. A little arithmetic here shames us into a sense of guilt. Our good fortune—how we take that for granted. The advantages we possess, the privileges we have, the ease with which we are permitted to do some things—all these we accept as though they were our rights and we had really earned and deserved them; yes, as though we had bought them by the "sweat of our brow." And yet there are countless men and women—as deserving as we are, as able and as gifted—with none of these things.

For a moment consider success. Whether it has come to us late or early, it is not all due to the skill of our hands or the cleverness of our minds. Nevertheless, we take it for granted, as though others were only a part of our social climate and had not abetted us or lent us encouragement or given us of their wisdom, and in a deeper and more spiritual sense, surrounded us with their concern. Have we ever asked ourselves how much of what we have is due to the spiritual agony of those who love us? Will any of us ever know?

But—BUT—if there is someone who alone is responsible for his success, to whom no one has ever contributed one iota or lifted one finger on his behalf, if there is someone like that, should he not then be the more grateful for whatever courage and skill and insight God has given him? How can a man be so thoughtless?

For years I have had the joy and the sorrow of entering into the lives of married people. How often I have heard one or the other say, "I really did not mean it. Had I known what it would come to, I would never have done it, I would never have said it." But it was done and it was said. Those of you who have been with me during our premarriage counseling know how I say again and again, "Do not let a day pass by on an angry word or a thoughtless deed." Of all the hurts which come in marriage, none cut deeper or leave the heart more desolate than those which come from thoughtlessness. How much people who love each other can hurt each other—parents and children, children and parents, husbands and wives, wives and husbands, friends and friends. How the bond of affection can be frayed by thoughtlessness.

I am driven to deep reflection when I think of all this. This past summer we walked again along the wall of Berlin. We stood in front of the Church of the Reconciliation in East Berlin. The front is completely walled in, so that no one from the West may enter. I think of a small group of Protestants in a theological seminary south of Lisbon. Overnight, twenty-four students, all Angolans, disappeared. No trace of them has been found.

How much we take our religious privileges for granted. You may come to church; you may worship here. In some lands men would give their very souls to be able to do what you and I are doing today—worship. There is no member of the Gestapo in this congregation, taking down your names, filing them away. There is no one waiting outside to arrest me for what I am now saying. Yet we take it all for granted. The perils of thoughtlessness!

Yes, the peril of thoughtlessness is the peril of immediacy. Even the law of the land recognizes this, for it speaks of mitigating circumstances where there was no intent to kill, just thoughtlessness. A man is just as dead in one instance as in the other. We speak in anger. The anger passes away but the words—they stay and haunt and pursue us. We act in panic. We respond to the prompting of our emotions. We act out of the misery of sheer boredom and never think of the consequences. We mean no evil. We intend no harm. We are just thoughtless. At that time we live for the moment and we live for the day. We forget that each day has its sequel. The reckoning for today is always tomorrow. The hasty word spoken *now* haunts us *then*. The hurt is just as deep and the guilt is just as great.

So we are left to survey the wreckage thoughtlessness has caused. Peter is standing by the fireside. He denies his Lord. There are bitter tears. How much he would have given to undo it all. Did he mean to deny his Lord? Was there evil in his heart? Was there hatred? He was thoughtless! What did men talk about on the night of the crucifixion? They must have talked about some things that were done that day. They saw an innocent man scourged; they saw him spat upon; they saw him die. Were there some who said to others and to themselves as the shadows passed into the darkness, "I didn't know it would turn out that way. I didn't think he would die on a cross"? But he died on a cross as though they had spat upon him and been the executioners.

So I plead with you, as I plead with my own heart, not to be thoughtless—not in our homes, not with our fellow men, not in matters of the Church, not with our God. Rather let us say with the psalmist, "If I forget thee, . . . let my right hand forget her cunning. If I do not remember thee, let my tongue cleave to the roof of my mouth." There is so much we do because we cannot help ourselves. But knowing how much hurt we can bring to others, let us never, never be thoughtless, lest He, looking at us, has to say again, "Father, forgive them, for they know not what they do." We ought to know.

Sermon Fourteen

THE CHURCH AND THE KINGDOM OF GOD

REVEREND CHARLES A. TRENTHAM, TH.D., PH.D.

Pastor, First Baptist Church, Knoxville, Tennessee

Charles Arthur Trentham was born in Jefferson City, Tennessee, on July 2, 1919, and later moved with his parents to Knoxville, Tennessee. He attended Mars Hill Junior College and Carson-Newman College. While in college he served as president of the Philomathean Society and as pastor of the Piedmont, Benton, and New Market Baptist churches. He received the Th.D. degree from Southwestern Baptist Theological Seminary, where he graduated with honors and was speaker for his class. During his student days at the seminary, he served as pastor of the Sycamore Heights Baptist Church in Fort Worth. He has taught in the Department of Religion at Baylor University, and has served at Southwestern as student assistant to Dr. W. T. Conner and later as professor in the Systematic Theology Department for seven years. Dr. Trentham received his Ph.D. from the University of Edinburgh, Scotland.

Since 1953, he has been pastor of First Baptist Church, Knoxville, Tennessee, and combined with this pastorate, he has served as dean of the School of Religion at the University of Tennessee since 1958. He is a trustee of Carson-Newman College, a member of the Executive Committees of the Southern Baptist Convention and the Tennessee Baptist Convention. He has served as a member of the Sunday School Board of the Southern Baptist Convention and the Survey Committee of the Tennessee Baptist Convention.

His published writings include adult and young people's Sunday school lessons; young people's Training Union programs; contributions to *The Baptist Student* magazine, *The Baptist Training Union Magazine, Open Windows,* and the books, *Christian Faith in Action* compiled by Foy Valentine and *Southern Baptist Preaching* compiled by H. C. Brown, Jr. He is author of the 1960 Bible Study book, *Studies in Timothy,* for the Southern Baptist Convention (translated into Korean and Spanish), and of *The Shepherd of the Stars* (1962).

Dr. Trentham has preached on the Columbia Broadcasting System's "Church of the Air"; in 1958 he delivered the Theological Lectures at Golden Gate Baptist

Theological Seminary, and in 1963 delivered the H. I. Hester Lectures on Preaching at Midwestern Baptist Theological Seminary. Dr. Trentham's preaching reflects his long and careful scholarship and his deep personal faith. This sermon was preached at the Southern Baptist Pastors' Conference at San Francisco, California, June 5, 1962. His discussion of loneliness and the problems of the church will be welcomed by many.

THE CHURCH AND THE KINGDOM OF GOD

A great English preacher tells of the tiny church of St. Ennadoc which stood in a lovely spot among the sand hills of Cornwall. People worshipped there and offered God their simple vows. Then, slowly the attendance fell, until one Sunday, the door was not opened. Sand blowing against the building mounted higher and higher till only the stony finger of the spire remained visible to remind men and women of vows now ruined, prayers now silent, and hope now dead.

The winds of change and controversy are blowing through our Southern Baptist Zion—winds that may drive the sands of suffocation and death against the windows and walls of our denomination. We have lost the way of worship and have suppressed the drawing power of the Spirit of God with organizational pressures. We are now turning in upon ourselves, imagining that our spiritual dearth may be traced to our doctrinal differences and that all of our maladies may be healed by making a scapegoat of our seminaries. The schism among us is pulling us farther apart and farther away from our mission.

The word I hear everywhere from pastors is this, "I am exceedingly lonely." The mood of the world has infiltrated our churches. Dr. Paul Tournier, the Swiss physician and author of the widely discussed book, *The Meaning of Persons,* in his more recent book, *Escape from Loneliness,* has called loneliness the major malady of our time. Coming from a man whose life is given to psychotherapy, this should call us all to attention.

Loneliness is everywhere. Here is a secretary who turns on the radio only that she might hear a human voice bidding her goodnight. Here is a mother who has no adult companions; she is so desperate for amusement that she terrorizes her child with a doll dressed as a devil. Here is a well-educated career woman who draws apart from society because she is ashamed of her small-business-man husband. Here is a psychology professor who cannot understand his wife or win the attention of his children. More shocking still: here is a pastor who unburdens his soul to a priest because he has no close ties among his colleagues or his congregation. In a day when the population explosion is so unbelievable that some tell us that if it continues at the present rate, by the year 2080, if the earth's surface were equally divided, each person will have only one square foot of ground, is it not madness that causes anyone to be lonely when the masses press upon us from all sides?

Does this not rather point the truth that physical proximity apart from spiritual kinship only drives us deeper and deeper into ourselves?

I. Causes of Loneliness

What has caused this loneliness? Well, first of all, in the economic realm, we have allowed free enterprise to degenerate into ruthless exploitation which causes us to suspect one another and to push one another around as pawns in the game whose only goal is personal success.

In the social realm, we have isolated ourselves by the false belief that freedom means independence to live our own lives regardless of what happens to others. Such freedom is only negative self-affirmation.

We exclude each other by our possessiveness, grasping after happiness as if it were something we may keep to ourselves, forgetting that by its very nature, it is a community property which can only be had as it is shared.

Racial majorities destroy community by driving wedges between themselves and racial minorities. We forget that when we insult any man because of the color of his skin, it is not the man we insult but his Creator. Racial minorities destroy community with a distorted sense of justice, contending that God and humanity are obligated to give us all equal gifts, demanding equality when our real need is gratitude and love.

Within our denomination we destroy community by allowing our insecurity to turn into hostility toward all who differ with us.

II. Cure for Loneliness

The only way to put an end to our cravings and combats and to heal our loneliness is to come back to the fellowship for which we were created—the fellowship of love in the Kingdom of God made manifest in His church. We shall then see that neither individual nor state nor any social structure nor any denominational structure can be an end in itself; that no life reaches its truest and highest fulfillment until it shares in honest and open relationships with all other men whom God has created. "For none of us liveth to himself, and no man dieth to himself" (Romans 14:7). We live unto Christ and there is only one place where we may live in the fellowship of Christ and that is where all others in that fellowship live.

The most devastating result of sin, even for the redeemed, is not only that it separates us from God but that it separates us from one another. If we are separated from one another, this may be prima facie evidence that we are also separated from God, for God refuses to bind any man unto himself unless he is willing to be bound to his fellowman.

Luke tells us, of the early church, that the multitude of them that believed were of one heart and of one soul (Acts 4:32a). To read the works of J. B. Phillips, for many, is like receiving a special delivery letter from Heaven. It breathes with the fresh, pure air of direct, straightforward communication. Notice how he puts this passage: "Among the large number who had become believers there was complete agreement of heart and soul."

Now this had not always been true in the church and it was not always to remain true. God has come upon the scene with the sound of a rushing, mighty wind and with this boisterous gale from Heaven, the deep-seated prejudices and limited ideas of men were blown out of the church. Had it not been for the constant blowing of this wholesome wind from Heaven, the Christian church would have become a Jewish sect despising every man outside the land of Jewry.

III. The Way to Unity

What united this early church was not a mind closed upon arbitrary articles of faith, but hearts open to the fresh blowing of the gales of God. Early Christians knew that there was truth in Christ which they had not begun to fathom. This kept them alive and alert. The difference between a dead church and a living church is that the dead church thinks it has already understood and performed the will and work of God. The living church realizes she is only beginning to discover the boundless depths of the wisdom of God in Christ and that she is indebted to every man of God who is the channel through which truth is made clearer.

That which united the early church was not her pride of achievement and self-sufficiency. It was rather the deep recognition that she was called into being by the grace of God. Is it not a strange fallacy that we who believe most strongly that the individual cannot be saved by works believe that the church must be saved by works? It has always been so with God's people. Many have imagined that in the Old Testament men were saved by works, while in the New Testament they are saved by grace. Yet it was not to the Judaism of the Old Testament which Paul referred when he wrote, "not of works, lest any man should boast" (Ephesians 2:9). He was refuting the decadent distortion of the Old Testament by the Judaizers of his own day. God has always dealt with men by grace. It was God's grace that held them together, not their ability to obey the law or to agree on creedal statements.

The Kingdom of Israel was continually stabilized by God's grace. When Saul died a suicide on Gilboa, all that he had worked for was lost. It was David—the fair-haired darling of Saul's court, the military hero and giant killer—who reversed the fortunes of Israel. Yet the Scriptures make it plain that it was not his native gifts but the "charisma" (the gifts of God's grace) that enabled him to reign. Israel saw his achievements as the evidence that God's gift of the Spirit has passed to David.

When David's wars were over his dominion stretched forth from the Gulf of Aquabah in the south to Central Syria in the far north. His was the most powerful nation in Palestine and Syria. His flourishing trade in horses and chariots between Egypt and Cilicia filled the royal coffers with unprecedented wealth. His vast copper smelteries, which boiled and blew their smoke to the skies in Eziongeber, were the largest in the ancient world. Then under Solomon Israel became decadent for he came to the throne not because of charismatic qualities (not because of the gift of God's grace of the Spirit) but by a palace plot. Religion was then made into the instrument of the state.

Religion in Israel became sick and there is no plague on earth like a sick religion. Now this sickness was not openly apparent. All the shrines were thronged with worshippers. The temple coffers overflowed. However, most of the religious activity was a nauseous attempt to purchase the favor of the Almighty and to manipulate Him to keep the balance of power on Israel's side of the iron curtain. No rebuke was spoken against the grossest immorality. Prophets chose to soothe the royal ear with smooth sayings. The feverish activity was not a sign of life but the dance of death. This kind of righteousness was like "a morning cloud, like the dew that goeth early away" (Hosea 6:4).

Yet herein we see the overarching grace of God. Israel's righteousness would fail but not God's. He would not leave her in her loneliness. He would raise up a repenting remnant through which the Kingdom of God would come. "I will betroth thee unto me forever; yea, I will betroth thee unto me in righteousness and in judgment and in loving kindness (hesed) and in mercies. I will even betroth thee unto me in faithfullness, and thou shalt know the Lord (Yahweh)" (Hosea 2:19-20).

A new covenant would be made and the Kingdom of God would come at last. Do you wonder then that all Jerusalem went out with high anticipation to the banks of the Jordan to hear John preach when he declared, "the Kingdom of Heaven is at hand"?

The new day dawned with the coming of the Christ and the New Testament speaks with one voice, declaring that all who have obeyed the voice of Christ are his true church and will inherit all the promises given to Israel (Romans 4:13-15, Galatians 3:29, Titus 3:7). In his Ephesian letter, Paul calls the church "the body of Christ" (1:15-23), "the temple of God" (2:20), "the household of faith" and "the family of God" (2:19), and "the bride of the Christ" (5:25-33).

I shall not soon forget hearing that lovely young girl from one of our college campuses, a summer missionary to Hawaii. As she stood early in the morning to read the morning watch, she told us of an old lady who was constantly talking about her confidence in Christ, her assurance that she was held in the hand of Christ until, one morning, a cynic said to her, "Suppose Christ should let you slip through his hand?" And she smilingly said, "But that could never be for I am a part of His hand."

No greater devastation has come in Christianity than the schism which results from dividing things which belong together. Too long have we oversimplified our position on the church by saying that while our Roman Catholic friends say we come to Christ by the church, we contend that we come to the church by Christ. Neither of these is true. We are drawn to Christ by the gift of his grace made known to us through the church which Christ has chosen to call his body. The Apostles did not separate Christ from His church and speak of them as unrelated. Christ has so drawn His church to Him and united it with Him that Paul saw that to persecute the church was also to persecute Christ. As he was breathing out threatenings and slaughter against the church, he heard the Christ say, "Saul, Saul, why persecutest thou me?" (Acts 9:4b).

The church belongs to Christ. The church is broken into fragments today because we have forgotten that the church belongs to Christ. It is not ours. We have forgotten that the heart of Christianity is not a creed but a person who is the living word of God and that He sits in judgment upon all our creeds and is higher and greater than all. We should then put down our judgment of others and submit to His judgment.

The wisest words I ever heard from the lips of Dr. John Baillie were these: "When Jesus said, 'he that is not for me is against me,' he was laying down the maxim by which I must judge my own relationship to Christ. When he said, 'he that is not against me is for me,' he was laying down the maximum by which I may judge every other man's relation to Christ."

Christ builds His church, not as we take it upon ourselves to convene the Sanhedrin to sit in judgment upon those who disagree with our private opinions, but by creating compassionate bonds between us so that when we err the long loving arms of the church may draw us back and lift us by love out of our error. Christ does not build the church by fashioning a Colossus with organizational men manipulating people with the latest Madison Avenue methods. Christ builds His church, first of all, by spreading His healing hands of forgiveness upon us that we may become a healthy body through whom the same healing hands that first touched those ailing, fevered brows in Galilee may still be spread upon our world.

Doctrinal rigidity cannot heal us. Our beliefs, or at least our interpretation of our beliefs, have always been imperfect for the church is not only a society of forgiven sinners, it is also a society of deluded sinners. The first men who followed Jesus followed through faith, not knowing very clearly who He was, yet trusting His word. "Follow me and I will make you" (Matthew 4:19). Everything that they came to believe about Him they learned in fellowship with Him. Even at the cross and after the resurrection there were times when the Apostles disagreed, i.e., Peter and Paul.

There real faith came through action. Theirs was a unity of service. Our unity will be restored as we put down our prideful pretention to omniscience and personal adequacy. We have even distorted the doctrine of the Priesthood of Every Believer making it mean that every man is his own high priest before God, concluding that he doesn't need his fellow Christians. This doctrine does not emphasize a man's personal adequacy but his dependence on other believers. I am not my own priest. I am responsible for being a priest for others. There is nothing of smug self-righteousness in this doctrine to cause me to trust in my own ability to go up before God. It is a doctrine to make me assume my responsibility to be a priest for others and to be willing to acknowledge my dependence upon my fellow believers to make intercession for me.

Our unity will be restored as we accept our dependence upon and our responsibility for one another.

We must be wise enough to remember that just because some of us claim to be working for pure doctrine does not of itself prove that the doctrine we advocate is pure. We must be sincere enough to allow love to transcend our differences and thrust us into the work which our Lord has given us.

If the broken body of Christ is to be healed in our time, it will come, not as we reopen the wounds of the Redeemer by strife and controversy, but as we unite in serving men for whom Christ died.

Perhaps if we spent less time in acrimonious committee meetings debating doctrinal issues and more time close to our people, the world would feel again the great compassionate heartbeat of the Son of man and we would know the meaning of that great passage of Revelation: "His servants shall serve him and they shall see his face" (22:3).

Sermon Fifteen

"YOU CAN'T GO HOME AGAIN"

REVEREND FOY VALENTINE, TH.D.

A Minister of the Southern Baptist Convention and Executive Secretary-Treasurer, The Christian Life Commission, Nashville, Tennessee

Using Thomas Wolfe's book as his introduction, Dr. Valentine discusses problems facing the Protestant Church today. His insight is based upon a knowledge of the development of the church in early America, plus wide experience and observation of the church in our own time. His use of words should stimulate many younger men to a wider use of the dictionary and his coining of words will bear careful study.

Dr. Valentine was born July 3, 1923, in Edgewood, Texas, attended Baylor University, then Southwestern Baptist Theological Seminary, Fort Worth, where he took his theological training and earned his Doctor of Theology in 1949. While a student, he held pastorates in Jonah and Golden, Texas; during 1947 and 1948 he served as special representative in race relations for the Baptist General Convention of Texas, and in 1949 and 1950 he directed Baptist student activities for the colleges in Houston.

Called to the pastorate of First Baptist Church, Gonzales, Texas, in 1950, Dr. Valentine served there until he became Director of the Texas Baptist Christian Life Commission in 1953. On June 1, 1960, he became Executive Secretary of The Christian Life Commission of the Southern Baptist Convention. He is a member of the Southern Baptist Convention's Public Affairs Committee, of the Southern Baptist Committee on Baptist Jubilee Advance, of the Executive Committee of Protestants and Other Americans United for Separation of Church and State, and of the Executive Committee of the Board of Directors of the National Temperance League. For three years he has served Southern Baptists as the official Observer at the United Nations.

He was the compiler and editor of *Christian Faith in Action* in 1956. He has written for *The Baptist Student, The Review and Expositor, The New Christian*

Advocate, *Home Missions*, and the *Baptist Standard*. He is the author of *Believe and Behave* (1964). He preaches four times a week and his sermons have been widely printed within the Southern Baptist Convention. He is a frequent speaker at student meetings and on college campuses.

As Director of the Christian Life Commission of the Southern Baptist Convention Dr. Valentine gives direction to a program designed to help Baptists to carry the whole gospel of Christ into every area of life. The Commission renders its ministry in the field of applied Christianity in the general areas of family life, race relations, moral issues, daily work, and Christian citizenship. Dr. Valentine believes that all men are responsible for making Christian faith effective in daily life and personal relations. This sermon was preached to the entire Southern Baptist Convention in 1963.

"YOU CAN'T GO HOME AGAIN"

In one of the most poignantly insightful titles in American literature, Thomas Wolfe makes the point that you can't go home again. The point is at once practical and profound, mundane and philosophical, somber and joyous, bitter and sweet, devastating and exhilarating. Most of us have tried it a thousand ways and know with Thomas Wolfe's George Webber, ". . . that you can't go home again.

". . . You can't go back home to your family, back home to your childhood, back home to romantic love, back home to a young man's dreams of glory and of fame, back home to exile . . . back home to lyricism . . . back home to aestheticism . . . back home to the ivory tower, back home to places in the country . . . back home to the father you have lost and have been looking for, back home to someone who can help you, save you, ease the burden for you, back home to the old forms and systems of things which once seemed everlasting but which are changing all the time—back home to the escapes of Time and Memory." [1]

The Hebrew children spent forty fruitless and futile years trying to go home again, to what was in reality an alien land. Their experience is recorded with brilliant clarity in Numbers: "And all the congregation lifted up their voice, and cried; and the people wept that night. And all the children of Israel murmured against Moses and against Aaron: and the whole congregation said unto them, Would God that we had died in the land of Egypt! or would God we had died in this wilderness! And

[1] Thomas Wolfe, *You Can't Go Home Again*, New York, Harper & Brothers, 1941, p. 706.

wherefore hath the Lord brought us unto this land, to fall by the sword, that our wives and our children should be a prey? were it not better for us to return into Egypt? And they said one to another, Let us make a captain, and let us return into Egypt" (Numbers 14:1-4).

For trying in her own faithless, circumscribed, feminine, human way to go home again, Lot's wife turned into a pillar of salt.

The wise man in Ecclesiastes was saying that you can't go home again when he said "Say not thou, what is the cause that the former times were better than these? for thou does not inquire wisely concerning this" (Ecclesiastes 7:10).

T. S. Eliot spoke with poetic precision when he had J. Alfred Prufrock say, "I have seen the moment of my greatness flicker, and I have seen the eternal Footman hold my coat, and snicker, and in short, I was afraid." I do not propose that we make Bildad, Eliphaz, and Zophar our heroes because they sang our song. I should like, nevertheless, to suggest that there are signs that we, like Prufrock, have seen the moment of our greatness flicker, we have seen the eternal Footman hold our coat and snicker, and in short, we are afraid. This is a critical time. It is critical for Christians generally, and it is critical for Southern Baptists particularly. We will forfeit the future if we continually bathe ourselves in nostalgia and expend our energies in vainly trying to go home again.

It is in order for us to focus briefly on the home from which Southern Baptists have come.

We were a country people, but, like the rest of America, we have moved to town.

We were an uneducated, even ignorant, people, but we are now learning a few things.

We were a provincial people in confident control of our province, but to our anguish and dismay our cogs no longer seem to engage the gears of any real power in our culture. We find ourselves an isolated and waning force in the court house, the state house, the White House, and the Glass House on the East River.

We were, at least in ecclesiology, a radical sect, but we are tending to become another Church.

We were racially, historically, economically, politically, and culturally homogeneous, but we are fast becoming irreversibly heterogeneous.

We were revival-oriented, but revivalism as known and practiced by Baptists when I was a boy is dead. It is dead in spite of our frantic mouth-to-mouth breathing over it and even though we still respectfully hold one-week and even two-week memorial services in loving tribute to its memory.

We were poor, but now, by any reasonable standard on earth, we are affluent.

We were ill-housed in our sorry, one-room, crowded, frame meeting houses, but now we meet in splendid, uncrowded sanctuaries for which we are gloriously in debt.

We were fervently convinced of the rightness of our cause, but now we harbor all the questions and doubts that normally accompany a measure of sophistication.

We were stoutly and vociferously opposed to the institutionalism of the old-line churches, but in only a hundred years we have established institutionalism of every shape, form, and fashion; and all the web is not yet woven.

We were rooted in the soil, but now from the cradle to the grave we roll around on the pavement.

We were a brash and lusty adolescent denomination bulging with unguided muscles, but the aging process has worked its unwelcome work on us and we are now politic, cautious, meticulous, respectable, proper, aging.

We lived in a settled, unchanging world where we knew even as we also were known, but now we live in a world where the winds of change blow with devastating fury across the face of all the earth.

We lived in an isolated, marvelously moated land where men never dreamed of mastering the black arts of nuclear war, but the time has come when men in a fantastically shrunken world have both dreamed that dreadful dream and actualized it.

This has been home for Southern Baptists. For us to go home again would be to go back to the country, back to ignorance, back to provincialism, back to radical sectarianism, back to homogeneity, back to revivalism, back to poverty, back to isolationism, back to our cabins in the clearings, back to the frontier, back to all this and much, much more.

Why are Southern Baptists trying to go home again? Because it is the natural thing to do. Because it is inevitable when growth has come. Because we cannot help it when we have aged a bit. Because we are caught in a world in travail and we are badly disoriented. Because we have not yet found ways of adjusting to industrialism, unionism, urbanism, statism, socialism, or for the most part even capitalism. Because we have discovered that our old formulae for success are no longer producing results and we are in shock about it. Because we have not learned to speak today's tongue. Because we are really not at home in this brave, new world.

How are we trying to go home again? By reproducing country churches in the city suburbs. By resorting to the use of artificial stimuli to produce results like we used to have. By hiding the fact that while we are fierce of visage we are actually faint of heart. By maintaining the pretense that we are as brave as bulls when we have actually become as timid as mice. By cultivating a mood that says, "Hang the facts. Give me a cliche." By our compulsive activism.

What is going to come of the effort to go home again? The effort will win some battles but it will lose the war. It is not a mean and ignoble thing to try to go home again. In fact, it has certain truly sublime elements. It is simply not starred to succeed. We cannot turn back the clock or even stop it no matter how dramatic our histrionics. We cannot recapture our past. We cannot recall yesterday. We can't go home again.

If we can't go home again, then where can we go?

Like Abraham, we must seek that city whose builder and maker is God. We remember, however, that while the City is in eternity, the seeking must be done in time. Christ was teaching us something very near to the heart of his gospel, not just a bit of pretty ritual, when he taught us to pray, "Thy kingdom come. Thy will be done in earth, as it is in heaven" (Matthew 6:10). Believers are not free to flag or fail until "the kingdoms of this world are become the kingdoms of our Lord, and of his Christ" (Revelation 11:15).

It is the two-fold thesis of this sermon that we can't go home again and that we can move measurably toward that true home which God is preparing for them that love him. Here and now, with God's help and by his grace, we are to be moving consciously, conscientiously, and consistently toward this ideal home. Its final consummation we necessarily await, but its distinct outlines and chief characteristics we need already to be getting familiar with.

In order that we may neither waste precious time in looking back at the home whence we have come or in looking bewilderedly for the wrong city, let us give attention to some of the distinctive features of our true home, the city of God. Any home which is satisfying and adequate for God's people here must approximate in outline and foreshadow in form the qualities of the home hereafter.

How can the eternal home be identified? What is heaven like? It is a family. It is a brotherhood. It is a moral fortress. It is a workshop. It is a kingdom. Let us consider these characteristics.

The ultimate home which Christians seek is a family. In it God is Father, Jesus Christ is elder Brother, and the Holy Spirit is eternal Comforter. In it, the family of God's redeemed children shall ever dwell together in unity. The home we seek is characterized by love, joy, peace, patience, kindness, goodness, faithfulness, gentleness, self-control.

In view of that home which is our ultimate destination, let us, as an earnest of our intent, begin here and now to make of our human homes little colonies of heaven where we dwell together in Christian love, Christian joy, Christian peace, Christian patience, Christian kindness, Christian goodness, Christian faithfulness, Christian gentleness, and Christian self-control. If my profession of interest in the home to come is genuine, then there must be a reflection of that interest in my home housed on Torrington Road in Nashville.

The concept of family in our Christian faith eschews too-early dating, immature marriages, feminine fathers, masculine mothers, undisciplined children, absentee parents, juvenile delinquency, promiscuity, divorce, materialism, and all the other forces that fragment today's families. It is a concept that embraces careful preparation for marriage, spiritually solid foundations for marriage, and marriage that is both initiated and lived out "in the Lord," where believers are not yoked unequally together with unbelievers and where husband and wife and parents and children are so caught up in a dream bigger than themselves that they strive through the years to make the dream of a truly Christian home come true.

Christians seek a home characterized by brotherhood. It is a city without walls. Outside walls are not necessary in the home where we are headed because there are no enemies there. And inner walls are not required because the redeemed who dwell together in brotherly love have no selfish interests to protect, no evil to hide, no exclusiveness to relish, no psychological complexes to nurture by shutting out somebody else.

In view of the city without walls sought by the saved, it behooves us to begin here and now to build such cities of brotherhood. The middle wall of partition which still divides believers is a wall Jesus Christ died to tear down. To the extent that we worship that divisive wall, we recrucify Christ. To the extent that we tolerate it, we deny Him who came to break it down. To the extent that we cherish it, we dishonor Him who hated it and who hates the pride and prejudice it still stands for.

To pretend that our prejudice in maintaining the walls of racial segregation, class consciousness, economic exclusiveness, and social snobbery does no violence to the gospel of Jesus Christ our Lord and the altar of God, our Savior, is to close our eyes to the real purpose of the life and death of Christ.

We need to abolish racial discrimination in our country and in our churches, not because of a clause in the Constitution, nor because of the communist challenge, nor yet because we need the votes of the watching world. We need to conquer race prejudice because it is a sin against almighty God and a rejection of the precious blood of Jesus Christ, his only begotten Son.

Let us then cease shouting at each other across Kipling's "seas of misunderstanding." Let us rather undertake to learn, in preparation for the brotherhood beyond, to call God, "Father" and all his people, "Brother" so that God's city without walls begins to look attractive to us here and now.

Christians seek a home which is a moral fortress. It is that bastion of ultimate integrity, that impregnable mother lode of rectitude, that veritable quintessence of righteousness which John the Revelator described as the city where "there shall in no wise enter . . . anything that defileth, neither whatsoever worketh abomination, or maketh a lie" (Revelation 24:27).

As we seek the city "wherein dwelleth righteousness" let us "follow righteousness" on our way there. As we seek the city where no immorality in any form shall ever be, let us make our profession of religion a morally relevant and ethically meaningful thing here and now. Christian morality demonstrates its genuineness only when it authenticates itself outside the church house in the rough-and-tumble, everyday world in which we daily live.

In this world's moral gloom let us not idly tolerate the erosion of all moral standards until our churches become like Robinson Crusoe's goat pasture, so big that the goats inside are as wild as the goats outside. Let us rather in the moral realm become "Christ's men from head to foot and give no chances to the flesh to have its fling" (Romans 12:14, Phillips).

Christians seek a home which is a workshop. The old rocking chair won't get us there. The notion that in heaven we will be stretched out on flowery beds of ease to do nothing forever has an unquestioned appeal when we are tired, but the fact is that the notion is extra-biblical and grossly inaccurate. Our true home will be a place of creative and satisfying work for God where "his servants shall serve him" (Revelation 22:3).

As we seek the home which is the Christian's ultimate workshop, let us perform our daily work, here and now, "As unto the Lord." In the beginning God assigned Adam the work of tilling and keeping the Garden of Eden. In the decalogue He commanded his people "Six days shalt thou labor." Even so he wills for us to work. Paul proclaimed this principle when he admonished, "If any one will not work, let him not eat" (2 Thessalonians 3:10 RSV). The Christian's approach to work involves seeking to find God's will concerning what work to do, experiencing something in the work itself which is significant before God and meaningful to man, cultivating a spirit of responsibility which takes honest pride in the work done, and in finding through daily work the highest self-development of which we are capable. Daily work, rightly understood, is no onerous chore but a holy task.

Christians seek as their permanent home the city of the Great King where our final citizenship is.

As we await the final papers for our future citizenship, let us honor that future with a significant Christian citizenship where we now live.

In the last presidential election when interest in citizenship reached a new high, only 64.3 percent of the qualified voters in the United States bothered to go to polls. If we find corruption in government we cannot honestly put all the blame on the so-called professional politicians. The blame must be shared by those who refuse to work in the normal processes of citizenship. In recent years many a good man has sought elective office only to be defeated by the apathy and inertia of his friends—equally good men who did not bother to get involved. Plato rightly said that the punishment suffered by the wise who refuse to take part in the government is to live under the government of bad men.

The Christian citizen recognizes that civil government is of divine appointment. He prays for those in positions of authority. He pays his taxes. He obeys the laws. He conscientiously casts his ballot. When the situation requires it, he presents himself as a candidate for public office. He remembers to use moral discernment in his support of governmental programs, bearing in mind that his ultimate loyalty is to the King of kings. The responsible Christian citizen will not even try to wash his hands of politics. He will rather try to get redemptively involved in the whole realm of citizenship.

If Christians bear clearly enough in mind the open portals of the eternal Home and hold well enough in focus the beckoning arms of the heavenly Father, then we will avoid both crippling commitments to the home of yesterday and debilitating compromises with the home of today. We must ride light in the saddle if we are to avoid injury when the horse stumbles.

We must, if we are to manifest spiritual vigor and moral thrust, maintain a structured tentativeness with regard to this present age. Indeed, "It is people for whom the navel cord of this world has been cut who can give themselves most joyously to its redemption." [2]

This does not mean, however, that we are to retreat into stained glass sanctuaries, cutting off all concern for and commerce with the world. Quite the contrary. If we fail to leaven the lump, we fail Christ.

This emphasis on the Christian's responsibility in this world is based on the understanding that God himself cares about what happens on this earth. Jehovah God was portrayed by the prophets as being concerned about such things as military alliances, the selling of debtors into slavery, the plundering of the poor by the rich, the cheating of the buyer by the seller, and the oppression of the weak by the strong. The God of the Bible, the God Christians know through personal faith in Jesus Christ, is no abstract First Cause or Prime Mover or Great Unknown out in the Great Somewhere who can be placated by a bit of discreet crying in the chapel. He is a personal God who is very deeply and very definitely concerned about military alliances, racial segregation, the unconscionable profits of the drug industry, the indefensible price fixing that honeycombs big business, and the criminal corruption that persists in organized labor. He is concerned about tax evasion, padded expense accounts, the exploitation of violence as entertainment, the toleration of senseless killings in the boxing ring, family fragmentation, and the unsolved problems of the aging. He is concerned about the unemployment which has been almost six percent of our labor force for the past five years (the U. S. lost more time last year from unemployment than we lost in the past thirty-five years from strikes), and the one hundred billion dollars a year (or about eight percent of its gross annual product) which the world now spends on weapons. He is concerned about the hideous inanities preached as a sorry substitute for the Christian gospel, the infuriatingly bland and crashingly dull church programs calculated to produce an attitude of profane indifference, the immensely absurd spectacle of loving the souls of Negroes in Africa and hating their guts in Nashville, and all the other moral flotsam and spiritual jetsam that could be orchestrated into this melancholy tune.

God cares. God is concerned. And since God is concerned, his people have an obligation to be concerned, too.

---

[2] Karl A. Olsson, *Passion*, New York, Harper & Row, 1963, p. 91.

The demand of Christ our Lord is not that we should take a sentimental journey back home. It is rather a demand for us to take a bold and visionary giant step toward our Christian destination. What God wants of us today is not an eviscerated, all-things-to-all-men, formal confession of creedal correctness. What He wants is a quality of life that demonstrates to this world and to the great cloud of witnesses above that we have been with Jesus.

Sermon Sixteen

BLESSED IS HE THAT COMETH

REVEREND ROBERT E. CUSHMAN, PH.D.

Dean of Duke University Divinity School and Professor of Systematic Theology, Durham, North Carolina, and a minister of the Methodist Church

Robert E. Cushman was born in Fall River, Massachusetts, the son of Maud E. Cushman and the late Bishop Ralph S. Cushman. He was educated in the public schools of Rochester, New York, and graduated from Wesleyan University in 1936. He completed his studies for the Bachelor of Divinity Degree at Yale Divinity School, 1940, and received his Ph.D. degree from that institution in 1942.

Dr. Cushman was minister of the South Meriden Church, South Meriden, Connecticut, 1936-1940. He was for a short time pastor of the Park Methodist Church, Hamilton, New York, before returning to Yale as instructor in Systematic Theology. From 1943-1945 he was Professor of Religion and Director of Religious Activities at the University of Oregon, and went to Duke as Associate Professor of Systematic Theology, becoming Professor in 1948. He was elected to the deanship in 1958.

Dean Cushman was Methodist delegate to the Third World Conference on Faith and Order, Lund, Sweden, in 1952, and to the Fourth World Conference, Montreal, Canada, in 1963. Instrumental in the inauguration of the Commission on Ecumenical Consultation of the Methodist Church, he has continued a member. He has served on the North American Commission on Worship of the World Council of Churches. He is a member of the North Carolina Conference of the Methodist Church and of its Board of Education. He served as an official Observer of the Methodist Church to the Second Vatican Council in Rome in 1963.

Dean Cushman is an author of numerous articles published in learned journals and the author of a volume entitled *Therapeia: Plato's Conception of Philosophy.* Dr. Cushman is presently Director of the Wesley Works Editorial Project, sponsored by four American universities. He is a frequent lecturer and preacher, both within and without the University.

In the previous volume of *Best Sermons* Dean Cushman was represented by another Easter sermon, "Lift Up Your Hearts." In the following sermon he again shows his understanding of the meaning of Easter as the apex of Christ's life. This was the Palm Sunday sermon in Duke University Chapel on April 7, 1963.

BLESSED IS HE THAT COMETH

Scripture Lesson: Matthew 21:1-11

* * *

> And the multitude that went before him, and that followed cried saying, Hosanna to the Son of David: Blessed is he that cometh in the name of the Lord; Hosanna in the highest.
>
> Matthew 21:9

As, in the season of Lent, Christians retrace the toilsome steps of their Lord to the Mount of Calvary, they do not forget that in some mysterious way Palm Sunday is a glad day in the long memory of the Church. From the first it was such a day; it was a day of rejoicing for the pilgrim throng that accompanied Jesus into Jerusalem.

Coming up for the celebration of the Passover, the pilgrims from Galilee and beyond Jordan swelled the company of Jesus' followers. As they recognized the prophet of Galilee with his disciples, they broke into noisy acclaim, hailing Jesus in words of historic Messianic import. Somehow the ancient phrases formed on the lips of one or two, were passed along to become a chorus: "Blessed is he that cometh in the name of the Lord; Hosanna in the highest!" Evidently the contrast between the kingly role they ascribed to the prophet of Nazareth and his lowly mount quite escaped them. Seemingly, they took no notice that he rode upon a donkey, a humble beast of burden, an immemorial symbol of patient service and uncomplaining endurance. It did not occur to them that Jesus, after the fashion of the older prophets, might be enacting the meaning of his message and mission, and that the words of Zechariah might be the clue:

> Rejoice greatly, O daughter of Zion;
> Shout, O daughter of Jerusalem;
> Behold, thy king cometh unto thee;
> He is just, and having salvation;
> Lowly, and riding upon an ass,
> Even upon a colt, the foal of an ass.
>
> Zechariah 9:9

The throng was excited and in festal mood. It mooted no question of Jesus' real identity or the hidden meaning of his attested kingship. Crowds do not reflect; they react. It was enough to be carried on the upwelling tide of their own spontaneous enthusiasm. They rejoiced in the reputation of the celebrated prophet of Nazareth in Galilee, their own countrymen, with whom for this moment and with high expectations they gladly identified themselves.

But we know that the tumult and the shouting died and that the exultant gladness of the first Palm Sunday was soon to pass. The fidelity of a crowd is as substantial as the measure of its understanding, and of understanding this crowd had not enough. And shortly, in retrospect, Jesus' disciples had to view the acclaim of their master on Palm Sunday as only a passing interval or welcome relief in Jesus' fateful and relentless march to Jerusalem and to Golgotha.

From the north country, the Mount of Transfiguration, you will remember, Jesus had steadfastly set his face, like flint, to go to Jerusalem. Here was the seat of theocratic authority and power. Here was the citadel of unbending and hostile resistance to his mission, his message, and his person. Here was Mount Zion, the Temple that enthroned established culture, law, and practice. Here, in Jerusalem, Jesus was set to make his final appeal for the obedience of Israel to the imperatives of God's kingdom. Here he was to confront decisively and climactically the forces of reaction. And here also was to be settled for all time to come the question of his own identity and the real meaning of his kingship.

And now the moment of arrival is at hand. The long way is behind him; and before—beyond the brow of the Mount of Olives—lies the walled city of Jerusalem, the ponderous gates, the glistening Temple; and around Jesus and his followers is the throng of pilgrims converging on the Holy City—the city of David. We do not know what sparked the recognition of the prophet of Nazareth by the festal throng. As he rode astride a lowly beast of burden, accompanied by the disciple band, he was recognized and hailed in language that recalled the long awaited messiah of Israel's ancient hope: "Hosanna to the Son of David. Blessed is he that cometh in the name of the Lord." None knew better than the one acclaimed the hidden mockery; yet it was all so spontaneous and, withal, so right, even if for the wrong reasons, that when the Pharisees enjoined Jesus to rebuke his disciples for their scandalously exorbitant praise, Jesus justly replied: "I tell you that if these shall hold their peace, the stones will cry out." (Luke 19:40)

Our Lord fully understood that the joyous acclaim of the throng was based upon some misunderstanding and misidentification of his role and purpose. Yet that he found in it a right instinct is attested by his adroit and perfectly calculated reply to the complaining priests and scribes: "Did ye never read, Out of the mouths of babes and sucklings thou has perfected praise?" (Matthew 21:16). Jesus' irony is crystal clear in all this episode, and yet he knew that the untutored and half-childish recognition of his mission and message by the pilgrim throng was, nevertheless, a partial comprehension, however inadequate. It was plainly to be honored for such truth as it comprehended and much to be preferred to the purblind, obstinate, and crafty obliquity of rulers, priests, and scribes whose minds were fast closed, indeed, impervious to new truth. Yes, "out of the mouths of babes and sucklings thou has perfected praise!" "Except ye become as a little child, ye cannot enter the kingdom of heaven." If there had to be a choice, then Jesus had always made it clear that over-sophistication, not simplicity, is the great deceiver.

And so we may confidently believe there was for Jesus, on that first Palm Sunday, a measure of satisfaction and joy in the glad recognition of the crowd. And for Jesus' disciples it doubtless *was* a "triumphal entry," however transient. For them it was at least a momentary fulfillment of hopes they had half abandoned or no longer dared to entertain in view of Jesus' repeated warnings of his own eventual betrayal, rejection, and death. Never quite to be forgotten were the shouted hosannas, the palms, and the crowd's acclaim. But in accordance with their worst misgivings and against their irrepressible and deepest hopes, the disciples were to learn that the exultation of the crowds was only a brilliant, deceptive, and fleeting interlude.

It was like a shaft of glorious sunlight momentarily illuminating a darkening landscape in the face of an advancing storm. As we know, the storm broke; and we move quickly out of the joy and gladness of Palm Sunday into the deepening gloom and menacing shadows of the final days of Jesus' earthly ministry. So rapid is the descent into the darkness of Gethsemane and Golgotha that it is easier for us, as it was for the disciples, to account the hosannas of Palm Sunday as hollow mockery than as honest praise. And we peer in vain among the things that followed Jesus to his crucifixion on Friday for some remnants of the pilgrim bands that on Sunday had hailed his entry with words of messianic acclaim. If there were remnants present, they were silent and inconspicuous now; had they been mistaken about Jesus' real identity?

The answer is plainly, yes: they had expected an overpowering deliverer, not a prisoner under sentence of death. But the prevailing witness of the gospels is that, not only were these mistaken about Jesus' real identity, so was everyone else—not the foes of Jesus only, but even his intimate disciples. The fear, the uncertainty, the indecision, and the desertion of Jesus on the part of his disciples in the hour of crisis, and Peter's denial following upon his vehement protestations of loyalty—all of this points to imperfect understanding of Jesus' mission and, consequently, of his identity.

And not only Peter, but such other prominent disciples as James and John—and at a late hour in Jesus' ministry—these, too, reveal a painful misunderstanding of Jesus' intention and mission. Almost at the last, they secretly ask for places of pre-eminence in the messianic age about to come. It was then that Jesus disclosed with rare and unaccustomed directness the nature of his ministry. It is a ministry of uttermost service, not that of rulership, of earthly prerogative and supremacy: "The Son of Man," he said, "came not to be served, but to serve, and to give his life a ransom for many." (Mark 10:45)

Doubtless to the disciples these words were veiled in mystery—a mystery that was shortly to be embodied in the cross. But even in the cross, the embodied mystery remains. It remains for us to this day when we enter into it and take in the magnitude of the spiritual achievement it enshrines. When we do, we know and in reverence confess that we stand shamed and overpowered by the supreme moral event in the history of our race. In its spiritual vision and majesty it remains incomprehensible and unapproachable. It is the sign of the cross, incomparable, and hung mysteriously between heaven and earth and somehow as a bridge between them. In the cross somehow we know that God becomes identified with man and man with God; and in this coalescence the identity of the prophet Jesus is given. Who does not feel this is not to be blamed but to be pitied, for he has lost the capacity of deeper moral sensibility, and often not through grossness of life, but through atrophy of his powers.

The truth is none could know the identity of Jesus before Calvary; it could not be seen in prospect. The simple pilgrim did divine a charismatic greatness in the prophet of Nazareth, attested to them by his word and work in Galilee. Within the slender limits of their vision they might exult in his entry into Jerusalem. But neither they nor the disciples, much less the secularized Sadducees and fanatical Pharisees, could prove the dimensions of Jesus' vision of his vocation under God. It was appropriate that all Jerusalem should be stirred, saying, Who is this? But none could expect an answer.

The fact is the answer was not available; it had not yet been given. It could be given only by Jesus himself as the outcome of an inward struggle, the issue of which was still pending and was to be settled only by a deed of final victory over all temptation. It was to be a deed of absolute and indefectable commitment to God on behalf of deviant and wayward men. When, therefore, on Palm Sunday, Jerusalem asks saying, Who is this? the answer is not available. It is only in the making; yet it was already in the making long before the entry into Jerusalem.

If, therefore, we look at the events of Palm Sunday in the light of the deed of Good Friday, we may find a clue to the meaning of the triumphal entry because our Lord purposely put it there:

Why did Jesus ride into Jerusalem on a donkey? There is no evidence that Jesus ever before transported himself on land save on foot. Now, on his entrance into Jerusalem, he forsakes his custom and takes, not to horseback, the manner of princes and warriors, but to donkeyback. Do you not see the irony, even the whimsy in it? The prevailing conception of Messiah is that of king. Can you imagine a king making entrance to his royal city, not on a donkey merely, but a donkey's colt?!

For those who might have eyes to see, the irony, the whimsy, and, withal, the purposiveness of Jesus' action is plain. To all who can perceive, he is saying what he says to Pilate: "My kingdom is not of *this* world," that is, your world of claims and counterclaims, of status seeking, of prerogative, and enforced supremacy over men's wills. The kingdom I represent is God's, not man's.

But the point was missed by the disciples and the pilgrim throngs. Sensing that they were in the presence of prophetic greatness, it was enough for them that Jesus rode and did not walk. It was only in retrospect, in the after-days of the early Church, that Jesus' meaning was recovered from the writings of Zechariah and recorded in Matthew's version of the triumphal entry. Only then was it seen to be a triumph, but of humility:

> Tell ye the daughter of Zion
> Behold, thy *king* cometh unto thee,
> Meek, and riding upon an ass,
> And upon a colt, the foal of an ass.

By now the early church was divining the identity of Jesus. Now they knew, in the light of the Cross, that he came, as he said, not to be ministered unto, not to claim prerogatives, but to minister and to serve. In truth, his kingdom was not of this world. But he was revealed as the King in the realm of the spirit. There, he was King of kings and Lord of Lords, that is, in perfect obedience unto God and in entire service to man. He was Basileus, king; but he was the meek king, *Basileus prāos.* For Jesus himself had taught in word, enacted in life, embodied in death, and received in the Resurrection the truth of the beatitude: "Blessed are the meek, for they shall inherit the earth."

On that first Palm Sunday all Jerusalem was stirred, saying, Who is this? The answer was not fully available. Jesus was in process of making answer. We know him or may know him as the ironical, whimsical, and mysterious one, not simply the prophet from Nazareth of Galilee. For in the Cross he everlastingly identifies himself for those who will stop to see, to gaze, to ponder, and to learn. In the Cross of his entire self-offering he is, in the centurion's words of dawning and fulfilled realization, truly the Son of God. So, likewise, if we can come to see, and with the centurion at the foot of the Cross, enter somewhat into the mystery that is embodied there, we will be better able than the pilgrims on that first Palm Sunday to declare: "Blessed *is* he that cometh in the name of the Lord."

Sermon Seventeen

THE DYNAMIC PERSONALITY OF CHRIST

REVEREND LESLIE D. WEATHERHEAD, PH.D., D.D., LITT.D., C.B.E.

Minister Emeritus, The City Temple (Congregational), London, England, and Honorary Chaplain to Her Majesty's Forces

In *The Dynamic Personality of Christ,* Dr. Weatherhead speaks with a progressive spiritual force which captures the imagination and holds the attention to the last word. There are places where he reminds us of John Wesley or Jonathan Edwards, yet he is as modern as today in his choice of words and the content of his message.

Born in London in 1893, Leslie Weatherhead studied at Richmond Theological College, London University, and Manchester University. During World War I he entered the military service of his country and served as a second lieutenant in India, Mesopotamia, Kurdistan and Persia. In 1919 he returned to Madras, India, for the English Methodist Church, and in 1922 was invited to Manchester and Leeds.

After serving as Minister of Wesleyan Methodist Churches for some years, he was called in 1936 to be the Minister of City Temple, London, and remained there until his retirement in 1961. When City Temple was destroyed during World War II he kept the congregation together for eleven years in rented church quarters. He helped to raise funds for the new building, part of which was contributed by the Rockefellers, and in 1958 the congregation moved into the beautiful new church building of stone and stained glass.

Dr. Weatherhead has written a number of significant books, including, *After Death, Psychology and Life, Jesus and Ourselves, How Can I Find God?, Who Do Men Suffer?, Personalities of the Passion, Discipleship, A Plain Man Looks at the Cross.* The value of his work has been recognized by the honorary doctorate of the University of Edinburgh, Pacific School of Religion, and the College of

Puget Sound. Over the years he has been popular as a preacher in England, the United States, and in various other parts of the world. He has always possessed the ability to bring fresh meaning to religious truth and encouragement to his hearers.

THE DYNAMIC PERSONALITY OF CHRIST

From time to time I am sure it is a good thing to spend part of a service in what I call "looking at Jesus"; for the heart of the Christian religion is our personal relationship with Him, and thus it is of supreme importance that we see Him as clearly as we can and from time to time look at Him from a different angle.

Let us go back to the origin of Christianity. Let us imaginatively do away with a lovely building like this, the architecture of which has the one aim that men shall be helped to worship God and to listen to Christ's message. Let us wash out imaginatively all the aids to worship, the comfort and warmth of this place, the lovely music, the book in front of you which contains a thousand hymns, the language of the prayers, some of them sanctified by centuries of use. Let us imaginatively see twelve young men who companioned with Jesus. None of them is highly educated or socially important. To us now they would look like a group of uncouth young fellows, little more than boys.

I want you now to make a mental picture of your fishmonger, the man who last Friday wrapped up some cod in a newspaper and handed it to you! Don't think I am criticizing fishmongers. Ours is a friend. But if on the way home somebody said to you, "Do you know that the man who wrapped up your fish today will one day be known by his Christian name to every educated person in the world? The most influential church in the world will be named after him and he will write words that will be read in every church for two thousand years. In some people's minds he will not only be called a saint, but be regarded with the deepest reverence. People will not only revere his statue, but kiss its toe?"—would you not laugh and say, "Don't be so ridiculous"? But all this is true of Peter who wrapped up in leaves, parcels of fish and sold them to men and women in Galilee. And what was the transforming power that changed Peter, the fisherman, into Peter, the most famous apostle in the world? The answer is the dynamic personality of Christ.

You may remember that when you returned from the Continent, a dull and rather stuffy little man, who peered at you through thick glasses, made you open your bag at the dock and declare what your luggage contained. If somebody said, "He will one day be a world-famous saint and his words will be read and revered throughout Christendom for all time," you would find it hard to believe. But, you see, Matthew, the customs clerk, met *Jesus*.

Luke was only an ordinary general practitioner as far as we know, but nobody else recorded the parable of the Prodigal Son, or the detailed story of the Way to Emmaus, or the parable of the Lost Coin and the Lost Sheep. You see, Luke, the doctor, wrote about *Jesus*.

Pilate was only a very ordinary governor of a very ordinary province, in a very ordinary country at the wrong end of the Mediterranean. But every time an Anglican says the creed, he speaks the name of Pontius Pilate. Pilate's name would long since have been forgotten. But one of his prisoners was *Jesus*.

As for the half-crippled, probably epileptic tent-maker, of whom we read that "his stature was unimpressive and his speech contemptible" (II Corinthians 10:10), the power that turned Paul round and changed him from a narrow-minded ecclesiastical fanatic into the great missionary of the Gentiles was the dynamic personality of Jesus Christ.

* * *

When we write to our friends we begin with our address and the date. Has it ever occurred to you why the year is dated thus? Have you ever paused to consider what power it was that changed the centuries out of their course? It was the dynamic personality of Jesus Christ. After all, many attempts had been made to change the calendar. It was suggested that the calendar should date from the building of Rome. It was decreed that after the name of the year should appear the magic letters A.U.C. (ab urbe condita)—from the building of the city. But it lasted so short a time that, if I may say so, you had never heard of it, had you? "Let us count time from the French Revolution," said men of great power in Europe's affairs. It lasted thirteen years. "Let us count time from an important conjunction of the planets," said La Place, the astronomer. It lasted three years. The most amusing illustration of all came my way a few years ago when a distinguished Mohammedan wrote to me. At the top of his paper at one side was the number of the years as Mohammedans reckon them, viz. the Heggira, or flight of Mohammed from Mecca to Medina, but at the other side of his notepaper was the number 1960, as though in having to write both numbers he confessed the small power of Mohammed compared with the might of Jesus Christ. "One name alone is stamped on the brow of the hurrying centuries," said Dr. Fitchett, "and it is the name of Jesus Christ." He adds, "Here is a peasant in the darkest age of the world; He lived in a subject province; He never wrote a sentence which has been preserved, He died when He had scarcely reached manhood and He died cast out by His own race and abandoned by His scanty handful of followers, and yet twenty centuries after He hung on the Cross, His birth is accepted, by believers and unbelievers alike, as the point whence all the centuries must be counted. . . . He has lifted, with His pierced hands, empires off their hinges, turned the stream of the centuries out of its channel, and still governs the ages." The dynamic power of Jesus Christ!

Many a newspaper today will fill its columns with attacks on everything Jesus Christ stands for, but at the top of the page, in printing the date, it will pay tribute to His power.

* * *

Let us look at Him again tonight, for one of our dangers is that we have become sentimental about Him. If you were away for Christmas and went to church, I expect some of you at least heard a sermon on the text, "There was no room for Him in the inn," and the preacher frequently (and legitimately, of course) pleads that Christ should be given a place in the human heart. Thousands of sermons have been preached on the picture of Christ gently knocking at the door. We have all seen Him depicted for us as the Friend of little children, the gentle Shepherd with the lambs, the lonely Man outcast by His fellows, the tragic Figure Who hangs on the Cross—and all this is true.

But wait a moment! Do you remember a word of His that begins, "Women of Jerusalem, weep not for Me!" We have seen pictures of Jesus in a beautiful pastoral landscape, with His men following behind, or Jesus teaching and preaching, with people lounging on the green grass in front of Him. We have seen pictures of Jesus in a spotless robe, healing a young girl with lovely flowing hair of some invisible disease. But sometimes I wish I could smash the stained-glass windows and tear up the sentimental pictures. If you could see the stinking Jerusalem bazaar even as it is today, and if you could imagine Jesus walking through that with its bug-infested beggars exhibiting their revolting sores and discharging ulcers; if you could have taken in the harshness of some of His sayings, it would correct your perspective. As Donald Miller said in his book, *The People of God:* "The sentimentalized Jesus of our time is not One before whom men would fall on their faces, and certainly He would frighten away no devils! He is One whom nobody would crucify, and for whom few, if any, would be willing to die. He could not have brought the Church into being, nor could He have sustained it through all the tortuous course of the long centuries." And I invite you to listen while I read some grim passages to you.

I came not to bring peace, but a sword! For I came to set a man at variance against his father, and the daughter against her mother, and the daughter-in-law against her mother-in-law: and a man's foes shall be they of his own household. He that loveth father or mother more than Me is not worthy of Me; and he that loveth son or daughter more than Me is not worthy of Me. And he that doth not take his cross and follow after Me, is not worthy of Me. (Matthew 10:34-38)

Ye generation of vipers, how shall ye escape the damnation of hell? Woe unto you, scribes and Pharisees, hypocrites! (Matthew 3:7, 23:13)

His eyes were as a flame of fire; . . . His voice was as the sound of many waters. . . . Out of His mouth proceeded a sharp two-edged sword and His countenance was as the sun shining in its strength. And when I saw Him, I fell at His feet as one dead. (Revelation 1:14-17)

Let us remember that although the idea of hell was caricatured by the vicious spiritual sadism of our grandfathers, the origin of the idea of hell lay in the words of Jesus. It was He who spoke of a door that was shut and of an agelong flame, and of weeping and gnashing of teeth.

Let us remember that it was He who said, "If thine hand offend thee, cut it off, and if thine eye offend thee, pluck it out" (Matthew 5:29-30). Certainly the words are not to be taken literally. But there is nothing sloppy or sentimental in the teaching of Jesus, for in these words He is really saying that if your job (that which your hand finds to do) imperils your soul, throw it up. He is saying that it is no good talking about "seeing life," if it imperils the soul to do so. It is better to live a one-eyed life and put up with your alleged frustration.

No one in the world ever spoke such tender, gentle, kindly words to sinners as Jesus did, but no one in the world ever said such dreadful things about sin. Even the tender parable of the Prodigal, you see, contains words like these: "This, my son, was dead and is alive again; he was lost and is found." *Dead! Lost!* So these are the words that describe what sin can do to you!

I have heard people in their prayers, and ministers in church, plead that they might have a vision of God: "Reveal to us Thy presence and show to us Thy face." I know that I have often used similar words myself. But if you are a slum landlord; if you have just chalked a swastika on a Jew's front-door; if you have blackened by gossip somebody's name; if you have been cruel to a child; if you have encouraged some young person in sin, if you have, by your flirtation, broken up a home and smashed another's marriage, I don't think you will be very happy about seeing His face and you will not be able to sing sincerely:

> Jesus, the very thought of Thee
> With sweetness fills the breast;
> But sweeter far Thy face to see,
> And in Thy presence rest.

Sweetness! I think you would be amongst those who cry to the hills, fall on us, and to the mountains, cover us, and as for resting quietly in His presence, I think you might feel like John on Patmos:

> His eyes were as a flame of fire, and from His mouth proceeded a sharp two edged sword, and when I saw Him, I fell at His feet as one dead.

* * *

There are two types of men who make me more angry than most. I hope you will think my anger is righteous indignation and not just personal hostility!

1. The first is the conceited egotist who seems to have forgotten the best definition in the world of egotism, viz. "it is the anaesthetic which God allows us to take in order to deaden the pain of feeling fools." I think of the egotist who frankly thinks of Jesus as an easy-going, weak personality. Gentle Jesus in fact! Such an egotist imagines that in that inevitable encounter which must come to us all when the soul is confronted by Christ, Jesus will pat him on the back and say, "Let's all be matey in heaven. I know you never lifted a finger to help another person, and I know you made your money in ways better forgotten; that you made your wife hate you, and your children dreaded the sound of your voice; I am aware that no one ever found out about this and that and the other. But never mind, it is all over. You didn't mean any harm. Come along into heaven and be happy." Oh, it won't be like that, you know, not when you see His face! You won't be able to say "Gentle Jesus" then. You will "fall at His feet as one dead."

Why, some of these self-important egotists actually patronize Jesus! I have heard them do so. They will say to me, "Yes, I have heard somewhere about the City Temple. I will come along one Sunday and hear you." Do they want me to say, "Oh, how very kind of you!" May I say, with throttled down anger, that I do not want them to hear *me?* I want them to get in touch with *Him*. Many do not realize that they are on the way to hell and that their stained-glass picture of gentle Jesus is just as misleading as it could possibly be. But nothing, nothing can break the shell of their complacent egotism. The eyes of the soul are so heavily bandaged that nothing will make it see, until at last the ruthless hand of Reality, in some dreadful day of judgment, tears the bandage from those eyes and men see themselves—which they may be able to bear—and see the *awful* face of Christ and feel the impact of His terrible purity, which will surely bring them flat on their faces. What other posture is possible for them, for even the *saint* said, "When I saw Him, I fell at His feet as one dead"?

2. The second class of person I find it hard to bear is the pimply young man who mutters that religion is all right for women: as much as to say, of course, that for he-men, like himself, it has really failed to appeal. It is effeminate and sentimental and credulous and feeble and a kind of crutch on which the weak may lean, but which strong men like himself do not need! Oh, you little puppy! So now you can feel with your finger the faintest down on your upper lip and you can smoke half-way through a pipe without being sick, and you think of yourself as a he-man! Indeed, one such puppy, to whom I was introduced, told me that he was a scientist! I looked at him in amazement for he was about nineteen. I thought the word scientist was a word one applied to men like Einstein and Dr. Bronowski and Professor A. C. Lovell, but I find that if you have taken chemistry and physics in your General Certificate of Education you may now call yourself a "scientist"! And this little pathological specimen talked as though the Christian religion was not a strong enough, manly enough thing for him!

Of course Christianity *is* all right for women. It has given to some of the finest women in the world the qualities we admire. When I look at the weedy youth before me I wonder how he would have reacted to the tests and trials and temptations of some of the great women in the world like Perpetua, St. Teresa, the Maid of Orleans, Florence Nightingale, Nurse Cavell, Mary Slessor, Amy Wilson Carmichael and Ida Scudder.

But if he means that Christianity is not a manly enough religion, I can only deduce that he has never seen the real Jesus. I wonder how long our puppy would have stayed with Paul in his trials, tortures and imprisonment. I wonder if he regards Augustine as a real man, Augustine whose thought dominated the mind of Western Europe for centuries! I wonder if Livingstone would have tolerated our "scientist" in the forests and swamps of Africa. And I wonder where he would have been when Latimer said to Ridley, as they were both burned at the stake for Christ's sake, "Be of good cheer, Master Ridley, and play the man, for this day we shall, by God's grace, light such a candle in England as shall never be put out." No, I think our little puppy had better go back to Peckham in a nice warm train and creep into bed with a bag of peppermints and his hot-water bottle, and a copy of one of our modern, sloppy love-stories and keep his mouth shut about Christ's religion. He isn't big enough for it yet. God help us, who amongst us is?

Oh, men and women, let the wind of Reality—bleak and cold though it may be—blow away our silly egotism, our foolish pride, our futile excuses, our cowardly hide-outs. Let us remember together that the day will come when no excuse will hide us any longer.

When I am introduced to a worldling, it is really amusing to me the way in which he will try to make contact with me. As soon as he knows I am a parson, he will rake up some uncle of his who once wanted to be a missionary, or he will tell me that he once had an aunt in Bloomsbury who was a big Baptist! Isn't it pathetic, and isn't it dreadful when you think that one day he will be face to face with Reality, and that all of us will have all our excuses and disguises and pretences, and silly, futile mannerisms stripped away from us? Yes, my friend, hold your head as high as you like! It will be bowed before Him at last, "for in the name of Jesus every knee shall bow and every tongue confess that Jesus Christ is Lord, to the glory of God the Father."

Do not imagine that you can hold any door closed against Him at the last. Your hidden motives, your business life, your secret sex life, your family life, your social life will all lie open before the eyes of Him with whom we have to do, and no Bluebeard hand of yours will be able to keep any door shut against Him.

What is your definition of a fanatic? I think my description of one would be a person who becomes very excited and emphatic about things which are really of no importance. Do you think Jesus was a fanatic? Do you think He used the language we have been quoting about things that really do not matter? If He were no more than a man, however loving and gentle and kind, Who walked across the stage of history two thousand years ago, saying beautiful things and doing lovely deeds, well, we may be able to escape His challenge. But if this Man is as much of God as can be poured into a human life without disrupting its humanity —and this is how I describe divinity; if He really had the values for us of God Himself, and if what He says is not a human opinion, but a divine revelation, then remember He is standing just as near to you as He was to the Scribes and Pharisees and the people of His day. Remember that what He said to them He says to us, and the God He revealed to them is the God with whom we still have to do. The challenge He made to them He makes to us.

I enjoy talking to you about the love and forgiveness and gentleness of God, but do let us sometimes look at another side of His nature. There lies before each one of us, if we have not reached it already, the point at which there is an inescapable encounter with Reality, an inevitable meeting with God. I should like to think that tonight you are making up your mind not to pretend, or pose, or hide, or try to escape any more, but that you have looked at the real Christ tonight and decided to respond to His challenge.

> He hath sounded forth the trumpet that shall never call retreat;
> He is sifting out the hearts of men before His judgment seat;
> O, be swift, my soul, to answer Him; be jubilant, my feet!
> For GOD is marching on.

Sermon Eighteen

THE LIGHT THAT SHINES FOREVER

REVEREND CARL F. H. HENRY, TH.D., PH.D., LITT.D.

A Minister of the American Baptist Convention, and Editor of Christianity Today, *Washington, D. C.*

Carl Henry is highly respected as a preacher and as Editor of *Christianity Today* he exercises a wide influence over a large section of Christian thinking today. He began a writing career as editor of *The Smithtown Star* and the *Port Jefferson Times-Echo,* two Long Island weekly newspapers. He was also a suburban correspondent for *The New York Times, The New York Herald-Tribune,* and the *Chicago Tribune.* In these busy years he was converted to the Christian faith and felt the call to become a minister of the Gospel. He therefore attended Wheaton College to take two degrees, then took his first theological degree at Northern Baptist Theological Seminary in 1941, followed the next year by his Th.D. at the same institution. Ordained to the Baptist ministry in 1941, he did further graduate study at Loyola University, Chicago; Indiana University; took his Ph.D. at Boston University in 1949, then did more graduate study at New College, Edinburgh, in 1953. Seattle Pacific College conferred the honorary Litt.D. upon him in 1963.

Dr. Henry was Chairman of the Philosophy of Religion department at Northern Baptist Theological Seminary, Chicago, 1942-47; Professor of Theology and Christian Philosophy, Fuller Theological Seminary, Pasadena, California, 1947-57. He has also been visiting professor at Wheaton College, Gordon Divinity School, and Winona Lake Summer School of Theology. He has been Editor of *Christianity Today* since it began fortnightly publication in 1956.

He has written a number of distinctive books, including: *A Doorway to Heaven, Remaking the Modern Mind, The Uneasy Conscience of Modern Fundamentalism, Giving a Reason for Our Hope, Fifty Years of Protestant Theology, The Drift of Western Thought, Christian Personal Ethics, Aspects of Christian Social Ethics* (to be published in 1964). He has traveled widely, visiting Burma, Thailand, Malaya, the Philippines, South America, Germany, Switzerland, Africa.

This sermon was delivered at Asbury Theological Seminary Alumni Association, Wilmore, Kentucky. Its evangelical spirit is strong and clear.

THE LIGHT THAT SHINES FOREVER

And the light shineth in darkness; and the darkness comprehended it not.

John 1:5, A.V.

The contrast of light and darkness is a familiar Biblical motif. In Genesis it appears in the created sequence of night and day; elsewhere in the Pentateuch, in the cloud by day and pillar of fire by night; and in the Prophetic Writings, in the light to arise and shine upon the Gentiles. The motif remains throughout the Gospels, in the Book of Acts, in the Epistles, and even into the Book of Revelation. One can, in fact, summarize the story of creation, of revelation, of regeneration, of sanctification and of final glorification, each and all, in these few words: "And God said, Let there be light . . . and there was light."

In the prologue of John's Gospel this motif appears in one of the most familiar yet most elusive passages in the Bible: *And the light shineth in darkness; and the darkness comprehended it not* (1:5, A.V.). Here two elements of special interest stand out: the first, a matter of tense—the tense of the Greek verb *phainō* in the first clause of the sentence; and the second, a matter of meaning—of what for the moment we may call "the mystery" of *katalambanō*, the Greek verb in the closing clause.

The light *shines* in the darkness, writes John. The Greek tense is present: the light *is shining* in the darkness—or, as The New English Bible has it, "The light shines on in the dark." The shining Light of John's Gospel is, of course, the Logos, the divine agent in creation, and the divine agent in redemption. As the eternal Christ once lighted the primal creation when it was a desolation and a waste ("without form and void"), so too He illumines the darkness of the fallen world of sin and shame. He said not simply "I was" but rather "I *am* the light of the world." "The light shines on in the dark." The Light of the World is shining still, even here, even now.

In translating the verb *katalambanō*, the translators seem to tumble over each other. The Authorized Version has: "and the darkness comprehended it not" (that is, failed to grasp the light, hence remains darkness still). On the other hand, the Revised Standard Version has: "and the darkness has not overcome it" (put it out). And The New English Bible: "the darkness had never quenched it" (hence the light is inextinguishable). At the heart of the difficulty is the Greek word *katalambanō*, which bears a variety of meanings—among them, to perceive, apprehend, overtake. Is the Apostle John then simply telling us that the darkness hasn't perceived the light, or rather, that the light keeps shining still despite every effort of darkness to quench it? Is John simply commenting on the character of the darkness or is he also making an affirmation about the light? Does he merely affirm the depth of iniquity, or does he declare also the inextinguishability of the light?

We are forced to do exactly what the translators themselves must do whenever they are unsure about the precise meaning of a word—and that is to search its context for a clue. A translator goes first to the writer's immediate context, then to the larger context of the whole gospel or epistle, and then to an author's other writings.

I

There is much in context to support the emphasis on the darkness as stubborn and uncomprehending of the light. Surely you will recall some of the important ingredients of John's Gospel: "He came unto his own, and his own received him not" (1:11)—His own creation, His own people. "The light shineth . . . and the darkness comprehended it not." Even His brethren in their unbelief repeatedly urge Him to go to Jerusalem and manifest Himself openly (7:3 f.). "The light shineth . . . and the darkness comprehended it not." Jesus is betrayed and scourged, and the Jews cry out, "Away with him, away with him, crucify him." "The light shineth . . . and the darkness comprehended it not." One recalls the Saviour's biting comment to Nicodemus: "This is the condemnation, that light is come into the world, and men loved darkness rather than light" (3:19).

"The light shineth in the darkness and the darkness comprehended it not." We need to hear afresh this emphasis that the light shines *in the darkness.* Modern man minimizes the depth of this darkness. By calling the darkness light, he tries to dispense with the need for supernatural light.

Hegel and the pantheists said (and some of the religious cults are still saying it) that everything that is, is a part of God. What man is doing, God is doing; what man is saying, God is saying. Everything is light; there may be shadow—the light turned low—but never darkness! Protestant liberal theology was influenced by such speculations in its denial of Satan and of original sin, and of man's need of regeneration and atonement.

Darwin and the evolutionary naturalists said that from an animal past all history is automatically moving higher toward a golden age. The darkness is far behind us; the light is becoming ever brighter. Liberal Protestantism was misled by naturalistic rationalism in its denial of the divine creation of the world out of nothing, of the fall of man, and of man's need of supernatural salvation.

Modern scientism says that the darkness is mere ignorance. Ours is the dawn of the human mind, not the black midnight of the soul, and our human ingenuity can illuminate the whole universe. We can put men into orbit, we can put Telstar into orbit, we can put a man on the moon —all magnificent achievements of modern technology. But it is not "He that is come down from heaven" (3:13) but the man we propel into the heavens who becomes the secularist hope of the space age; not the eternal word of the Logos, but the new era of human communication we can establish—in such progress men rest the hope of a new world.

Even the Church sometimes is misled by contemporary speculations about the social order, and acts to transform its essential nature by merely improving the environment, by relying on legislation more than regeneration. We are prone to trust all the change-agents for a new and better world except the only one the Bible commends, the grace and power of God who gives the gift of repentance.

John writes of *darkness* and he exempts no generation of fallen history from his phrasing. He writes of a world wherein generation after generation has been in the grasp of perverse men (in our time, Hitler, Mussolini, Khrushchev, Mao-Tse-Tung); where human nature is in the clutch of corruption and in the service of Satan. He speaks of mankind as lost not only in inhumanity and bestiality, but in moral rebellion and spiritual wickedness. And he does not exclude a land like ours, gripped by the passion for money and leisure and sex and status. *Darkness* is John's word for the ambiguous enterprise that we so often dignify by such terms as human culture and civilization of which we are often tempted to speak only good. Darkness is his word for the whole gamut of human life insofar as it is without God and without grace.

We Christians easily overestimate the potentialities of the unregenerate world, because we read it through the lenses of our partial sanctification. One night in Chicago the blind evangelist Walter Kallenbach was preaching during a violent thunderstorm. He could not see the flashes of lightning that probed everywhere through the night sky, but he could hear the thunderbolts and the wailing fire sirens. At one point he sensed—by that sixth sense that providence seems to have given those who lack one of the customary five—that the lights had gone off in the auditorium.

As he detected an invisible audience's restlessness, he stopped preaching and made a disarming comment. "Now," he said, "you are all in the world in which I live all the time." Do you know the character of the world in which the world itself lives all the time? *Darkness!* That is the way John the Evangelist puts it: "The light shines in the darkness."

Think of the darkness of our century:

The rise of Communism in a single generation sweeping into its totalitarian orbit three-fifths of the world's land mass and half the world's population, including the heartland of the Protestant Reformation.

The rise of the Nazis with their inhumane concentration camps, and the anti-Semitism symbolized by Eichmann and the slaughter of six million Jews. During the brief period of the Eichmann trial I attended in Jerusalem, witnesses told how the corpses of slain Jews were suspended from hooks in a slaughter house and displayed there beneath signs that were marked Kosher—in civilized Europe, in the twentieth century.

The missionary flow now runs from East to West, reversing the great nineteenth century missionary movement to win the Orient for Christ. Today missionaries from the pagan religions of the East (Buddhists from Burma, Hindus from India, Moslems from Arab lands) are sending missionaries to the "dark continents of the West"—the United States included—to offer spiritual light. There is a Bahai Temple in Evanston, a Moslem mosque in Washington. Strange new cults are on the move. In the United States, the Black Muslims now number more than 200,000 members. In Japan there are 20 million devotees in 120 new cults.

In Latin America, 88 percent of the population are baptized Roman Catholics, yet the vast majority seldom see the inside of a church, and spiritualism is sweeping many countries. In England, the land of the Wesleys, of the 26 million baptized Anglicans, less than 3 million are on the church rolls.

Darkness—that is John's term for the sweep of history without God. The corruption of human nature, the pursuit of false gods, the willful dimming of the light of the Logos—this is what he sees in the human enterprise. Our generation seems, like every other, to be marching into the night, plunged into the terrible depth of the darkness.

II

But is this really the emphasis John has most in mind: the dread reality of darkness? Or does he go beyond the fact of darkness to say something about the light—its persistence and inextinguishability?

Recall the immediate context again. "The light shines in the darkness.

. . . There was a man sent from God." In the midst of fallen history there is saving history, there is redemptive history, there is the proffered grace of God. Recall the larger context of the Gospel. "But to as many as received him, to them gave he power to become the sons of God" (1:12). As the Revised Standard Version has it, "the darkness has not overcome. . . ." Even the Greeks come saying, "Sir, we would see Jesus" (12:21). "The darkness has not overcome. . . ." Even in the Sanhedrin Nicodemus rises to his defense: "Does our law condemn a man before it hear him?" "The darkness has not overcome. . . ." The centurion owns him as the Son of God before the soldiers at Calvary. "The darkness has not overcome." Even when impaled upon the cross, He establishes a new family on the basis of redemption rather than of human blood: "Woman, behold thy son," "Son, behold thy mother." "The darkness has not overcome." And when every last blow has been struck against the Son of God, the crucified Christ rises in triumph from the tomb. "The darkness has not overcome." "The light shines on in the dark, and the darkness has never quenched it." The darkness has not put out the light, has not extinguished it.

Even in our times! Not only after Herod, after Judas, after Pilate, but after Hegel, after Darwin, after Marx, after Bultmann!

Do you recall how in the lean years when liberalism ruled the American pulpits Charles Fuller, venturing alone under God, preached the Gospel on radio until his voice was heard world-wide in the proclamation of good news? The darkness had not overcome the light! In my college days some extreme dispensationalist preachers declared that the Church had moved so far into final apostasy that the pulpit could only engage in a holding operation until the Lord's return, and insisted that there would never again be a great response to mass evangelism. But Billy Graham was spurred on by the Spirit of God until he touched every continent for the Gospel, and found an opportunity to witness even to presidents and kings and queens, and not long ago Chicago—the so-called graveyard of evangelism—gave him the largest crusade to date, while television has carried his message to millions. "The light shines on in the dark, and the darkness has never quenched it."

Do you recall how, after China fell and other smaller Asian lands began to topple to the Communists, missionaries despaired that all of Asia might be sealed to the Gospel? But Bob Pierce shuttled his pastors conferences across the Orient, gathering together national workers from the big cities and from the hill country along the Communist frontiers, and in this evangelical fellowship the Christian task force got new steel for its spirit in obedience to Christ's commission. In Burma I ministered to 1200 national workers whose Bibles were open in 20 different languages, many of them Karens from the Communist-infested mountains of the North. "The light shines on in the dark, and the darkness has never quenched it."

Do you recall how for a generation multitudes of ministers lamented the fact that *The Christian Century*, left-wing in its theological and liberal positions, was the only intellectually influential Protestant journal on the American scene? Then eight years ago a tiny band of Christian leaders met on a Labor Day week-end in New York City and launched *Christianity Today*, dedicated to the New Testament evangel, and today it has the largest circulation in the world to the Protestant ministry on an interdenominational basis. "The light shines on in the dark, and the darkness has never quenched it."

God is at work in the history of our times. The ancient prophecies are being fulfilled. The Jews are regathering in Palestine . . . in unbelief. Signs of Christ's coming multiply. "The light shines in on the dark, and the darkness has never quenched it."

Even here, even now, God is at work in your life and mine, miserable sinners though we were, justifying us by His grace, sanctifying us by His power. "Christ in you the hope of glory." So "the light shines on in the dark, and the darkness has never quenched it." Remember that He answers our prayers, that He promises strength sufficient in our weakness, that He pledges to conform us at last to His glorious image. "And they shall see his face. . . . And there shall be no night there . . . for the Lord God giveth them light" (Revelation 22:4-5). "And the light shines on"—verily, it is light that shines forever.

Sermon Nineteen

CHRISTIANITY AND FREEDOM

REVEREND EDWARD HUGHES PRUDEN, TH.M., PH.D., D.D.

Minister, First Baptist Church, Washington, D. C.

Dr. Pruden was born in Virginia in 1903, graduated from the University of Richmond in 1925 and from the Southern Baptist Seminary, Louisville, in 1928. During 1929-30 he did graduate work at Yale and in 1931 received his Ph.D. from the University of Edinburgh. The University of Richmond conferred the honorary D.D. upon him in 1932.

Ordained to the ministry of the Baptist Church in 1935, he was pastor of the church in Petersburg, Virginia, 1930-35, and in 1936 was called to be minister of the distinguished First Baptist Church in Washington. Here his sermons have won him great respect and his congregation has become a challenging one, where men and women from all walks of life, senators, representatives, world leaders, occasionally one of the presidents, attend.

In 1935 and 1936 he was a guest teacher at the University of Shanghai and is a member of the board of founders of that university, a trustee of the University of Richmond, a member (and past president) of the American Baptist Convention, formerly a member of the board and president of the American Baptist Foreign Mission Society, a member of the board of Trustees of Southern Baptist Theological Seminary. He is a director and past president of the Washington Federation of Churches and a member of the Washington Office of the National Council of Churches.

He is the author of *Interpreters Needed*, has contributed sermons to several books, served as Washington correspondent for the Christian Century, contributes to religious journals and has been represented in *Best Sermons* several times. This sermon touches freedom on many various social, political and religious aspects and gives spiritual direction for life today. His statement on the misrepresentation of freedom is important.

CHRISTIANITY AND FREEDOM

Dr. Frank P. Graham, former President of the University of North Carolina, and a former United States Senator from that state, was the principal speaker recently at a dinner in Washington which was sponsored by the editors of the Upper Room devotional booklet. He paid glowing tribute to the ideals of human freedom which our Founding Fathers wrote into our Federal Constitution, and then, referring to the current struggle to make full citizenship available to all our citizens, he called this present struggle an effort to complete "the unfinished business" of our democratic form of government.

Our late Secretary of State, Mr. John Foster Dulles, speaking before the General Assembly of the National Council of Churches several years ago, said: "The dominant American theme, both domestically and internationally, has been human freedom. Our nation was born as a revolt against despotism. That freedom concept caught the imagination of the world. It was called the 'Great American Experiment.'" And just a little further on in the same address, he declared: "Today, freedom is threatened as never before." It behooves all of us, therefore, to recognize the dangers besetting human liberties today; to redefine our concept of freedom; and to intensify our efforts to strengthen the foundations of freedom in our own country while providing every possible encouragement to the struggle for freedom in other lands around the world.

Let it be understood that as Christians our pronounced interest in freedom is by no means purely academic, sociological, or political, but primarily spiritual. However, it will be recognized immediately that any genuinely spiritual approach to the principle of freedom will inevitably have academic, sociological and political implications, for the relationship which the Christian has with his Lord must affect his total existence. Freedom looms large in every area of our program of Christian service. It is impossible to think of evangelism without thinking of freedom from darkness and despair. It is impossible to think of Christian education without thinking of freedom from ignorance and superstition. It is impossible to think of growth in discipleship without thinking of freedom from pride and prejudice and all the limitations of the natural man. It is impossible to think of the humanitarian phases of our ministry, such as orphanages, hospitals, homes for the aged, and social centers, without thinking of freedom from neglect, loneliness, pain and fear. And certainly it is impossible to think of world missions without thinking of the multitudes who are waiting to be freed from the meaningless worship of false gods, and the tragedies which inevitably occur where the message of the Christian gospel has not been proclaimed.

Let us consider first of all the misinterpretations of freedom which we must avoid at all cost. The first of these is that glorification of man which ignores the limitations within which his freedom operates. Dr. Elton Trueblood has written: "Millions, when they assert their faith in freedom, mean to say that they believe it is the natural right of every man to do exactly as he pleases under all circumstances. The popular position in the West is the opinion that freedom, in the sense of the elimination of all inhibitions on personal action is a natural right and ought not to be denied to anyone." From this shallow interpretation of human liberty we would recoil in horror and strenuous disapproval.

We fully recognize that the warning of Paul to the Church at Galatia is still needed by us today. "For you were called to freedom," he said, "only do not use your freedom as an opportunity for the flesh, but through love be servants of one another." This is not only a recognition of the misuse to which sinful man may put his freedom, but is a reminder that within the framework of a free society we are confronted by the obligation to serve one another in true Christian humility.

The second misinterpretation of freedom which we must scrupulously avoid is the tendency to glorify freedom as an end in itself, which could be interpreted as an invitation to anarchy. Dr. Reinhold Niebuhr has said that "Man is most free in the discovery that he is not free." Confronted by any suggestion that man is ever absolutely free, we would reaffirm our belief in the sovereignty of God. Kierkegaard has made it plain that the individual is indeed free to determine what his response to God shall be, but he cannot determine, by his own choice, what God's offer is.

Some one has suggested that our struggle against the totalitarian concept of government would be more enlightened and more Christian if we recognized that an extreme emphasis upon individualism represents just as great a departure in one direction from the Christian ideal as totalitarianism does in the other. The restraints laid upon individuals in the formation of our national government recognize the natural tendency of men to misuse the liberties to which they have fallen heir. In his farewell address, George Washington supported his belief in constitutional restraints by referring to "that love of power, and proneness to abuse it, which predominates in the human heart." To quote Dr. Trueblood again,

"The most trustworthy judgment is always the judgment of those who have submitted themselves, not only to discipline, but to the appropriate and relevant discipline. Until this is understood and accepted, the desire for freedom, far from being a boon to mankind, is always a source of confusion and ultimately of despair." We regard with pronounced disapproval any concept of freedom which might appear to be an invitation to anarchy.

The third misinterpretation of freedom to be avoided is the temptation to assume that freedom is an encouragement to isolation or irresponsibility. Archbishop William Temple once declared: "Membership of family and nation is not an accidental appendage of my individuality but a constitutive element in it . . . membership such as carries with it a share in a common weal and woe is an essential element in our nature." It has been pointed out that when Socrates had been condemned to die, one of his friends encouraged him to attempt escape. After reviewing his relationship to the state, and the many years he had enjoyed the benefits of its law and order, he decided that he was actually not free to renounce his relationship to the state. His very residence within its borders constituted for him a moral contract which no good man would dare violate. We like to feel that this attitude has become a part of our spiritual heritage. Our freedom must never be considered an invitation to isolation or irresponsibility.

When France collapsed during the early months of World War II some of its more discerning citizens saw in this tragic event the result of a freedom that was spiritually irresponsible. Freedom is always a temptation to declare one's independence, even of God, yet this is the very means by which the basis of freedom is destroyed. Only as men accept a responsible freedom, and relate themselves to God in obedience, is freedom guaranteed.

What has been said thus far would indicate that we entertain no illusions as to some of the results of man's freedom. Since men are free to do so, some will oppose the right and uphold the wrong; but it is through trial and error, success and failure, and the other phases of human experience that we learn what is true and good and eternal. Perhaps we would become too complacent and suffer moral and intellectual decadence if we were not being constantly prodded and challenged by those who do not share our opinions nor appreciate our efforts. We are reminded of that portion of Socrates' defense of himself before his fellow Athenians when he referred to himself as a gadfly, constantly annoying the state with his criticisms and rebuke. The citizens of Athens probably thought they were protecting the interests of the state by condemning one of its critics but no more serious mistake could have been made. It is in the freedom of the critic to express his view that progress is assured and abuses ultimately corrected. Our belief in freedom then is not based upon any assurance that such freedom will bring peace and quiet, but rather with the knowledge that freedom may lead to the encouragement of dissenting opinions and harsh criticisms, all of which, when offered intelligently and constructively, serve a useful purpose and contribute to the common good.

Consider, too, our obligation to avoid any tendency to become so obsessed with political and religious freedom that we ignore man's bondage to attitudes of mind and spirit which rob life of its higher meaning. Some of those who are politically free are morally in chains; and many who have inherited the right to worship God according to the dictates of their own consciences choose not to worship Him at all. It is perfectly proper that we should be concerned over the plight of those who suffer political and religious hardships under despotic forms of government, but it is utterly distressing to realize how nonchalant we can be over man's slavery to pride, fear, intemperance, prejudice, and sense of guilt. These too are cruel taskmasters from which men need to be liberated. We do not present a very impressive picture when we concentrate on the external disabilities of others while refusing to recognize to what extent many of us are willing tools of the world, the flesh, and the devil.

It is worthy of note that Jesus, who lived in an occupied country, and was constantly speaking to men and women who were restive under the authority of Rome, had very little to say about political bondage, but a great deal to say about the tyranny of sin. Much emphasis has been given to the words of Jesus concerning the fact that when one knows the truth, the truth will make him free, but such references usually overlook the words which were uttered just prior to this particular quotation and which are a vital part of it. "If you continue in my word," He said, "you are my disciples, and you will know the truth, and the truth will make you free" (RSV). The inference here is quite clear. General knowledge is not the thing about which Jesus is speaking. Rather he is speaking of a particular kind of spiritual discernment which comes through obedience to His word, and the vital relationship which one enjoys with Him as His disciple. This particular passage in the New Testament is followed by a further reference to the enslaving effects of transgression. When those to whom he was speaking protested that they were descendants of Abraham and in bondage to no one, Jesus replied "Truly, truly, I say to you, everyone who commits sin is a slave to sin. . . . If the Son makes you free, you will be free indeed." It is quite evident that in the midst of our enthusiasm for political and ecclesiastical freedom, far more needs to be done by way of confronting men with the extent to which they are enslaved by unworthy concepts of life and distorted views of man's relationship to his fellow men.

Now let us consider for a moment the three-fold nature of the freedom we seek, and which we gladly champion. First of all, it is the freedom which has its source in God. As Thomas Jefferson once put it, "The God who gave us life gave us liberty at the same time." And Felix Morley, commenting upon this statement, has said that "Governments can establish conditions, like those of freedom and slavery, which are favorable or unfavorable to the quality of liberty. They can also secure the blessings attendant on that quality, but while the state can do much to destroy liberty, as it can do much to destroy life, it is powerless to create either of these individual qualities, for they are the gift of divine —not human—authority."

The second characteristic of the freedom we seek to champion is a freedom which finds its purest expression in community. While we have had a great deal to say about man's right to differ, we need to say a great deal more about his right to cooperate. There is so much that he needs to be doing with his fellow men in establishing and maintaining worthy institutions, and in creating the moral climate in which such institutions flourish. Men must be constantly reminded that their freedom does not necessarily find its best expression in being different, and certainly not in being difficult. There is too much to be done in this tragic world of ours for one to exhaust his energies in opposition to principles with which he is in disagreement. By the exercise of a small amount of effort, all of us can discover in our contacts with others vast areas of spiritual agreement and countless ways by which those areas of agreement may find practical expression in service rendered for the common good. We have our various denominations as a constant testimony to our right to be different; we need to address ourselves increasingly in the years ahead to the more dramatic and substantial means by which our similarities may be readily recognized and usefully employed. Most denominational traditions have something of value which can be used to enrich the sum total of a more vital spiritual experience. The time has come for us to exercise our freedom in the interest of harmony, cooperation, and constructive achievements.

And the third characteristic of the freedom we seek to champion may appear to be a contradiction in terms but is nevertheless a spiritual reality; it is the true freedom which we find in absolute bondage to Christ.

In commenting upon the words in the 119th Psalm, "How I love Thy law" Dr. Lynn Harold Hough has said that "Law itself is thus seen to be most regal when it is suffused by love, and love has this creative quality because law ceases to be an abstract principle, and is found concretely glorious in a living person. The transformation of law through joyous love is seen in its full meaning in the New Testament, where all goodness and truth and excellence are alive in that great Person, Jesus Christ. Loving Him, we love all that is excellent, and what might have become a harsh and slavish obedience becomes a living joy."

When Christ declared to the disciples that He would no longer call them servants but friends, He was indicating to what extent their personal relationship to Himself had now produced in them those qualities of character which the law had never been able to inspire. They had thereby attained to a new freedom, not by a revolt against authority, or a determination to violate the law, but rather by a personal encounter with Christ which had resulted in a new experience of life and all its thrilling possibilities. True freedom, then, is actually a kind of divine captivity. As a line in a well known hymn has it, "Make me a captive, Lord, and then I shall be free." No man with the staggering burden of sin upon his conscience can ever pretend to be free, but having met the Savior and accepted His redeeming grace, there comes to man a sense of freedom he never knew to be possible. The joy of such an experience is due not only to the fact that we are now assured of God's acceptance of us, but that we have also become acceptable to ourselves. This experience of self acceptance is entirely different from defiantly asserting "I am quite all right just as I am." It actually means that in spite of our genuine sinfulness, we have found forgiveness with God through Christ, and that because God accepts us, we are therefore able to accept ourselves. Having become the disciples of Christ, and having committed ourselves unalterably to the doing of His will, we thereby have access to the truth which makes us free. It is this freedom which we seek for all men and without which life never acquires its true meaning.

Sermon Twenty

PICTURES OF JESUS

REVEREND ROLAND H. BAINTON, PH.D., D.D.

A Minister of the Methodist Church and Professor Emeritus of Church History, Yale University Divinity School, New Haven, Connecticut

Dr. Roland Bainton is Professor Emeritus of Church History at Yale, where he taught in the Divinity School for forty-two years. The chair which he filled had in a century only three incumbents, the other two being Williston Walker and George Parker Fisher. Dr. Bainton was born in England in 1894. His father, a Congregational minister, moved to Canada in 1898 and to the United States in 1902.

He attended Whitman College, then took his divinity degree at Yale in 1917 and his Ph.D. in 1921 in the field of Semitics and Hellenistic Greek. He is an authority on the Reformation and most of his writing has been in this field. His best known book is *Here I Stand: A Life of Martin Luther*, 1950. He also wrote a life of his father, *Pilgrim Parson.* His interests have included work with the Quaker Unit of the American Red Cross and he is a member of the American Church Historical Society. *The Church of Our Fathers* is a history of the church for young people.

Pictures of Jesus presents a series of stimulating and different portraits of Christ in the style for which Dr. Bainton is so highly respected. His use of Renan's *Life of Jesus* in the French edition of 1863 is worth noting.

PICTURES OF JESUS

"Who do men say that I am?" To this question of Jesus the answers have been legion. A list of books about him issued a generation ago contained five thousand titles and since then many more have appeared. There is no one in all history about whom so much has been written as about Jesus. Napoleon per chance might be second and Luther third. Each of these pictures of Jesus has its own peculiar slant. There are however certain broad groups into which the portrayals fall. Let us look at some representative examples.

The first is the romantic type which presents an idyllic, poetic Jesus. Such is the figure painted by Ernest Renan.[1] He draws for us a gentle Jesus radiating an infinite charm of person and of speech, gathering about him a simple and joyous following of the poor, the outcast, and the young, preaching in a land of great natural beauty and in an atmosphere of simple and devout belief. Here are a few touches from Renan:

> We cannot conceive the intoxication of a life which thus glides away in the presence of the heavens, the glow, mild yet strong which this perpetual contact with nature gives, the dreams of these nights passed amid the brilliancy of the stars, beneath the azure dome of the illimitable depths. It was during such a night that Jacob, his head pillowed upon a stone, saw in the stars the promise of an innumerable posterity, and the mysterious ladder by which the Elohim came and went from heaven to earth. In the time of Jesus, the heavens were not yet closed, nor had the earth grown cold. The cloud still opened over the Son of man; angels ascended and descended upon his head, visions of the kingdom of God were everywhere; for man carried them in his heart . . . Jesus lived with his disciples almost always in the open air. Often he went into a boat and taught his hearers crowded upon the shore. Sometimes, he sat down upon the hills which border the lake, where the air is so pure and the horizons so luminous. The faithful flock went also, cheerful, wayfarers, receiving the inspirations of the master in their first flower . . . His preaching was sweet and gentle, full of nature and of the perfume of the fields. He loved flowers, and he took from them his most charming lessons. The birds of heaven, the sea, the mountains, the play of children, were used by turns in his teachings . . .[1]

The Jesus of Renan has thus a feminine gentleness and charm enshrined in the idyl of the Galilean hills.

---

[1] Ernest Renan, *Life of Jesus*, first French edition, 1863.

How vastly different from all this is the Socialist picture of Jesus as we have it in Bouck White's book *The Call of the Carpenter*. He reminds us that Jesus was born at the time of the census and for what was the census? To serve as an aid for taxation. For whom? For Rome, the exploiter. The situation burned deeply into the soul of Mary and when she learned that she was with child and should bear the redeemer of her people she burst into singing of how God had cast down the mighty from their seats and had exalted those of low estate. Jesus grew up a worker in a poor land and a poor home. It was a land in which people had to put their treasures where moths and rust would not corrupt. The loss of a tool by rust would be a domestic tragedy. If a bottle developed a leak, or clothes a hole, they were not thrown away, but patched. If a coin was lost the entire house was swept and the finding of it was an occasion of rejoicing with the neighbors. There were brigands between Jericho and Jerusalem. The strong man had to guard his goods. When the rich man built greater barns, White imagines the mob of hungry peasants saying to him, "This night is thy soul required of thee." The disciples of Jesus did not fast. Why not? Because they were hungry all the time. Jesus came from a home so poor that when his parents went up to the temple to sacrifice, they could not afford sheep, goats or bullocks, but brought only a dove. All the little economies mentioned in the parables of Jesus were drawn from the experience of his home.

Jesus felt deeply the indignities of the poor. He cried out "Woe unto you that are rich. Woe unto you that are full now, for ye shall hunger. Woe unto you that laugh now for ye shall mourn and weep. Blessed are the poor. Blessed are ye that hunger now. Blessed are ye that weep now."

Why was Jesus crucified? Because he attacked a piece of graft, the monopoly of the money changers who made a racket out of changing the coins brought up by the Jews from the gentile world into the coinage of the temple. Because he attacked this exploitation the rulers of the people trumped up against him the charge of political sedition which alone the Roman government would consider.

Set over against these two portrayals is another very different, that of the businessman's Jesus as delineated by Bruce Barton in his book, *The Man Nobody Knows*. According to Barton, Jesus was an executive who as he passed by called Matthew. There was no argument, no appeal. This strong man simply said a word and at once was obeyed. Jesus was an outdoor man. Why was he able to prostrate the money changers? Partly because of his surging indignation, but partly because of his muscles of iron. He had worked in a carpenter shop. He was a sociable man who went to a wedding and made wine to save a poor mother from the failure of the great social event of her life. He was an advertiser. He went into the market place where people were gathered and said arresting things. Had he lived today he would have been a national advertiser. He was the founder of modern business which is based on his principle of service.

These three types by no means exhaust the varieties. Kagawa portrays the humanitarian Christ, going about doing good. Mazumbra, the Indian, pictures the contemplative Christ, the incarnation of the cosmic spirit of life. Many a modern scholar has sought to divest himself of all of the presuppositions of our time and to place Jesus back in his own century as a wandering Jewish rabbi.

Surely we must not forget the medieval picture of Christ as the great lover suffering for mankind. A painting portrays his love in that his arm is about the shoulder of his bride, the church. In this mood we have the hymn, "O Jesus, the very thought of thee with sweetness fills my breast." But above all he was the agonizing Christ suffering for the sins and the redemption of mankind. This was a peculiarly medieval theme. We do not find it in the early church. In the catacombs there is no portrayal of the cross but only of the resurrection, symbolized by Jonah emerging from the whale. When the crucifix appeared in the century after Constantine, Christ was fully draped and utterly without emotion. His expression was that of eternal serenity untouched by time and pain. But in western Europe in the thirteenth century we have the Christ naked save for a loin-cloth, writhing in pain upon a cross. This type of crucifix hung in the cell of the monk, in the church and in the cloister and from the cross the Savior was believed almost to reach forward to signify his curse or his blessing upon his followers.

When the English mystic Marjorie Kempe was sitting alone in a church weeping before the crucifix, a priest came to her and told her not to be so distraught because after all Christ had been a long time dead. She replied that one ought to feel as if his pangs were being inflicted here and now.

The very diversity of these pictures prompts the suspicion that Christ of necessity completely eludes us. We are able to portray him so differently because he is the man nobody can know. We read in the gospels that the soldiers at the time of the crucifixion dressed him in their own clothes. They did it in mockery, we in reverence. But still Christ is only a manikin whom we dress as we will. In time of war the militarists place him in a uniform. At any time the laboring man gives him overalls, the advertising man a gabardine, the socialite a tuxedo, and the mystic robes him in the flowing garments of an oriental sage. Thus we end our quest with skepticism as to the possibility of finding him whom we seek. But such skepticism is not warranted. The truth is symbolized in a mosaic of Christ in a church at Constantinople. When the Turks came in they covered it with plaster, but in the intervening centuries the plaster has cracked and the features of the Christ show through. So is it also in every one of these portrayals. Each has vitality and an element of truth. Every one is related to that which was most profound in the experience of the writer. We are able to lay hold of Christ only at that point at which he has laid hold of us. We read that he touched the eyes of the blind men and their eyes were opened. Only where we are touched are we able to see. Let us review again the first three examples and we shall discover in each instance a close relationship between the picture of Jesus and the deepest concern and experience of the author.

Take again Renan. His picture of Jesus may be thought to have been patterned after the likeness of his sister Henrietta. She was an older sister who had been a mother to him. She was a very sensitive spirit and when they went to a village fair and some peasant women came bedecked with excessive finery and some rough yokels jeered at them, Henrietta broke into tears. She accompanied Renan on his trip to Palestine and assisted him in the writing of the book. He records the sequel:

> In the midst of these sweet meditations Death struck us both with his wing; the sleep of fever seized us both at the same hour; I awoke alone! . . . You sleep now in the land of Adonis, near the holy Byblus and the sacred waters where the women of the ancient mysteries came to mingle their tears. Reveal to me, O my good genius, to me whom you loved, those truths which master Death, prevent us from fearing, and make us almost love it.

Renan's Jesus is modeled after the grace and sensitivity of Henrietta. But it is not therefore false. After all, the character of Henrietta was modeled after Jesus and he was characterized by charm and feminine sensitivity. Renan saw him through her and discerned correctly.

Take Bouck White.[2] He was the pastor of a poor church on the east side of New York. When the Ludlow massacres occurred in the mine fields of Colorado, it was learned that John D. Rockefeller had extensive holdings in these mines. White thereupon sent a letter to the pastor of Rockefeller's church saying that on the next Sunday he would appear in the church service and invite that church to join with his church in appointing representatives of each to meet together and to discuss the ethical implica-

---

[2] Bouck White, *The Call of the Carpenter*, 1912.

tions of the massacre. When White appeared the following Sunday, he was taken in hand by the police and was given a prison term for disorderly conduct. This is the account as given by White himself. One would hope that the other minister could place a more favorable light upon his behavior. But this at any rate is plain, that White was the pastor of a poor congregation and that he did serve a prison term. All of this obviously affects the tone and character of his portrayal of Jesus. But one cannot deny that every text which he quotes is there in the gospel. He too had laid hold of something, the truth of which cannot be impugned.

As for Bruce Barton he was the son of a minister and was less concerned to turn Jesus into a businessman than to bring businessmen to the master.[3]

Are we to conclude then that the difficulty with these portraits is their lack of completeness? The apostle Paul spoke of Christ as the fullness of the godhead and precisely what is lacking in each of these is fullness. We are tempted then to suggest that we shall obtain a true picture if we combine them all. Jonathan Edwards at this point came nearer to adequacy when he described the Master as the Lion and the Lamb. In the squalor of his birth—he was born in a stable not because there was no room in the inn but because nobody would give up a room—in the simplicity of his life, in the shame of his death, he was a lamb. In his power over his disciples, in his forgiveness of sins, in his triumph over evil, darkness and death, he was a lion. Here one has a feeling for the fullness of God in Christ.

And yet mere addition will not suffice because in many of the portrayals of Jesus there are elements which are definitely false. We do need some criteria of truth if we are to achieve a correct portrayal. The scholars are right that we cannot press rigidly the details in our gospel because they were not written until some thirty years after his death. But we do have the impact which he made upon his disciples. We do have the church and the picture of Jesus which created the church, sustained the church, and was perpetuated by the church and in this total portrayal, which we find throughout the whole New Testament, there are certain traits of Jesus which must be included if any portrayal is to be sound.

And first of all we are never to forget that Jesus is the reproving Christ. In his own day he deflated the pompous, punctured the proud, berated the exploiters, exposed the hypocrites, expelled the racketeer, put probing questions to the rich young ruler and even in silence by example shamed

[3] Bruce Barton, *The Man Nobody Knows*, 1925.

those who fell short of his standards. The medieval monk was right in feeling that the eyes of the crucifix were ever upon him in his cell, searching the inmost recesses of his heart, discovering his secret sin, and causing him to fall upon his knees in shame and contrition.

At the same time there is another note also never to be forgotten that he was the comforting Christ. "Come unto me all ye that labor and are heavy laden." "My peace I give unto you." He relieved men of intolerable burdens, he forgave their sins; when he beheld the multitude he was moved with compassion; over Jerusalem he wept and in his very last hour promised paradise to a dying thief. In him we find hope, confidence and cheer.

Once more no portrait of Christ will be adequate which fails to see in him the Redeemer. The early church based its very life upon the experience of redemption. They believed indeed that Christ had introduced a new historical era. Old things had passed away. The old Adam had been succeeded by the new Adam, the old covenant by the new covenant, and the Christian himself had become a new creature. Peter Marshall in his book, *Mister Jones, Meet the Master*, has a vivid picture of the way in which Jesus redeemed and transformed his first band of disciples. Peter is described as blustering, blundering, clumsy, impulsive and smelling of fish. James and John were called sons of thunder, who after they became disciples wished to call down fire from heaven and desired for themselves the chief seats in the kingdom. Judas was a leader of the underworld of revolt. Nathaniel a day dreamer. Thomas wanted to wait and see and Matthew was a collaborator with the Roman imperialists, a collector of taxes. Out of such raw materials Jesus forged a little band of world conquerors. The early church father Origen, writing in the third century, could say even in his day that no philosopher of antiquity, no general of Greece or Rome had ever exercised such power over the wills of men as had the crucified Galilean.

No picture is adequate which does not make one feel that at his name every knee should bow and every tongue confess that he is Lord of all.

Sermon Twenty-one

WHAT DIFFERENCE DOES IT MAKE?

LEE H. BRISTOL, JR., HH.D., LITT.D., MUS.D., LL.D.

President, Westminster Choir College, Princeton, New Jersey, and a Layman of the Protestant Episcopal Church

Lee H. Bristol, Jr., has had several varied and successful careers in his forty years of life—businessman, writer, composer, civic and religious leader. As an educator, he heads Westminster Choir College, an interdenominational institution which prepares young men and women for positions of musical leadership in churches and schools. As a religious leader he is vice-chairman of the General Division of Laymen's Work of the Second Province of the Episcopal Church, a trustee of Berkeley Divinity School in New Haven, Connecticut, and a past president of the Laymen's Movement for a Christian World.

As a musician-composer he has many published works in the choral and organ fields and specializes in sacred music. As an author he wrote *Seed for a Song*, the biography of Bishop Robert Nelson Spencer. As a businessman he formerly directed public relations for Bristol-Myers.

He is a graduate of Hamilton College, holds the Licentiate in Organ from Trinity College of Music, London, England, and has received five honorary doctorates for his work. His many musical works are played in churches everywhere.

WHAT DIFFERENCE DOES IT MAKE?

When Bishop Stephen Bayne recently went to Russia, he attended a number of church services. After one of these, a young girl came up to him and asked all about the Church in America. The Bishop gave her as complete a picture as he could. Then the girl, with sincerity and no trace of sarcasm, asked him, "But what difference does it make? What difference does it make in the people?"

Quite a question, isn't it? Disarming and strangely reminiscent of one Jesus raised in the Sermon on the Mount when He asked: "What do ye more than others?" (Matthew 5:47).

Said He: "For if you love them which love you, what reward have ye? do not even the publicans the same? And if you salute your brethren only, *what do ye more than others?* do not even the publicans so?"

When we do so, however, we want to remember what Jesus meant by the question. He did not mean that He was interested in the number of things a person did but rather in the quality or spirit a person brought to what he did. We know, for example, that He could get very angry with the Pharisees who indulged in any number of religious practices, and yet He could be compassionate with a prostitute who had a change of heart and wanted to start a new kind of life. No quantity but quality concerns our Lord; not what we claim our faith to be but how much that faith has changed us.

Isn't the acid test of a faith, after all, how much it changes us? Do we radiate a difference where we live and move and have our being? If we are not different husbands and wives and parents, if we are not different business and professional people, if we don't meet awkward situations differently because of what we believe, can our faith really be said to mean very much?

You and I profess and call ourselves Christians. We attend services and take part in church activities. We see that our children are baptized and that they go to Church School on Sundays. But, as the Russian girl put it—just what difference does it make, what difference does it make in the people.

I

Take the home, for example. Why is it that there seems to be little or no difference between the Christian home and any other? I am not just speaking here of the way many so-called Christian homes may be without family prayer, regular Bible reading, or grace at meals. I am speaking as much about how members of a Christian family may fall short in the way they treat one another—husband, wife, parents and children.

Haven't you known married couples where husband and wife seemed to lead two separate lives with no attempt to share one another's concerns? Haven't you watched families eating at a restaurant and noticed how often children seem to have trouble getting their parents—especially their fathers—to listen to them?

It is easy to let outside interests or being overtired cause us to be inconsistent or unfair with our children. It is easy to make demands on our families which were never made on us. It is easy to forget even just to listen to one another! The Christian answer lies not necessarily in giving up more time to our children or wife or husband, it seems to me, so much as it lies in what we do with the time we do give.

Shortly before Joseph Welch died, his son told him, "Dad, when we were growing up, your most influential moments were your most inadvertent ones. We were apt to imitate what you really were, not what you said you were, or even what you may have believed you were."

How can one be the perfect parent or husband or wife? We Christians don't know all the answers but I like to think our faith gives us a keener sense of unquestioning responsibility to our families, a keener sense of unquestioning responsibility to those at home who often look at us as if to ask, "What do ye more than others?"

II

Or take the world of our daily work. We know our faith has much to do with our jobs. The Bible mentions work, I believe, about a thousand times. The Scriptures teach us that Our Lord called all of us, laymen and clergy alike, to be His ambassadors to the world. And, quite frankly, just what do most of us do about it on the job?

I think it is helpful for us laymen to bear in mind that all work can be sacred, not just what we do in Church on Sundays. What we do on the job the rest of the week can be just as sacred, for work is not sacred or secular in itself. It becomes sacred or secular in terms of the spirit you and I bring to it.

The other day, a woman I know telephoned Grand Central Station for information and was surprised at the courtesy and helpfulness of the man on the other end of the line. "My, but you're helpful!" she said.

"I try to be," said the man, with conviction.

My friend was intrigued. "What is your position?" she asked.

"Oh, I'm just a dispatcher. You might say my job is giving out information, but I like to think it's more than that. I like to think my job is trying to make travel easier and pleasanter for people. Guess it's all in the way you look at it."

I think he's right. It *is* all in the way you look at it. "For some clergy their work is a chore; for some cab-drivers their work is a ministry."

Living our faith on the job may not mean instituting hymn sings at the coffee break—chances are we might meet with a little sales resistance! But it may very well mean seeing the sacred side of situations which others overlook—like how human beings may be affected by that proposed lay-off or whether our company's services are everything that our ads claim them to be.

Don't you think it could be said that what matters is not how many committees a Christian is on but what he brings to the committee he *is* on. Someone has said our Lord is not so much concerned with whether you're the Board Chairman or the night watchman as He is concerned with what kind of person is that man who just happens to be Chairman or night watchman.

I don't mean, of course, to suggest that it will always be easy to see the sacred side of our work. Often it won't be. Often I suspect our work will seem dreary, mechanical, meaningless. At such times we'll want to remind ourselves that no matter how routine or boring a job may seem, it still gives us the opportunity to serve God—if not in the work itself, at least in the way it offers us a chance to touch the lives of those working to our right and to our left.

I don't think we hope for the kind of man I know who owns a small business and literally compels his employees to attend a prayer meeting first thing each morning. I like to think we're more interested in someone like a sales manager I once knew. He had to fly out to the Coast to reprimand one of his salesmen severely. After he had done so, my friend made a point of remaining out in the man's territory for three weeks just to see how the man survived the experience. Would he fold, or would he pick himself up and start over—a better person? The story in this case had a happy ending, but its significance to me lay in the fact that here was a man who saw the job of sales manager as the kind of ministry it can certainly be. He cared that much about his people.

A friend of mine driving in Michigan the other day came to a three-way fork in the road and found all three roads blocked. One sign said "Road Closed," another said "Do Not Enter," the third road had a large arrow, showing that the road was one way—the other way! My friend had to turn back and go another way.

Many of the decisions a Christian faces in his work will be like that. There will be times when all three roads seem blocked, times when he has to turn back and perhaps follow another route he's tried before. At other times there will be three open roads with no signs to guide him. Instead of being black or white or clear, many decisions will be gray and confusing. It won't be easy to face decisions like: is it worth the risk to disagree with the boss? Wouldn't it be easier just to go along? Here again, hopefully, the Christian's faith will give him a sense of responsibility to those related to him, a sense of responsibility that helps him face up squarely to such questions.

Day in and day out, consciously or unconsciously, there may be those where we work who look at us in situations on the job as if to ask, "What do ye more than others?"

III

But it is not enough that a Christian tries to be a good husband or wife or parent, important as this may be. It is not enough that he tries to live his faith on the job. What completes the picture of the Christian is the fact that above and beyond what he does at home and at work, he recognizes his unending responsibility to serve his community.

The other day, a fine man who is rector of a large Western parish said, "I'm teaching a new course for laymen in the evening, and the response in my parish has been wonderful. Why, do you know some of my key laymen have actually resigned from the school board, the hospital board, and political committees just to take it?"

That rector's course is undoubtedly important and helpful, but—as some of his clergy friends suggested to him: couldn't he have rescheduled the course, so that those laymen could have taken it at another time and yet continued their work on the school board, the hospital board, and those political committees? After all, isn't it through dedicated laymen that the Church is able to broaden its ministry and have greater impact in the world? Archbishop Temple once said, "Nine-tenths of the work of the Church in the world is done by Christians fulfilling responsibilities and performing tasks which in themselves are not part of the official system of the Church at all."

The Christian views his community differently. He doesn't say, "I pay taxes. I give to the hospital and the United Fund. Let me alone!" He is deeply conscious of his responsibility to the others who make up his community. He knows the wisdom of the old Toc H motto: "Service is the rent we pay for our place on earth," and he knows, too, that community problems can be so complex these days that they call for joint effort. He may well have seen for himself how the same number of concerned citizens working in proper collaboration can often achieve far greater results than the same number of citizens working independently. Scientists call this potentiation. I suppose you and I might call it a kind of two plus two equals five proposition.

"Seek ye first the Kingdom of God and His righteousness" was not a call for us to go out of this world. It was a call for you and me to stay in this world but to see it all differently, sensitized to needs around us which others overlook, putting first things first.

It may mean working for laws that are more just, helping the poor, rescuing the fallen, or simply bringing people together. The opportunities are limitless. Oftentimes the service which a Christian may do in his community will be the same service an agnostic "do-gooder" might do. The difference will lie not so much in the service as in the motive behind it. And that motive for the Christian wants to be a grateful sense of concern, mutual responsibility, love—proving that our Lord is counting on us and that we cannot let Him down.

Are there people in your neighborhood community and mine who look at us and at the decisions we make in social, political, and economic affairs, are there people who look at us to ask, "What do ye more than others?"

IV

Let me leave you with just a word or two about deepening our spiritual lives. As I see it, there are three simple essentials: (1) really wanting to grow; (2) letting God know that you do; and (3) keeping everlastingly at it—continuing to try. That's exactly what I might tell my children, and it's what I am suggesting to you.

Trying to grow spiritually won't be easy. We laymen will find it frustrating at times. We're bound to have our ups and downs. But remember: *we laymen do not have to do it alone*. Jesus did not leave us a book. He didn't just leave us a lot of principles to follow. He left us Himself, His Spirit to help us. All He asks is that we really want Him enough.

God knows what we really are—better than we do ourselves. He knows how we rush about, doing too much and often meaning little by it. He knows how much our lives are governed much by what others do and say and think, rather than by any thought about what God might hope for us. He knows all that, and yet patiently He waits for us and for the day we sense our own inadequacies and seek His help.

Says Our Lord: "Give Me your strengths and weaknesses, your triumphs and failures; give Me everything, and let me give back to you power beyond yourself to become what all along I hoped you might be."

Wouldn't it be wonderful if more of us were like a young mother I know who had to grow when illness hit her suddenly? She prayed for strength, and that prayer was answered—not only with strength for herself but a kind of strength she was able to pass along to others. Even her little boy noticed the change. "I don't know what's happened to you, Mommy," he said, "but you're different. You're different, and I think it's wonderful!"

We profess and call ourselves Christian. What difference does it make in the people—in you and me? What do *we* more than others?

Sermon Twenty-three

OUR CHRISTIAN HERITAGE IN THIS SPACE AGE

THE HONORABLE LUTHER W. YOUNGDAHL

District Judge of the United States, District Court for the District of Columbia, Washington, D. C.

Judge Youngdahl is one of the high-minded, spiritually-inclined leaders of our country whose deep and profound faith in God, his integrity and justice to his fellow man is nationally recognized. In his religious convictions he is a Lutheran, but he believes in religious freedom for all.

Born in Minneapolis in 1896, he was the son of Scandinavian parents who settled in Minnesota and established a grocery store. The motto of the Youngdahl family was "religion, work, education," and his father worked long hours to rear and educate his family of ten. As a boy, Luther Youngdahl delivered groceries and ran a newsstand to help pay his school expenses. He attended the University of Minnesota and Gustavus Adolphus College. His college days were interrupted by World War I, which he spent in the Field Artillery, then re-entered Gustavus Adolphus for his A.B. degree. In 1921 he received his LL.B. degree from Minnesota College of Law, then taught there for twelve years and became assistant dean.

He was appointed Assistant City Attorney of Minneapolis in 1921, then became a partner in the law office of Judge M. C. Tifft and practiced before the bar. In 1930 he was appointed Municipal Judge in Minneapolis, then was elected District Judge, and in 1942 was elected to the Minnesota Supreme Court. In 1947 he was elected Governor of Minnesota, an office he held for three terms. Known as Minnesota's "crusading governor," he wiped out the rackets in Minnesota against terrific opposition, and his political philosophy was "honesty and humanity in government." In 1951 he was appointed Judge of the United States District Court for the District of Columbia and has served continuously ever since.

The Judge has worked for improvement in all phases of human relations. In his private and political life he evidences a special interest in young people, and as Governor, secured the passage of the Youth Conservation Commission by the legislature of Minnesota.

Many honors have come to Judge Youngdahl through the years, but the following indicate the nature of those garnered by one whose life is wholly dedicated to others: The Boy Scout Silver Antelope, National Big Brother, the Grand Cross of the Royal Order of the North Star, presented by King Gustav V of Sweden, and the award of Layman of the Year by the Washington Federation of Churches.

Judge Youngdahl is the author of a book entitled *The Ramparts We Watch*, published in 1961. The message given here was delivered before the Chicago Sunday Evening Club on October 29, 1961.

OUR CHRISTIAN HERITAGE IN THIS SPACE AGE

Fellow Christians, I recall the man who said he was born a Lutheran; he is living a Lutheran; and he is going to die a Lutheran. The Methodist responded, "Haven't you got any ambition, my brother?" Moreover, it is related that when a certain group of people came to heaven, they were met by St. Peter. As they were shown a beautiful meadow, they saw people gathered there, and one of the group asked who they were. Saint Peter responded, "The Presbyterians." As they journeyed on, they came to a beautiful babbling brook and one asked who were the people gathered there, and Saint Peter said, "The Congregationalists." Then they came to a tremendously high wall, and one asked who were behind that wall, and Saint Peter said, "Please be quiet, the Lutherans are behind that wall—they think there're the only ones up in this place and we don't want to disillusion them!"

We are grateful that we can gather here this evening with no particular emphasis upon any one denomination, but as fellow Christians, ready to reaffirm our faith and to give thanks to our God for our Christian heritage.

A Scandinavian bishop came to our country recently and said a most significant thing: "I have always tried to play my instrument of Lutheranism skillfully and well, for I love its notes and its tones, but I would like to play my instrument in harmony with other and differing instruments so that out of these differing instruments would come a symphony of God."

In that spirit we are met to dedicate ourselves anew to our heritage of faith.

First, let me say that I value my Christian faith as my most prized possession in life. I would be remiss if I did not acknowledge how fortunate I have been to have had Christian parents whose lives were centered at the cross—parents who considered it their sacred responsibility to give their children religious education and to rear them in the atmosphere of a Christian home. At a very early age we were not only enrolled in the Sunday school, but also attended church services with our parents on the Sabbath. Moreover, a deep impression was made upon us as we participated with the adults at the family altar.

There are many parents who do not bring their children to church services because they are of the opinion they are too young to get any benefit from them. However, I can testify from personal experience that these services have a significant effect upon the lives of children.

One of the great Christians of this era, Albert Schweitzer, puts it this way, "From the services in which I joined as a child, I have taken with me into life a feeling for that which is solemn, and a need for quiet and self-recollection, without which I cannot realize the meaning of my life. I cannot support the opinion of those who would not let children take part in grownup people's services until they, to some extent, understand them. The important thing is not that they understand them, but that they shall feel something of what is serious and solemn. The fact that the child sees his elders full of devotion, and has to feel something of devotion himself, is what gives the service meaning for him."

I have prayed many times that I would be worthy of our parents in endeavoring to pass on to our children that same sturdy faith so characteristic of their lives, for there is nothing that will as adequately equip this generation for the challenges of the space age as the Christian heritage. This age of intercontinental ballistic missiles and travels into space demands a new reformation—greater vision, greater courage, greater consecration to Christian principles in all realms of life than ever before.

In 1517, on the church door at Wittenberg, Martin Luther fanned into flame the smouldering thought of generations. Luther emphasized the liberating truth of the forgiveness of sins and ushered in a new era of freedom, light, and life.

It is of significance that at the time Columbus discovered America in 1492, Luther was being prepared for his great crusade. It is also of great significance that the printing press was invented about that time, so that the first book printed was the Holy Bible.

One of the pillars of the Reformation was known as the supremacy of the people and the spiritual priesthood of all believers. Martin Luther advanced the proposition that Christian laymen have spiritual faculties and powers of the same sort as the clergy. He believed that they may feel, in all natural relationships, a spiritual dignity like that of the priest. He said it is also accomplished in honest toil, in the affairs of government, in the institution of marriage, the home and parenthood.

To quote Luther's magnificent paradox, a Christian is not only the most free lord of all and subject to none, but in his newly-found liberty, he is the most dutiful servant of all, subject to everyone. In short, liberty implies obligation. It must eventuate in service.

Christianity is desperately in need of lay members who will give more than half-loyalty, secret discipleship and lukewarm fealty or lip service.

Clearly the lines are being drawn for a struggle between the Church of Jesus Christ and the godless materialism that would destroy men's souls. Leadership in this great moral struggle must come only from a revitalized church. In this fight, laymen are needed badly.

Luther stressed particularly the importance of effective laymanship in the home, in Christian activity in the community and government and at the place of prayer in personal communion with our God!

Scientists warn us that our hour is running out; that we are critically in danger of catastrophe unless we learn how to live together and to share the blessings of the world's resources. Dr. Compton, the great scientist and lay religious leader, has challenged us with the fact that the time is short to learn the lesson of living together and that only by the religious emphasis in the experiences of men can the lesson be learned.

He posed the question, "If scientists, engineers, employers, employees—a million people in this country engaged in the common task of building the atomic bomb—submerged their differences and succeeded in their task because they knew that freedom was at stake, why can we not now—when freedom is still at stake—join hands in the same spirit of unity and consecration to our tasks?"

On a humid summer afternoon, the wife of a farmer was ironing in the kitchen of her home. Her three-year-old youngster was playing nearby. Suddenly the mother noticed an accumulation of flies and that the screen door was open and the child missing. She searched about the premises but couldn't find her youngster. She called in her husband from the fields and they both searched, but to no avail. Over the country telephone went the urgent call for help, and all the neighboring farmers came in to join in the search. On the morning of the second day, one of the farmers suggested, "Our efforts so far have been futile. Let us all join hands together and cut a pathway a mile long, and then another pathway adjacent to it a mile long, and still another pathway adjacent to the second. We've got to find the child." So they all joined hands and cut a pathway a mile long, and another pathway adjacent to it a mile long, and finally they came to a gully and there they found the child. She was dead. She had struck her head against a rock. One of the men tenderly picked up the child and placed her in the arms of the hysterical mother who cried out, "Why didn't you join hands sooner—why didn't you join hands sooner?" That is the challenge that comes to us—to join hands in this age of space to make our Christian Heritage count in every phase of life.

The clock ticks steadily as God gives us one more chance to straighten out our human relations. How long must the world flounder before finding the way through a spiritual renaissance that stretches out to enfold all people and all nations in following the way of Christ? But the Church has not been as effective as it should be.

Pierre van Paassen points to the calling of the Church in this hour when he says: "Only by fulfilling her duty of confession—of speaking out at no matter what the cost or risk, in the language of our times—and on subjects or problems which directly and intimately concern the men of our times—can the Church save her soul and perhaps the world."

Archbishop Joost de Blank of Capetown, South Africa, recently spoke at the general convention of the Episcopal Church. He expressed concern over the tendency of the Church to wait on secular leadership in controversial problems involving inescapable moral decisions. Said Archbishop Joost, "Are we Christians moving quickly enough or are we allowing ourselves to be overtaken by events, so that the Church always has to go on acting as an ambulance whereas God designed it to act as a fire engine? Is the Church always to go on helping victims who have suffered in the conflagration, or is its function to put the fire out? Is it enough to sit down and pass pious resolutions—and then talk warily about precipitate action, no doubt mouthing such sententious phrases as 'God's good time'? We like to comfort ourselves with the reminder that with God a thousand years is a day but forget conveniently that a day is also with Him as a thousand years, and that what happens today may affect for good or ill the future of the world for the next ten centuries."

Dr. Robert McCracken, in a sermon at Riverside Church, said, "The plain fact of the matter is that Christianity no longer is at the hub of things. The chief influence is that of science and its mastery of the material world." Asserting that to make Christianity relevant, churches and churchmen must speak out forcefully on the larger issues, he added, "There is no use setting up a tepid Christianity against a scorching paganism—the threat of the demonic has to be met with the fire of the divine."

We need to be constantly reminded of the role the laity has played in the Church since Jesus first chose the motley band of twelve from fishermen, tax collectors and ordinary folk. The very word "layman" springs from the Greek word *laikos,* meaning belonging to the people—that is the chosen people of God. In this framework of reference, all members of the Church are "laikoi."

The New Testament has a word for disciple—*diakonia.* In its original sense, this Greek word, diakonia, means waiter on table. Jesus made this simple word with its humble origin the typical expression for the relation of His Disciples with the world. It should be our cue for what we conceive to be the role of the layman in the mission of the Church.

St. John points up the role of the layman in the mission of the Church as he describes the scene in the upper room with Christ washing the Disciples' feet. It is symbolic of what Christ expects of the laymen of the church.

Laymen today are surrounded by a great host of witnesses as to their important mission in the work of the Church. St. Luke, the physician; St. Paul, the tent maker; Tertullian and St. Augustine—now listed among the great Church Fathers—were all laymen. We recall the lay movement of the Waldensians and the Lollards in the revolutionary movement in the Middle Ages; they protested against a too worldly Church, recalling it to its true mission.

Martin Luther's Reformation was mainly a lay movement with princes and peasants catching a new look at the role Christ intended the Church to play.

John Calvin, who fathered the Presbyterian Church, an extraordinarily gifted layman, stepped from a specialized study of jurisprudence into the movement recalling the Church to renewal.

America was cradled in a lay movement—recalling the Church to freedom of conscience and dignity of the common man. The Christian faith of the laymen who spearheaded this movement is attested by their complete reliance upon God to aid them in resolving their difficulties.

In our day, we need but mention such a name as Albert Schweitzer to be reminded of the role a layman can play in making the Christian faith relevant in the lives of men.

Moreover, we could call the roll of countless ordinary folk who are dedicating their lives in the witness and ministry of the church. My church recently called a production foreman from a lucrative position in a caterpillar plant and sent him to the untouchables of India. He will teach the use of tools and open employment for a people to whom, heretofore, were open only menial jobs. This is a ministry of sharing under the leadership of a layman. This, too, dramatizes the relevancy of the mission of the church in world affairs.

This age of space in which we live demands an articulate, aggressive and dedicated laymanship. Doubt, despair and deterioration of our personal and public life appear beneath the thin veneer of our society—and this despite the unprecedented church and Sunday school attendance and accelerated building of church plants.

The real difference between the Soviet system and our system is that we profess that we are, and strive to live as *a nation under God*, and yet there are ominous signs we are straying from the path.

Let us look frankly at the record:

Consider the intensity of delinquency and crime. Since 1950 crime has increased in this country four times as fast as the population. For every dollar our churches cost us, our crime rate costs us $12.

In the field of fraud, in 1958, bad checks that came to the notice of the F.B.I. had a face value of eight million dollars.

Daily press releases of the Federal Trade Commission reveal misrepresentation by sellers of goods as to origin, quality and price.

Householders have found themselves the victims of slipshod work and padded bills for repairs to the home or the family car.

Unscrupulous persons on relief have fraudulently requested and received more money than the law permits.

Surety companies reveal that employee dishonesty can be safely estimated at somewhere between five hundred million and one billion dollars a year.

Collusive arrangements between business and labor and television scandals have been revealed in recent congressional investigations.

Corruption of law enforcement officers and other public officials and influence peddling have been disclosed in many quarters.

Our human relations have deteriorated, as is indicated by numerous incidents of bigotry and intolerance, and our world relations are at the lowest ebb in all our nation's history.

What's wrong? The torch of religion may be lit in the church, but it is not burning as it should in the family, in the shop, or on the street.

Democracy is in trouble today and only the Christian heritage can revitalize it.

We have been too smug and complacent about the freedom we have enjoyed. Because we had it yesterday, and have it today, many have assumed we will have it tomorrow. But the events of the last few years ought to awaken us from our lethargy.

We cannot afford to take a chance to win the struggle with the Soviets in the economic, political or military fields. We still must press forward, of course, in these fields and we have faith that the Soviets will not be able to excel us economically, politically or militarily; but it is in the moral and spiritual realm that we have a real chance for victory, and only as we continue to live under God will we have a chance to remain free. A revival of the dynamic faith that sparked the revolution is imperative.

But there are those within our churches, and they are sincere and well-meaning, who proclaim that religion and politics do not mix; that the purpose of the Church is to preach the Gospel and its business is not to be concerned with the social issues of the day.

Dr. Edwin T. Dahlberg, the former dynamic president of The National Council of Churches of Christ, has effectively answered this contention. Courageously he has stated that the prophetic voice of the Church will not be silenced; that pastors and laymen, alike, are compelled to interpret the Gospel in terms of moral and spiritual issues of our time; and that it is the responsibility of the church to speak out on these issues even before they become political issues.

On many occasions during my administration as Governor of Minnesota, when I was fighting for honesty and humanity in government; in eliminating the slot machine racket; in providing for humane care for mentally ill, and other programs, I told our church people, "We get just as bad government as we are willing to stand for and just as good government as we are willing to fight for." And I will say to the credit of the church people of Minnesota, when they were finally aroused out of their apathy and indifference, they became militant crusaders in helping us achieve these programs for better government.

If government is corrupt, inefficient and unprogressive, it is because Christian people have not sufficiently cared. On the other hand, if government is honest, humane, and progressive, it is because Christian people are alert to their citizenship responsibilities.

The Christian citizen must dedicate himself to a program that places human values first. He must fight for honesty and humanity in government. As Christ was most concerned with children and unfortunates, so must the Christian citizen see that government invests generously in education, health, and general welfare of youth. He must fight for humane care of the mentally ill and other fellow human beings in need of a helping hand. He must set an example of self-discipline and wholesome respect for law and order and fight vigorously for honesty and integrity in public life. He must work to put Christianity into practice by striving to foster and protect the heritage of citizenship for all of every creed, race and national origin. We laymen need the urgency of mission that was the mark of the Master.

We must rediscover the role of the laity in the mission of the Church. Part of the laity's responsibility, of course, is to operate the institutional machinery of the Church.

But in the dynamic Biblical sense, laity are the people of God abroad in the world. Laypeople in various segments of society are God's messengers for the releasing of grace and power for the healing of human life. As Luther put it, they are called upon to be little Christs.

Real Christians are the ones who are doing things, not just talking about doing things. Jesus was an activist in the best and well-balanced sense of that word. Thirty-three short years, but what years!

Henry Ward Beecher once spoke of men who thought that the object of conversion was to clean them as a garment is cleaned and that when they were converted they were to be hung up in the Lord's wardrobe, the door of which was to be shut so that no dust could get at them. A coat that is not used, contended Beecher, the moths eat, and a Christian who is hung up so that he shall not be tempted—the moths eat him, and they have poor food at that.

When one has been touched by Jesus, the place for him is out among others, amid the turmoil of life, expressing by his words and deeds what his faith has meant to him. He is to be a commissioned ambasssador—a living example all the time.

It is related that shortly after the last war, an American army outfit was given the task of reconstructing a small German village which had been practically demolished by bombs. With customary American efficiency, they rebuilt the village. As they were reconstructing a small church, they had completed their task, except for a statue of Christ. Search as they would, they could not find the hands of the statue and they seemed to be in a dilemma. Finally the captain of the contingent, who had been an active layman in the church, said, "I know what we will do, we will inscribe these words on the base of that statue: 'I have no other hands than yours.'" This illustrates, of course, that the Gospel of Christ can be disseminated only through his followers—the laypeople of our churches.

What a different Church it would be if it would frankly and aggressively challenge the modern paganism of our times. Yet that is the genus of our Christian heritage.

The missionary Apostles in the early years of the Church, as they preached in the market places of Corinth, the Forum in Rome, or the wilderness of medieval Europe, did not hesitate to hurl that type of challenge to their listeners.

America was founded by men who were bold. It cannot be maintained by men who are timid. The Church must have leadership and programs in rethinking our ministry to the world.

The beep, beep, beep of the satellite has been a familiar sound to one listening in an astronomy observatory in recent months. If one listened intently, it almost seemed the little satellite was saying to the people on earth, "Your time is short. You may have discovered a way to get to outer space, but unless you discover a way to peace, the conquest of space may well forecast the death of the world. It is the earth to which you should give importance. It has greater significance than the moon." The real issue is not whether one will get to the moon to beat any other nation, but will we get to the earth to save man from destruction?

Our problem has not changed with the coming of the space age. Though man should be successful in launching a bridgehead on the moon, or in finding possible living conditions on other planets, or perhaps in projecting a rocket into space with space pioneers ready to establish families and communities far beyond our earth in another solar system, our problem remains essentially the same—these courageous pioneers would have the same characteristics of human nature as those of the people they left behind. Our problem would still be man, himself.

True, it is a day of crises. But *crisis*—compounded out of two Chinese characters—means first, danger; second, opportunity. There is danger and there are many perplexing problems, but what an opportunity. The intriguing frontier of human values and human relations is yet to be explored.

Communism and every anti-Christian movement is demanding a wholehearted devotion and a loyalty bravely proclaimed. Nothing less will suffice for this generation of Christians.

Today the man who does not declare his loyalty to Christ is no more than an onlooker—a neutral in the face of Christianity's greatest test in all history.

When the French philosopher, de Tocqueville, visited America many years ago, he said, "America is great because America is good—and if America ever ceases to be good, America will cease to be great."

He has sounded forth the trumpet that has never called retreat.
He is sifting out the hearts of men before His judgment seat.
O be swift my soul to answer Him,
Be jubilant, my feet,
Our God is marching on!

Sermon Twenty-two

THE GREATEST POWER

REVEREND ERNEST GORDON, T.D., LL.D.

Dean of the Chapel, Princeton University, and a Minister of the Presbyterian Church, Princeton, New Jersey

This moving sermon on love is so full words and ideas fairly spill over—Ernest Gordon's tremendous experience in the war and his knowledge of people and life make it one of the distinguished sermons of the year. During World War II he was a Captain in the Argyll and Sutherland Highlanders, was wounded in Malaya, and on the downfall of Singapore made his way to Sumatra. Here he helped fifteen hundred men, women, nursing sisters, wounded soldiers, and children make their way to freedom. When the Japanese arrived, he escaped again in a sailboat with eight others, but after twenty-four days on the Indian Ocean, he was recaptured by the Japanese Navy.

For three and a half years he was forced to work on the infamous "Railway of Death" between Thailand and Burma. During this time he helped to organize and taught in "The Jungle University," which stimulated morale, and in addition, he served as lay minister to his fellow prisoners of war. After the war he was ordained at Paisley Abbey, where he served three years as deputy minister. For a year he was Chaplain to Presbyterian students at Princeton, and he was appointed Dean of the Chapel in July, 1955.

Ernest Gordon did his undergraduate work at St. Andrews University in Scotland before the outbreak of war in 1939. Later he completed his theological studies at Edinburgh University, Hartford Theological Seminary, and at Glasgow University. He is the author of *A Living Faith for Today* and *The High Way by the River Kwai,* and has conducted Religious Emphasis Week on various university campuses. He is the Founder and first President of the Church Service Society of the U.S.A.

Through the Valley of the Kwai has been published in England (as *Miracle on the River Quai*) and has also been translated and published in Dutch, Swedish, German, Danish, and Norwegian, and will soon appear in Hebrew and Chinese.

Many—in fact, most—of Dean Gordon's sermons are preached for the students and faculty of Princeton University. The present sermon was delivered at the Chicago Sunday Evening Club on December 8, 1961.

THE GREATEST POWER

I needn't remind you that this particular age is one in which people have become very conscious of power. Fifty years ago the man at the dawn of the twentieth century foresaw the day when the great advances in technology would be used for the betterment of mankind. He dreamed of a world where all the powers of the machine and of nature would be harnessed for the good of his fellow men.

We who are living halfway through the century realize that everything isn't just as rosy as it might be. We are living in an age of power. It is a devastating kind of power that we have to face.

The man of today looks back and sees the century which started off so full of hope ending with man being overcome by another power, a power that is demonic, destructive, and impersonal. The dilemma surely of modern man is that he has cut himself adrift from the spiritual source of power, that power which makes life possible, that power which restores and redeems mankind. Man has become the slave of the natural world instead of its master. That is why he can make all kinds of wonderful gadgets, including the hydrogen bomb, yet not know how to use them for good instead of evil.

Isn't it the case that we are so cluttered up with the cares and worries of the physical world that we forget about the personal, about the spiritual world, about the Kingdom of God? We are so busy groping around in the mud and the muck for we know not what that we forget to look up, to behold the shining glory of God's starry firmament. We are so concerned about scandals and fears and petty jealousies and hatreds and mean criticisms and fashionable hypocrisies and base prejudices, that we choose to ignore the greatest of all great powers, the love of God. Oh, it is something we have heard about. We have all heard about it, but so often we are content to leave it there, up in the air somewhere among the other abstractions of our minds.

Is this power, the greatest power of all, the love of God, is it nothing more or less than a pretty phrase, or is it a reality? I believe that it is. I believe that it is our only security, that it is the only power which can redeem the condition of man. Although it is not of the world, that is, it is none of our creation, it is in the world. Thank God it is, otherwise life would be too grim to be endured. Yes, it is there, all right, despite the fact that it is only now and then that we take the trouble to notice it. In times of tragedy it very often makes a sudden and mysterious appearance. Isn't it the love of God working in the hearts of men and women that makes them respond so generously to calls for help at times of personal, national, and international disaster? For a time at least, the clamor of the noisy world is silenced, and God's word of love, addressed to us, is heard in the depths of our souls. The desperate facts of life awaken us to the realization that love, and love alone, is the only redeeming power. Our hearts are made sensitive because we are caught off balance, as it were. We feel the pressure of the eternal all around us, and experience a moment of grace, a moment of insight into the nature of eternal reality.

And then what happens? Then we forget about it. For a second or two we allow our eyes to rise to the heavens, to behold the splendor of the light, but only for a second or two, as we hurriedly lower them again to the dimness and to the darkness to which we are so well accustomed.

Many of you will remember that during those dark years of the Second World War we found that all wasn't quite as terrible as we had at first anticipated. Our lot was made bearable by the friendliness of those around us. Fear unlocked our frozen hearts and allowed God's love to enter. One-time rivals became friends. Former lessers became equals. Pet aversions became bosom buddies, and our forgotten neighbors became our close companions. Even God was remembered.

Then the war ended, and with it the lessons that people were in the process of learning. Hearts were closed once again to the divine love, and people got down to the job of the daily round and the common task, the business of living in an all too materialistic world.

God and His love are in this world as our only security. There is no other. Of this I have absolutely no doubt whatsoever. This was the glorious fact which made all the difference to us who were prisoners of war of the Japanese in the jungle camps on the railroad of death in Thailand. Deprived of all that normally makes up our so-called civilized way of life, we were thrown into prison, forsaken by our government, forgotten by our friends, starved, beaten, and overworked by our captors. We were reduced to the stage where it was so much easier to die than it was to live. But God was there! He was there sharing our sufferings, and pouring out His love upon us in such quantity that it spilled over into the lives of us all. It was measured, not in words, but in deeds. The noble generosity and the sacrificial selflessness of our troops made me strangely humble, so that all that I could say of them was: "You have taught me more of what God is than ever I thought to know. I never knew He could come so close, or that I could love Him so."

How can we possibly know of this warm, living, creative, personal, dynamic, redemptive love, apart from the cross of our Lord Jesus Christ? When I think of love what do I think of? I think of the cross. And believe me, these days I've got to think of it time and time again, in order to lay hold of the only real security there is; for the cross of our blessed Lord stands at life's intersections to show us the way, the only way that leads to life in its completion and fullness. That cross is a perfect revelation of God's love for all men, for all are embraced within its outstretched arms. No one, no one at all is forgotten.

It is a pity, I think, that Oscar Wilde never found this truth until near the end of his life. You may remember how, in his "*Ballad of Reading Gaol,*" he tells the story of a fellow prisoner, a young guardsman who was awaiting execution. His crime had been that of murdering his sweetheart in a moment of overpowering jealousy. When Oscar Wilde thought it over, he came to the conclusion that all of us should be in the condemned cell, because we are all guilty of killing love, and so he writes:

> But each man kills the thing he loves, by each let this be heard,
> Some do it with a bitter look, some with a flattering word,
> The coward does it with a kiss, the brave man with a sword!

He may have been right in that assumption, but surely he was wrong in declaring this:

> The prison wall was round us both. Two outcast men we were:
> The world had thrust us from its heart, and God from out His care,
> And the iron gin that waits for sin had caught us in its snare.

No, no, my friends. He was wrong there. The world had thrust them from its heart but God hadn't cast them beyond the pale of His care. The security of His love was still there, waiting for them to accept it.

The cross, you see, tells us of the seeking love of the loving Father Who comes to us in utter humility in the Person of His Son. Standing alone and defenseless before the world, this Son declared: "God loves you. God cares." But the world didn't and the world doesn't want to hear anything so simple. As a result the Lord of Glory was, and is, trapped by man's cruel inhumanity, and crucified.

Can't you visualize that scene at Calvary? There is a soldier passing by. He spits in Christ's face because Christ is so weak. There is a politician passing by, and he sneers at Him because it's the right thing for him to do as a politician in order to keep in with his constituents. And there is a priest passing by. He jeers at Jesus and he says: "Look here, if you have all that power You claim to have why don't you use it and come down and show us that You are truly God's Son?" By the side of the cross a mother weeps.

Can anything take the place of this love? Of course not. It is the only real power there is, the only power that can transform us, to make us the kind of people that God intended we should be. All else may fail, but love, never.

Remember how Paul says in that beautiful poem of love of his: "Love never fails, but whether it be the gift of preaching, it will be done with. Whether it be the gift of tongues, it will cease. Whether it be knowledge, it too will be done with. Love never fails." It stands forth in the midst of a confused world as our only hope, as our only power. Like a friendly light on a dark, dark night, it shines through the storm of men's noisy selfish seeking, pointing the way, the only why which leads us home to God Himself.

All through the ages the cross stands as an eternal fact, witnessing to the love of God for the children of His creation. It is God's answer to us, the only answer against which there is no argument. Its appeal is to every man and to every woman in every age. No matter what language we may speak, or how high or how low our I.Q. may be, or whatever our economic and social standing, or whatever the color of our skin, we all can understand what God is saying to us through that lonely figure on the cross. It is the eternal, graven upon the face of time, that men may never dare forget the cost, the terrible cost, to God Himself. The stupendous mystery, the glorious mystery of it all is that, although we reject God's Ambassador of love. He still comes seeking us out, that although we crucify Him, He still loves us.

I think Herbert French has caught a glimpse of this mystery in that very poignant poem of his, in which he depicts the greatness of a mother's love, of a love that will never give up. It is a picture of the eternal love of God as it is depicted in the heart of a mother:

A poor lad one, and a lad so trim, gave his heart to her who loved not him.
Said she, "Fetch me tonight your mother's heart to feed my dog."
To his mother's house went that young man, killed her, cut out her heart, and ran,
But as he was running, look you, he fell. The heart rolled out on the ground as well.
And the lad, as the heart was rolling, heard
That the heart was speaking, and this was the word,
The heart was weeping, and crying so small:
"Are you hurt, my child? Are you hurt at all?"

Isn't this the reflection of our Father's love, of the love that cried from the cross, Father, forgive them, for they know not what they do."

Agnes Keith, in summing up her experiences during the time she was in the Japanese internment camp, said: "I knew this, that there are just two things which can break a heart: One is the terrible harshness of man, and the other is his transfiguring mercy." What is that transfiguring mercy but the love of God? I understand perfectly what Agnes Keith means. One of the things from my own Japanese prison camps that stands out clearly in my mind was in a camp, at the very end. We had been released and had been flown from Bangkok into Rangoon. When we arrived at the airport in Rangoon a group of ladies, flown out from Britain, were there to meet us and to give us some of the creature comforts that we had missed for three and a half years—comforts such as white bread and butter and tea. While I was drinking, I think it was my sixth cup of tea, I looked up, and there, standing in a corner of the marquee, were three comrades, three tall, gaunt, bearded men, who had been through hell. I looked at them. I saw that their Adam's apples were working overtime and that tears were coursing down their cheeks. I wondered what it was that caused them to do this. I looked. There was a lady coming to them, bearing a supply of tea and bread. That was all, yet the tea and the bread were symbols of love. These men were so overcome by that love that they were broken down. They had glimpsed the great and glorious purpose that is behind the universe. They had looked into the heart of the eternal and seen that it is love.

That reminds us of the story of the prodigal son. You remember how that young scamp went off into the far country, how he felt that he didn't need his old Dad any more, until one day he found himself in a pigsty. There in all that filth and squalor he suddenly thought to himself. "Why should I be here? Why shouldn't I go back home to my old Dad? I know I've cut myself off from him. I've done this on my own. I've taken my inheritance and I've estranged myself from Dad, but I know what I'll do. I'll go back and throw myself upon his mercy, and I'll say to him, 'Look here, Dad. I know I can no longer be a son but at least I can be a servant.' If I go back and be a servant on my father's farm, I'll be sure of three square meals a day and maybe four, and a roof over my head, and everything will be all right." Because of his need the prodigal went back home. When he was nearing home, you remember, his father came rushing out and embraced him and said: "My son! My son! At last you've come back!" He put the ring of sonship on his finger and he brought out the finest robe. He killed the fatted calf and he said, "My son!" And the son said,

"I'm no longer worthy to be called your son." This time he said it on his knees. He said it because he meant it. He had been overcome by his father's love. He was brought down to that place where he realized that he was no longer worthy. His father's love called him into genuine authentic humanity. It called him to be a man and more than a man. It called him to be a son, the son of the living God.

And that is the way God deals with us. He isn't angry with us. He loves us. I've seen an awful lot of anger in my time and I'm not scared of hell, no matter how fiery some people might think it is. But I'll tell you what I am scared of. I'm scared of the love of God. I'm scared of looking into the eyes of the crucified One and seeing that I've failed Him, that I haven't loved as I should have loved. God, you see, doesn't force anyone to love Him. We aren't dragged into His Kingdom by the hairs of our heads. No. He loves us into it, and because He loves us into it, that means the cross for Him. It is only when we stand at the foot of the cross and see ourselves in the light of God's love that we can say, "Love so amazing, so divine, demands my soul, my life, my all." God so loved the world that He gave all that He could give, He gave His Son, His only begotten Son.

Today, as we think of God's love for us and for all men, isn't it enough to break these all too mortal, all too proud hearts of ours? Think of the cross. Think of the love behind it. Think of that power, the greatest power of all, the power that transforms us. God so loved the world that He gave His only begotten Son, that whosever believeth in Him should not perish, but have everlasting life. Thanks be to God for His love.

Sermon Twenty-four

THE MINISTRY–MEN OF GOD

REVEREND ROBERT W. BURNS, D.D.

Minister, Peachtree Christian Church (Disciples of Christ), Atlanta, Georgia

During Dr. Burns' long and distinguished ministry at Peachtree Christian Church he has become famous for his sermons on marriage and the Christian home. Each year he has an anniversary service when the couples he has married in the last thirty-five years come back to renew their marriage vows. Every seat at these services is always filled, as Dr. Burns has married thousands of couples and these in turn often bring their families, children and grandchildren, with them. Part of the reason for the success of "his" marriages is that Dr. Burns emphasizes the importance of love and gentleness, of God, and of care for one's marriage partner. To be married by Robert Burns has almost become a symbol that the marriage will be lasting and happy! His new book, *The Art of Staying Happily Married*, discusses many of his rules for a good and successful marriage.

Robert Burns was born on January 20, 1904, and his family home was St. Louis, Missouri. His father and grandfather were for many years associated with the publishing business of brotherhood books. He grew up attending the Union Avenue Christian Church, St. Louis, and was baptized by Dr. B. A. Abbott during his pastorate.

He attended Drake University, 1921-24, and in 1923 became pastor of the Chesterfield Christian Church in Des Moines, Iowa, then took his degree at Washington University in 1924-26. He was a student at Eden Theological Seminary, 1926-28, and received his B.D. there. He has since taken graduate work at the University of Washington, at the Divinity School of the University of Chicago, and at Union Seminary in New York. He was pastor of the Webster Groves Christian Church in 1924, then for two years was pastor at Maryville. In 1930 he became minister of Peachtree Christian Church, Atlanta, Georgia, and has been there ever since—35 years. He was awarded the D.D. degree by Oglethorpe University in 1936 and by Drake University in 1963.

During 1926-31 he was active in the International Youth Convention of the

Christian Church, being president at Seattle and also in 1930 at Washington, D. C. He has been parliamentarian of the International Convention of the Christian Church for a number of years. In Atlanta he has been active in many phases of the city's life—president of the Evangelical Ministers Association in 1932, president of the Child Service Association 1935-40, Executive Trustee of the Atlanta Child's Home since 1946, plus a number of other responsibilities. In 1933 he was president of the annual convention of the Christian Churches of Georgia and was also Chairman of the state board of Christian Churches for several years.

In 1962-63 he was President of the International Convention of Christian Churches (Disciples of Christ) and has given local, national, and world leadership to his denomination. This address, *The Ministry—Men of God*, was given at the May, 1963, commencement of The College of the Bible.

THE MINISTRY–MEN OF GOD

A graduate of one of the leading centers of theological training in the ancient world, who was also a teacher-supervisor of field work by young ministers, used three interesting words in two of his letters to the beginning pastor. He called Timothy a "Man of God." If he had been writing to a group of ministers, he probably would have called them, "Men of God." Let us consider what he wrote to Timothy as a message to us today, "As for you, *Man of God*, aim at righteousness, godliness, faith, love, steadfastness, gentleness" (I Timothy 6:11), and along with that place these words from II Timothy 3:16, "All scripture is inspired by God and profitable for teaching, for reproof, for correction, and for training in righteousness that the Man of God may be complete, equipped for every good work."

You graduates are the largest class in the 98 years of The College of the Bible, . . . the main purpose of which has been to educate ministers for the preaching and pastoral service of the church. You have received superb training, but training is not enough. The plus element which is essential may be understood when we ask ourselves three questions as Men of God:

Do I really love God?
How does God know I love Him?
How do I share with others my love for God?

The academic year now closing has been the first year of a three-year period designated as the Centennial Observance Period, to culminate in

June of 1965. On behalf of our whole brotherhood I congratulate all who shared in the expansion of these physical facilities on their vision of the future. Room for additional growth is here. A serious financial crisis must soon be solved so that the approximately half a million dollars of operating deficit may be paid off to release this school for greater service. On this, frankly, I appeal for the help of all of you, but I do not choose to center this message on raising money which is the proper task of other men, except to say that when people really love God, they will want to do whatever is essential to the welfare of the work of God, and their reasons for giving will be such as to bring a double blessing—a blessing to The College of the Bible in receiving such gifts and a blessing to those who give as the expression of their love of God helps to increase their love of God.

I appeal to you graduates to give yourselves to the Ministry as Men of God as you enter the next stage in your chosen work. What do the churches really want from their pastors? Since "God created man in His image" (Genesis 1:27), all humans are persons of God, but there is a unique sense in the scriptures according to which a minister is a "Man of God"—a man who belongs to God, God's man, a human with his personality centered in God, living day by day in such God-awareness that we become in the mercy of God men of God.

Some of you in this Chapel are ministers. Many more are part of the general membership of the church. I desire to reach deeply into your hearts as all of us ask three questions today, each one of us asking and answering for himself each of these searching inquiries:

> Do I really love God?
> How does God know I love Him?
> How do I share with others my love for God?

Let us look at each question briefly and see how the Biblical phrase "man of God," applies to us as ministers, but is also filled with fruitful insights to the general membership in understanding their relationship to God.

I

What does it mean for a minister as a *Man* of God to ask himself this question, Do I really love God? Recently, the *Christian Century* quoted Dr. David Stitt, President of Austin Presbyterian Seminary in Texas at the February consultation on the ministry, as opening the meeting with these words, "I beseech you, Brethren, concentrate on this one task—take these students and make MEN of them." [1] The first word of this simple phrase is important—we are to be MEN not boys. Jesus said that the first and greatest commandment was this, "Love God with all your heart and soul and mind and strength." Yet it is right at this decisive experience where most of us fail most often in our ministry. I have had wide correspondence with all those leaving the ministry of our people since January 1, 1962. A few left their ministry because their health failed, but most of them left because their love of God was not strong enough to motivate them for the actual hard work of the ministry. The letters reveal the record of undisciplined, inadequate affection for God.

A basic assumption lies back of the functioning of all churches—that the general members and the ministry *know God and love Him.* This may not be true at all. Many gods may be, and probably are, worshipped in most congregations. Since last October I have been visiting many of our congregations, speaking in state and district conventions and engaging in personal correspondence with several thousand of our leaders around the world. More than anything else I am deeply concerned about the quality of our Christian experience among the ministry and the laity.

President Riley B. Montgomery on March 12, 1963, made this report to the semi-annual meeting of Trustees, "Young men with potentials to become spiritual giants are grown toward maturity here." This, according to the man who knows you best, is what is possible. How many of you will so minister that the potential becomes the actual? Will you be spiritually strong or ministerial midgets? The answer depends more on the response you make to this first question than to any other single factor. Do you really love God? Do you love Him more than you love yourself?

II

What does it mean for the minister, as a man of God, to ask himself this question, "*How does God know I love Him?*" God searches every heart. He knows our inner motives. From Him there are no hiding places.

Therefore, let us earnestly examine our own purposes in entering the ministry as they may look to God. *Why did we choose to serve God in the full-time, church-supported ministry?* Let us say an honest word, heart to heart, to one another. *Our motives are mixed, strangely mixed.* They

[1] *Christian Century,* April 24, 1963, p. 53.

will be mixed all through your ministry, but they should be less mixed as you grow older.

God knows I love Him when I spend time with Him in prayer and in diligent searching of the scriptures. If you ever get to the place where you no longer know God as both a Friend and a Foe, One who stands at your side to help and One with whom you grapple in never-ending struggle, it will not be because you are too busy, nor because He is no longer there. *He will be absent from you because you don't really want Him, and you'd better begin your ministry in the realistic facing of that fact.*

God knows I love Him when in my day by day work as a minister, I keep the will of God at the center of the church I serve. This will reveal itself in a multitude of ways, about most of which I may be completely unconscious. The naturalness of the tone of my voice when I speak to Him and about Him, the ways in which I recognize that I belong to Him and that His church belongs to Him, and the diligence with which I serve Him by helping people are all ways which tell God what means the most to me.

A few days ago I heard Professor Dwight Stevenson speak at the Texas Convention with great profit. He related an incident which occurred one Sunday within less than 150 miles of Lexington, where the pastor introduced Professor Stevenson with this sentence, "Welcome to my pulpit." Professor Stevenson told of his immediate response, jarred at the reference to the Lord's pulpit as "my pulpit." The church belongs to God. All the church belongs to God. None of the church belongs to us as ministers. We are servants, not masters, in God's House.

God knows I love Him when He is on my mind more than I think about myself. Your mind will need to be constantly alert to two voices that will speak to you—one the voice of other humans signaling their desperate needs, the other the voice of God trying to break through the crust of your pride and self-satisfaction. God knows we love Him when we listen to Him.

III

What does it mean for each minister, as a man of God, to ask himself this question, "*How do I share with others my love for God?*"

We communicate to others our love for God by conversation. On occasion this must be brief. Years ago I heard the story of a man examining candidates for the military chaplaincy who gave each prospective chaplain a box of matches and said, "Light one of these, and then tell me quickly, before the match burns down, what you would say on the battlefield to a dying soldier about God." We ought to be able to express in less than a minute what is the heart of our relationship to God.

Our casual conversations are very revealing to others about our own real attitudes. Do we assume superiority because of our training? We shall drive them away from God and the church. Do we express freely our own doubts? We shall destroy their faith. Do we spread defeatism? We shall quickly sap the strength of those around us. Do we like to build ourselves up by tearing other persons down? We can drive people from God as well as from ourselves.

We communicate to others even more our love for God *by consecration*. What we do speaks more clearly than what we say. Dr. Dan Poling's son asked him, "Dad, tell me all you know about God," to which Dr. Poling replied, "I don't know very much about God, but the little I do know has changed my whole life," and because his son knew the genuine devotion of the father's life in serving God, what he said was illustrated by his deeds.

The great new fact of science is that for the first time in the history of our race we have the possibility of self-extermination. This is a threat which will hang over all the years of our ministries. What we say about God will be only a lot of empty words unless we are filled with such abundant love of Him that we can stand firm in faith under the threat of extinction. Our ability to communicate depends on the reality and range of our own convictions.

During Dr. Harry Fosdick's first pastorate a youth from one of the finest families in the church, conquered by alcohol and in utter despair, said to him, "I don't believe in God, but if YOU do, for God's sake, pray for me, for I need Him." The incident closed many months later, "If you ever find anyone who does not believe in God, send him to me. I know." Such events will happen in your ministry only if you can share a love of God with others.

The ways in which we share with others our love for God change from century to century. After you have won the confidence of the members of the congregation you are serving, try some experiments in expressing to each other the love you have for God. Some services of worship are unendurably dull. Our conduct of weddings, funerals and baptisms may all too easily slip into a routine of meaningless words. The only way to prevent this is to open our hearts to the love of God until He fills us to overflowing with His presence. Then every act of our ministry will be done in the POWER of His ministering grace. We shall be channels through which His love reaches out through our love for Him to touch the hearts and change the lives of persons.

We communicate to others most of all our love for God *by Christ living in us.* The minister, as a man of God, is a new man in Christ. Those great phrases with which the apostle Paul appealed to the early Christians still appeal to us. "You are Christ's and Christ is God's" (I Corinthians 3:23). "You are the body of Christ" (I Corinthians 12:27). "For me, to live is Christ" (Philippians 1:21). "Christ in you, the hope of glory" (Colossians 1:27).

Sermon Twenty-five

THREE DAYS WITH ALBERT SCHWEITZER AT LAMBARENÉ

REVEREND DONALD SZANTHO HARRINGTON, S.T.D.

Minister, The Community Church (Unitarian), New York, New York

Since 1944 Donald Harrington has been minister of the Community Church in New York. For the first five years there he was junior minister with Dr. John Haynes Holmes; since 1949, following Dr. Holmes retirement, he has been in charge of the church. Dr. Harrington was born in Newton, Massachusetts, and attended Old First Parish Church (Unitarian) in Waltham. He attended Antioch College and the University of Chicago. He received his theological training at Meadville Theological School in Chicago and became minister of First Unitarian Church in Hobart, Indiana. In 1938 he was awarded the Cruft Traveling Fellowship and went to Europe to study at the University of Leyden for a year. While there he also visited the Universities of Marburg, Kolosvar, Oxford, and Cambridge. He has traveled through most of the countries of Europe. In 1939 he and the Reverend Vilma Szantho, the first woman to be ordained to the ministry in Central Europe, were married by the Bishop of the Hungarian Unitarian Church in Budapest. He and Mrs. Harrington returned to the United States in the fall of 1939, and he became Minister of the People's Liberal Church in Chicago.

During the winter of 1960-1961 Dr. and Mrs. Harrington made an intensive study tour of Eastern Europe and Israel as well as East, Central, South and West Africa. At present he is Chairman of the American Committee on Africa. He is also a member of the American Association for the United Nations' Commission to Study the Organization of the Peace. In 1959 he received the honorary degree of Doctor of Sacred Theology from Starr King School for the Ministry in Berkeley, California.

In 1961 he and his wife made their pilgrimage to Lambarené to visit Dr. Schweitzer and see the work he is doing for Africans in the tiny African village where he has built his hospital and home. Dr. Harrington preached this sermon, giving his impressions of his visit, in Community Church on January 14, 1962. His discussion of the achievements and personality of the Great Doctor and even his pointed remarks concerning the criticisms about Dr. Schweitzer's work are valuable. His meeting with Dr. Schweitzer is reminiscent of that between Stanley and Livingstone a century ago, but in a somewhat more modern setting.

THREE DAYS WITH ALBERT SCHWEITZER AT LAMBARENÉ

This morning at 7:30 A.M., against the background accompaniment of the myriad noises of the jungle birds and insects, the bleating of goats and crowing of cocks, the cries of babies and friendly murmur of conversation of a jungle village, a choir, not of angels but of lepers, gathered outside the long, low, screened-in dining room under the already fierce African sun to sing "Happy Birthday to You" in African to eighty-seven-year-old Albert Schweitzer of Lambarené.

I was there just about a year ago, and can see it all in my mind's eye. Dr. Schweitzer lifts his grizzled head and glances around the table, feigning surprise. The faces of his associates, many of them young but some of them deeply lined and haloed with silver, are all smiling. As a matter of fact, each one has hidden under his chair or plate some little gift, a token of his love and respect for Le Grand Docteur.

Albert Schweitzer pushes back his chair, stands up and goes outside to greet the singers one by one and each by name. Each of these, too, has brought something:—a little woven mat, a carved piece of wood, a small painting, a fragment of himself. Schweitzer receives these gifts gravely, thanks each giver warmly, and then returns to hear the spoken praises of the men and women who have laid the world away and come from east and west and north and south to share his burdens in the healing of the hurt in the midst of the African jungle.

It was just a year ago that Vilma and I were there and saw it thus, and we will always remember with gratitude those three days in 1961 spent with Albert Schweitzer at Lambarené.

Some have wondered why I have not spoken earlier about our visit to Schweitzer. I am quite frank to report that it has taken me a full year to know what I wanted to say, to gain some perspective and a penetration of understanding of what is really happening there in the forest primeval on the banks of the brown Ogowe. For a time I was not sure that I could understand it, or that I should have anything to say about our experience. But as the year has worn on, and I have thought and rethought every moment, every word, every detail, the things which I had not understood began to grow clear, and I began to feel as though I could speak, as now I shall.

The outline of the Schweitzer epic is well known. Here was a man who had everything, brilliance of intellect, depth of spirit, security of position in his world, and careers of greatest promise in music, the ministry, theology, so much so that by his mid-twenties he already stood at the peak of his profession, was principal of his theological seminary, and had published books of unusual creativity and originality.

But over the shining joy of his accomplishment and glory of his gifts, there lay the slightest shadow, a deep sense of personal obligation. He recorded how one morning in Gunsbach, as he lay in bed with the morning sun streaming in through the window upon him, and pondered the many gifts so freely showered upon him by his parents and society, there suddenly came upon him the conviction that he must share this bounty, must find some way in his lifetime to return to the less privileged of his fellow men a measure of the joy and happiness he felt at that moment. He determined that he would live for ten years for music, religion and art, and then would find some way to give the rest of his life in direct service of his fellows.

The next stage in Albert Schweitzer's spiritual development came with his decision to *live* Christian truth rather than to try to teach and preach it. Norman Cousins, in his excellent book, *Albert Schweitzer of Lambarené*, gives us Schweitzer's own description of this decision.[1]

As a young man, my ambition was to be a good minister. I completed my studies; then, after a while I started to teach. I became the principal of the seminary. All this while I had been studying and thinking about the life of Jesus and the meaning of Jesus. And the more I studied and thought, the more convinced I became that Christian theology had become over complicated. In the early centuries after Christ, the beautiful simplicities relating to Jesus became somewhat obscured by the conflicting interpretations and the incredibly involved dogma growing out of the theological debates. . . .

In my effort to get away from intricate Christian theology based on later interpretations, I developed some ideas of my own. These ideas were at variance with the ideas that had been taught me. Now, what was I to do? How could I, as a principal of a seminary, accept the responsibility for teaching young men that which I did not believe? . . .

---

[1] Norman Cousins, *Albert Schweitzer of Lambarené*, quotations by permission of Harper & Row, New York.

I decided that I would leave the seminary. Instead of trying to get acceptance for my ideas, involving painful controversy, I decided I would make my life my argument. I would advocate the things I believed in terms of the life I lived and what I did. Instead of vocalizing my belief in the existence of God within each of us, I would attempt to have my life and my work say what I believed.

This led directly to Schweitzer's Great Renunciation, his turning his back upon Europe, his splendid careers in music and theology, his comfort, his financial security, and all of the other dreams which would be natural to one of his station and stature in European life, and to his going to school to become a doctor. Then, forty-nine years ago, in March of 1913, he set sail for Africa. He chose Equatorial Africa, that part of Africa where disease is most rampant, the heat most terrible, conditions of life most primitive and medical care virtually non-existent. His first hospital was sponsored by a missionary society, but he found the theological restrictions too great, and after World War I, during which he was temporarily forced to suspend his work, he went back to Africa, relocated the hospital, this time all on his own, and from that time on he has been building it with his own hands and heart, and with such funds as those inspired by him throughout the world were willing voluntarily to send, and such as he could earn by his writing and publishing. So the hospital has grown until today the Albert Schweitzer Hospital and Leper Village at Lambarené constitute a thousand human beings, all of them needing to be cared for, governed, and fed by him.

One must experience the Schweitzer Hospital to understand it, and three days is not nearly long enough. That is about the time necessary for one to be shocked to the very core of his being by the magnitude of the problems and the primitive character of existence in this part of the world. Before one would have really earned the right to write critically about the Schweitzer Hospital, he would have had to spend at least a year there, testing his own fortitude against the fierceness of the heat, the loneliness of the isolation, the omnipresence of disease and death, and for this reason I speak, even now, hesitantly, and pray to God that I may not be unjust.

Our DC-6 plane landed on the red dirt airstrip at Lambarené after a wildly bumpy trip from Brazzaville which left everyone shaking with sickness. In some ways it was a fitting preparation, for we were to witness things during the next three days which would often make us feel sick.

Met at the airport by a genial African Major Domo from the Hospital, we were taken with our bags to the red edge of the river Ogowe, helped into the large, solid canoe and then paddled upstream against the current by three paddlers from the leper village. Two of them were middle aged men, whose leprosy had been, for the time being at any rate, checked. One was just a boy. All three bore their afflictions with good humored patience. The sweat poured from their faces and bodies as they grunted in unison with each stroke against the current, skillfully maneuvering back and forth across the river to take advantage of every eddy and the protection of every turn and twist. We had an inkling, however, of one of the things that was to puzzle us deeply at Schweitzer's Hospital when a similar canoe, with half a dozen Africans, went plowing past us powered with an outboard motor!

Our arrival at the hospital was a never-to-be-forgotten moment in our lives. As we approached the landing, we suddenly saw a familiar, stocky figure with the white sun hat, accompanied by doctors and nurses dressed in white, coming down the slope to meet the oncoming canoe, and then before we knew it, there we were, face to face with a living legend, with the man who in his own lifetime has become a myth and an integral part of Christian mythology, *the greatest man alive in the world today!* For once I found myself completely at a loss for words. If I had tried to speak, I know I would have burst out crying, for I saw in this old man's face a dearness that made me feel as though he were not only my own father, but a kind of father to the hopes of all mankind.

Fortunately there were things at once to do. The canoe had to be unloaded. We had to find our places in the long, barracks-like residential building, and lunch was waiting too. Before we knew what was happening, we were part of the routine, dressed like the others, and expected to find our niche and place in the ongoing life of the community. It was almost as though we had been there all our lives.

How shall I describe to you Albert Schweitzer's Hospital at Lambarené? First I must describe the heat. If you can imagine living in 110° to 120° of heat accompanied by about 98 percent humidity day and night, year in and year out, then you know what Lambarené is like. You are fortunate if there is just a little breeze to ease it and dry your sweat, but most of the time you become accustomed to being dripping wet, both day and night.

Everything at the Hospital seems very primitive. We lived in one of the rooms of a nurse away on leave. It had two white-washed walls, with the two ends, covered with screening, wide open to catch every breath of air. There was a white iron bedstead, a chair, a small writing table, a stand with bowl, a pitcher of water and slop pail, and that was all. All that anyone would need. The outdoor toilets were of the most primitive type. The dining room was open on every side with screens and lighted with oil lamps.

The Hospital itself should not be called a hospital. This is a misnomer. It is really a jungle village, very similar in basic spirit and facilities to any other jungle village in that area, overrun with goats, ducks, chickens, children. Each sick person has a little segment for himself, a wooden bunk with space beneath it for his luggage and travelling equipment and space above it for a hammock for his "gardien," the member of his family who has to come to cook his meals and take care of him. There were no sheets, mattresses or pillows. Food is distributed each day, and cooked in iron pots over the traditional three stones for each patient individually, and the smoke of the fires rises constantly casting a blue haze over the hospital area. Right in the midst of all this is a dispensary, pharmacy, operating room, nursery for babies, and the different clinics for the different kinds of illnesses. The patients line up in morning and afternoon for care. Those who cannot walk, of course, are visited by the doctors. The operating room is the only room there which has electricity, and when one hears the gasoline generator going he knows that an operation is in progress.

The dispensary and clinics are a scene of the most intense activity every day, with three of the four doctors hard at work seeing patients as rapidly as possible, and with the venerable Dr. Schweitzer sitting right in the midst of it all at his desk reading, writing, ordering supplies, paying bills, answering mail, turning from time to time to answer questions from the other doctors or to consult with them about an unusual condition, or getting up to comfort a squalling baby or child.

What can one say about this staff of almost twenty-five people except that, like Dr. Schweitzer, they have given up everything and are following in his steps. I think of Dr. Richard Friedman, the Czech-Hungarian, Jewish doctor, a man about fifty years old, who has already been at the hospital for five years and been away for only two afternoons when he went down to Lambarené Village to get supplies. Dr. Friedman, like the other doctors, is up early and goes to bed late, and over and over again, in the middle of the night, we heard, often through driving rain, cries of alarm, hurrying footsteps, and the doctors being awakened and hurrying down through the night into the Hospital with a lamp to attend to some emergency. There was the Japanese doctor who takes care of the Leper Village, who is up every morning at six and already has a good segment of work under his belt before the 7:30 breakfast. I remember our stopping over at the Leper Village, having walked across what Dr. Schweitzer whimsically calls his trail through the jungle from the hospital to the Leper Village, "The Philosopher's Walk," and seeing the Japanese doctor, wielding his instruments with his bare hands, cleaning the dreadful leper's wounds and sores of children and young people and older people in the Leper Village. I could not help asking him if it was not dangerous to work so constantly, day by day, close to this dread and contagious disease, and he looked up at me with a bland, innocent face and remarked, "Very, very dangerous!" and turned back to his work. I remember Ali Silver, a sweet, frail reed of a woman, the nurse upon whom Dr. Schweitzer depends the most, and whom he has called, "An angel from heaven." It was she who made the arrangements for our coming, and who handles a thousand details of the hospital life each day under Dr. Schweitzer's direction. Each of these, and so many others, is earning a sainthood here, whether he will or no.

Oh, and I must not forget the animals. After all, Schweitzer is the prophet of "reverence for life, all life!" So there are animals everywhere! Some of these have been rescued from the jungle. The chimpanzee and the young gorilla were found with dead parents, and have been rescued along with the other animals and people. There is the famous pelican, and dozens of cats and dogs, goodness knows how many hens, roosters, ducks, half of them lame, and literally herds of goats. One of my most vivid memories is that of the sound of a whole troop of goats dashing across the piazza of our sleeping hut at 6:00 o'clock in the morning.

Some of these animals are not well cared for. They look hungry, and even some as though they should be put out of their misery. But I know what Dr. Schweitzer would say to any such suggestion. He would say that the only one who has a right to say that he should be put out of his misery is the One Himself. For most of us, our misery is preferable to death any day, and the decision is not one to be made by another.

How is all this vast panorama maintained? The answer to this question holds the key to an understanding of many of the things which are going on at Albert Schweitzer's Hospital. This community of one thousand souls, engaged in the process of being healed or of healing, is all carried on by Dr. Albert Schweitzer's own efforts. He either earned or attracted the money to purchase the land, to build the buildings, the Leper Village having been built mostly by his own and African labor and the materials bought by the Nobel Peace Prize. The bills are paid by his power to attract unsolicited financial support, and he has no fund-raising organizations out working across the world for him except such as have been voluntarily set up by others and operate without his control or desire. His staff is drawn also simply by the power of his example to attract others to work with him, and to make the incredible sacrifice involved. It is hard to find any words adequate to express the real truth of how personal a thing the Albert Schweitzer Hospital is. He is the organizer of the work details, and one can see him after breakfast with the gathered "gardiens," those who come with their relatives to tend them, cook for them, and help carry on the work of the hospital. He is sending them out to the gardens, the orchard, the place where the new building is being put up to do the work of the day. He is the master builder, architect and carpenter. He is the feeder, the purchaser of grain, the distributor of goods. He is the treasurer and fund-raiser; he is the personnel manager, the governor, the recruiter of doctors and nurses at long distance. He is the minister-counsellor, who, after the evening meal, opens the Bible and reads a passage and then in simple, yet profound interpretation, says what it means. He plays the rickety old piano for the singing of the evening hymns, and somehow those few moments of the evening are all that one needs by way of recompense for the sustaining of his spirit!

Of course, this independence of the spirit, this insistence upon the voluntariness of the offering, has at times in the past been costly to both Albert Schweitzer and the Hospital. It means that income is irregular, and there were times during the last fifty years when the staff did not have enough to eat, when medical supplies were not adequate to the demand, times when Albert Schweitzer was driven to his writing for the sake of making enough money to carry on the work.

There were things at Schweitzer's Hospital which we found very hard to understand or accept. These were things we had heard rumors about before going to Lambarené, and which shocked us when we arrived there. I am going to face these frankly, and speak of them openly and straightforwardly, not only because it is the only honest thing to do, but because it is the only way to defend Schweitzer's good name and hard work.

The first criticism comes under the heading of general hygiene. Is it really necessary to have in this day and age a hospital with no running water, without electricity in the wards and staff buildings, with wholly inadequate outside toilet facilities, with no protection from the terrible heat, with no motorized transport along the river. Why can there not be at Lambarené a modern and well-equipped hospital which Schweitzer could build with the money which undoubtedly could be raised if he would use his influence to do so?

Secondly, he is criticized for being an autocrat and practicing paternalism in his methods and manners toward both the Africans and the Europeans who work with him. There is no question as to who is the boss at Lambarené, and Schweitzer is at times very stern in his giving of orders.

Thirdly, he is accused of being kinder to the animals than he is to the human beings, and on the surface I am sure this sometimes appears to be so. The daily rituals of feeding the antelopes, which come and lick his arms and face, the dozens of cats, the pelican, the gorilla and chimpanzee leave no question of his deep affection for them, which is not so manifest towards human beings. You will remember that when Adlai Stevenson visited him, and Mr. Stevenson slapped a mosquito on his forehead, Schweitzer remarked tartly. "That was my mosquito!"

Finally it is charged that he does not encourage the development of the African, and maintains segregated facilities at the Hospital and among the members of the staff.

All of these things are true, and at first they are dreadfully shocking. So great was my initial sense of shock, in fact, that I actually felt sick, and before I was through I got sick. Albert Schweitzer immediately came to see me, and prescribed for me, and I will say this for his prowess as a medical doctor, that within a few days I had thrown the illness off. I am glad that I had enough sense of humor left, despite the misery of my bowels, to say to him that I had gotten sick deliberately so I would always be able to say that the great Dr. Albert Schweitzer had been my personal physician.

But the more I have pondered what we experienced at Lambarené, the more I have come to understand what we saw there and why it had to be the way it was. I have even come to defend this great, good man and what he is doing. Not, incidentally, that he gives any indication of feeling any need to be defended, though I am sure he has read the criticism of him. He gives every impression of knowing what he is doing.

Why is it necessary that those who come to the Schweitzer Hospital should live in such unhygienic and very rough conditions? The answer, I think, is first of all that Dr. Schweitzer believes that most of the African villagers would not go to a modern hospital. One of their principal beliefs is that a person can't get well if he is lonesome and if his family isn't there to care for him. So Dr. Schweitzer has tried to duplicate, as nearly as possible, the actual conditions of an African village, and the patient comes with a member of his family to care for him, and lives in just about the same kind of conditions as he would in his own village.

Perhaps something more could be done to teach these villagers more hygienic ways and habits, and I suspect that Dr. Schweitzer has tried over the years to do so, and perhaps has failed and is doing what he can, quite aware of where he has failed.

And an even more important element in this, however, is, I believe, Schweitzer's decision to keep his witness in the work of this hospital personal despite our age of super-organization, of specialized administrators, fund-raisers, executive directors, personnel managers. While it would theoretically be possible for all that he has built here at Lambarené to be torn down, and a shiny, new hospital to be built, staffed, and financed, it would require his leaving this work, his going on world tours, his putting himself into the hands of fund-raisers, the hiring of administrators, and there is some question as to whether very many Africans would come to the hospital. There is a new, modern hospital a few miles down the river, but we were told that it was half empty. When I asked one of the African patients why he didn't go to the new government hospital, he said because it cost too much, the care was poor, he didn't trust the doctors, and the nurses required bribes. He preferred Dr. Schweitzer's Hospital without so much hygiene but with more help.

I believe that Dr. Schweitzer's refusal to modernize is probably intimately connected with his understanding of the fact that, whether he likes it or not, he has become the symbol of something of ultimate significance to human life, while still alive and conscious, a part of the ongoing Christian myth. I suspect, though he does not like to talk about this, that he feels this as a kind of incredible responsibility to be borne somehow wisely and bravely to the end without permitting its being tarnished.

Perhaps there is a dreadful tragedy here. Perhaps the march of world events, of mass organization, of modern methods has overtaken Albert Schweitzer and his hospital at Lambarené, but at the age of eighty-seven he cannot alter the character of his witness. Perhaps he and the hospital together are becoming anachronisms in an age which is replacing the person with the organization, but if that is so then that too somehow must be borne. Perhaps it was a sense of this that led him to remark to one of the other doctors, as reported to me, "Through most of its existence this hospital has needed me far more than I needed it, but now I need it more than it needs me." On the other hand, perhaps it is civilization that has gone astray. That, too, is conceivable!

So far as the electricity is concerned, it requires generators, and generators require a constant flow of barrels of fuel oil. Such a flow requires boats and money, money which Schweitzer does not have to spend.

As for the outboard motors, I know what his reply would be, "There are many over at the Leper Village with nothing to do who need to feel needed."

Yes, Schweitzer is something of an autocrat, but one must remember that he is an old German professor, and I wonder if we have any right to ask a man to forget the habits of a lifetime. I well remember from my own studies abroad how one could ask the professor a question, but could not question his answer. There is something of this in today's Albert Schweitzer, but I cannot condemn him for it.

I think we must also remember that a society of one thousand human beings, with all of their loves, fears, hates and jealousies, their anxieties and hopes, is not simple to maintain in harmony. I am not surprised that it takes a bit of authority at the top now and then to keep it all running.

Yes, and at times Schweitzer may seem to be kinder and more loving toward the animals than toward the human beings, though I must reject out of hand this charge in any serious sense. One cannot see him with the patients and not feel the kindness and concern that his life exemplifies. If his manner towards human beings is more reserved and at times more stern, it is, of course, because he expects more of human beings than he does of animals, and because he has spent a lifetime of battle fighting against the lethargy and apathy of chronically sick people in order to get things done. He once said that in Africa, fighting pain, sickness, death and the apathy of the ages, he had had no opportunity to be the saint his European admirers imagined him to be.

What of the segregated staff and facilities? Yes, the African patients are housed in one building and the Europeans in another, and this appears to be segregation. But, I think that one must realize that cultural differences here in Africa are very great indeed, and the motivation of the segregation becomes all important. This is not segregation for the purpose of segregation or domination, but simply and solely for the purpose of mutual comfort of the different communities. They would not be comfortable in the same kind of facilities.

Perhaps Albert Schweitzer has not done enough to change the African villagers' way of life, perhaps he has not adequately encouraged them to build different kinds of villages and to learn new ways, but I think that he would answer any such charge by saying simply that one man cannot do everything, and that he came out to Africa to try to use the skills of medicine to heal the African's body when it became sick and to teach the simplest rules of hygiene, and that someone else would have to do the revolutionary job of changing the basic African way of life.

I think I was hurt most of all by the fact that all around that table when we had our meals there was no dark face. Why has Schweitzer not been able to train some promising young African boy or girl to be a nurse or doctor? Several had become orderlies, taking temperatures and giving shots, dispensing pharmaceuticals, etc. Why had it not been possible for African young people to be sent to France for education, and then to come back to serve their own?

I don't know what or whether there is any answer to this charge. Perhaps it is in this area that frustrations became too great, and the good doctor gave up too soon. I will say this, however, that the criticism of some modern Africans and Europeans ill becomes them, for they are not willing themselves to make any similar sacrifice. I was told of one African doctor from Gabon who had been trained in Paris and who came back to visit Schweitzer's Hospital. When asked whether he would take up the practice of medicine in his homeland, the Gabon, he replied indignantly, "What, come back to this dirty, filthy, poverty-stricken country! Don't you know that I have a degree from the Sorbonne, and have a good practice in Paris?"

When the time comes that an African doctor or nurse is ready to make the sacrifice as did Schweitzer himself, then there will be time for criticism, and if there is not a dark face around the staff table at Lambarené I have to believe it is because Albert Schweitzer simply does not know how to build the bridge to make it possible.

Finally, I must say that nothing that happens at the Hospital now can hurt Albert Schweitzer or mar the magnificence of his Great Renunciation. Yes, he is a human being and he has made his errors. But, he has shown the world with his life that Christianity is not an impossible dream and the Nazarene a misguided fool. He has shown mankind for all time to come that a man can give up everything to serve the poorest and lowliest of his brethren, and in so doing be exalted. The countenance of this eighty-seven-year-old patriarch is the most serenely beautiful I have ever seen. It reflects and radiates the ancient admonition, "*Come unto me, all ye who labor and are heavy laden, and I will give you rest.*" To his European co-workers and to all subject to the power of the attraction of his example, he says, "Take my yoke upon you and learn of me, . . . and you will find rest unto your *souls.*"

This old man, immersed in pain and standing near the end of his age-long battle with Death, looks out at the world with confident and confidence-creating eyes. Perhaps he is the only one in the whole world today who truly can say, *"In the world ye have tribulation, but be of good cheer for I have overcome the world."* And that is why when one sits down in the soft lamplight at Lambarené for the evening meal, and above the murmur of the myriad insects and through the dreadful heat, hears that wise, old voice, strong and clear, invoking God's blessing upon His world, one somehow is aware that there is Something of Eternity sitting at that Table each evening, holier than any altar, more sacred than any church, the same Presence which roamed the hills of Galilee and stalked the streets of Jerusalem two thousand years ago, and one is silently, sweetly blessed.

And what would Schweitzer say to us, gathered here together in this church this morning to think of him on his eighty-seventh birthday? I think he would say something like he once wrote in a little book called, *Memories of My Childhood:*

> . . . I have struggled against facts and experience on behalf of belief in the good and the true. At the present time when violence, clothed in life, dominates the world more cruelly than it ever has before, I still remain convinced that truth, love, peaceableness, meekness, and kindness are the violence which can master all other violence. The world will be theirs as soon as ever a sufficient number of men with purity of heart, with strength, and with perseverance, think and live out the thought of love and truth, of meekness and peaceableness.

"As soon as ever a sufficient number of men. . . ."

Sermon Twenty-six

THE ANATOMY OF FREEDOM

REVEREND WILLIAM SAMUEL MEYER, D.D., LL.D., L.H.D., S.T.D.

Minister, Immanuel Presbyterian Church, Los Angeles, California

Dr. Meyer came to the pastorate of the Immanuel Presbyterian Church of Los Angeles, California, in March 1950. He is a native of South Dakota and held pastorates in Illinois, New York and Oklahoma. He was associated with the Fourth Presbyterian Church of Chicago, was pastor of First Presbyterian Church of Ponca City, Oklahoma, and from 1941 to 1950 he was pastor of Central Presbyterian Church of Rochester, New York.

He is a graduate of the College of Wooster, Ohio, and of McCormick Theological Seminary, Chicago. He received the Doctor of Divinity degree in 1938 from the College of Emporia, the Doctor of Laws from Huron College in 1947, and the L.H.D. from Wooster College and the California College of Medicine in the same year, 1957. In 1963 he received the S.T.D. from the University of Southern California.

Dr. Meyer has been a director of the Presbyterian Publishing Company, a writer in the fields of Hymnology, Christian Education and Missions, a member of the Hymn Society of America and the Guild of Organists, a director of the Los Angeles Federation of Churches, the Board of Church Extension of the Presbytery of Los Angeles, Moderator of the Presbytery in 1954, a member of the Executive Committee of the Los Angeles U.S.O., the Meals for Millions Foundation, and the Board of Governors of the Welfare Federation of Los Angeles.

In the summer of 1948 he was International Exchange preacher in Scotland, England, France, and Germany; he toured the Holy Land in 1959; and in 1961 and 1963 he was a delegate to Kirchentag, in Berlin and Dortmund, Germany. He was a delegate at the 1948 meeting of the World Alliance of Reformed Churches, and following this attended the first Assembly of the World Council of Churches in Amsterdam. Since 1957 he has been Chaplain of the Council of Regents of Forest Lawn Memorial Court of Honor.

This sermon on *The Anatomy of Freedom* discusses the gradual encroachments of government on the liberties of the individual and the nation and the need for strong religious faith in our national life. In this time when prayer has been taken out of public schools and the federal government is assuming more and more control over local life, Dr. Meyer shows ways to keep the faith of our founding fathers. The sermon won the Freedoms Foundation Award for 1962-63.

"THE ANATOMY OF FREEDOM"

> Ye are a chosen generation, a royal priesthood, a holy nation, a people for God's own possession, that ye may show forth the excellencies of him who called you out of darkness into his marvelous light.
>
> I Peter 2:9

St. Peter wrote a gospel, but it doesn't bear his name. It bears the name of his secretary, Mark. But he also wrote some letters and we have as our text this morning a verse from the first letter of St. Peter, the second chapter, the ninth verse. "Ye are a chosen generation, a royal priesthood, a holy nation, a people for God's own possession, that ye may show forth the excellencies of him who called you out of darkness into his marvelous light."

It would be trite for me to begin by saying that we live in a critical age, and a critical period in world history. Great forces are at work among the nations of the earth, and not the least of these is the upsurge of desire for freedom on the part of many who have not had it in the past. Strange it is indeed that at that moment when more men and women are desiring freedom and seeking it, at just such a time more people are losing their freedom, surrendering it to totalitarian powers, than in any other two decades in human history. Since this has become such a vital issue in our time, it seems essential that those of us who still retain at least a measure of freedom, though it is little by little being eaten away, should understand the fundamentals on which liberty is based. We should know the things in which it consists. Therefore we have as our theme this morning the title of the well known book, *The Anatomy of Freedom.*

It was Jesus who said, "Ye shall know the truth and the truth shall make you free." St. Paul said, "Now the Lord is the spirit and where the spirit of the Lord is, there is liberty." It was St. Peter who uttered the words we quoted as our text.

Twenty years ago one of the citizens of this community, Mr. Tuller,[1] wrote a dissertation on the subject of freedom and liberty. I should like to quote a few sentences from it. This is what he said, "For more than a century our people have taken liberty as much for granted as the air which they breathe . . . Liberty is the greatest achievement of the human race . . . It is not only the most priceless possession of a free people but it must be remembered that it is not automatic. Nothing more true was ever said than this, 'eternal vigilance is the price of liberty.' Once liberty is lost," he said, "it may never be regained. The preservation of our free institutions depends upon this understanding. The philosophy of totalitarianism is based upon the idea that the State is everything, the individual exists for the State. Our American philosophy, in which spirit our Constitution was written, is just the opposite of this. The State exists for the individual. It derives its just powers from the consent of the governed. The essence of liberty, therefore, consists of effective limitations upon the powers of government. Our founding fathers were greatly concerned that the powers of government should be clearly defined and effectively limited. The great purpose of the Constitution was to secure the blessings of liberty to ourselves and our posterity. This is the very antithesis of unlimited government. In America the people are as yet sovereign. The government is merely the agency of the people, possessing only those powers which the people have delegated to the government. Under totalitarianism the State is sovereign. It possesses all power. The people have not rights but only privileges which the government allows. In our case the State derives its just powers from the consent of those it governs."

Well, if this remains true, then our courts must remain independent of the other branches of government—the executive and the legislative—in order that they may see if either the executive or the legislative branch is seeking to exercise powers which the people have not granted them. The people in turn must exercise care that all three branches do not go beyond the prerogatives which the Constitution assigns to them. So let us not forget these four ideas which you will find running throughout the whole spirit and context of the Constitution of the United States.

First, government exists to secure the blessings of liberty for the individual citizen. In the second place, liberty can only exist insofar as there are effective limitations on the powers of government. In the third place, the Constitution prescribes the limitations on its powers;

---

[1] Quoted by permission of Mrs. Walter Kilbourne Tuller.

and in the fourth place, to make these limitations effective the courts must remain independent of the other branches in order that they may declare void any act of government which violates the limitations which the people themselves have put upon its power. This of course ascribes to the courts of our country a great responsibility. It ascribes to them a great power, and it is exactly in this regard that at this moment in our country we must be on our guard. It is time our elected officials remember their promises before election and be reminded that our founding fathers intended this to be a Christian country, not one where God was ruled out of schools, business and life.

I. The World Seeks Freedom

So let us note first of all this strange paradox: In a day when more and more people of the earth are seeking freedom, clambering for liberty, in just that same day there is going on across the world a mighty movement toward the vesting of greater and greater power in government. This is happening in our country, too, unfortunately. America is caught up in exactly this same type of movement. This week I read a statement that the new positions created by the Federal Government this year will require the tax payments of a million citizens, just to pay the salaries of the new jobs created since 1962 began. Soon, if this continues, more people will be employed by the government than there are people to pay the taxes to support the government. The moment we arrive at that point the whole American system is in extreme jeopardy. As a matter of fact it is right now. Few people seem to realize that when the powers of government are increased the liberties of citizens are thereby automatically reduced. Unless the man in office and the man back home (and this is where we come into the picture—the average citizen back home), unless the man in office and the people back home unite to stop this trend, the time may well be not far distant when we will have a government of totalitarian power. We as Americans, like so many others, will have lost the priceless thing for which our forebears gave their lives: in other words, freedom and liberty. All history unites to prove this thesis. You need but read the histories of the nations of the world and you will see that bureaucracy and freedom have never existed very long side by side. Either the one or the other takes over, and the great question is whether the bureaucracy of our country will soon engulf the total citizenry.

History also shows that when a people have given themselves to the heady wine of voting themselves personal benefits which are contrary to the best interests of the country, that this too has been the forerunner of collapse. That is exactly what is happening in the United States today, where it is a grave question as to whether or not a majority of people can be summoned who will help to defeat paternalistic measures, such as the Medicare Program, federal aid to education, and a host of other things of similar stripe. I for one do not want to see this happen in America. . . . If it does, another segment of our freedom goes with it.

II. The Greatest Danger Is Within

History also shows that this insidious inside danger is a far greater menace to the future than anything that comes from without. Now we are concerned about the foes without, but no foreign foe will ever be able to arise to defeat this country if we have not first undermined our own character from within. If we have done that, anyone can defeat us under those circumstances. In this connection we should note that liberty and democracy are not quite the same thing. It is possible to have a totalitarian democracy, and that is the direction in which we are headed. Redundant though this may sound, this is possible. The only difference between that and a totalitarian dictatorship is that in the latter case the totalitarian power is in one man or in a small committee, or a small group of men. In the other the totalitarian power is vested in a temporary and irresponsible majority. The important point to remember is that liberty is impossible without effective limitations to government and that is true whether it be a dictatorship or a democracy. So the thing we must remember as we think about this matter is that, if constitutional democracy and the representative form of government such as we have are to continue in the United States, such as we have had in the past, and if the blessings of liberty and freedom are to be preserved, then the majority can no more possess arbitrary and unlimited power than can a dictator. The powers of the majority must continue to be limited as they have in the past, with the rights of the individual as the question in point.

This is the same so far as pressure groups are concerned, even as it is in autocratic majorities. Our motto must be, not democracy instead of liberty; but our motto must be, democracy and liberty. We have said here before and we repeat this morning that unfortunately not all people of the world are capable of self-government. This may sound as a "holier than thou" statement, but the fact remains that history substantiates this idea. Read about it and see the many countries that have tried democracy, but didn't have the necessary character to keep it going. There are many such in the world today. Without naming names, there are countries where it is a grave question as to whether they have sufficient character to deserve to govern themselves. We know what Lincoln said about no man ever having a right to govern anyone else. But the question still remains what are you going to do about the people who can't govern themselves? Some say, let them fight it out until the last man dies! This is a poor choice, it seems to me. We must remember that it took thousands of years of sacrifice to create the freedoms and the liberties that we have in America. Our forebears in Britain and other parts of Europe struggled and bled and died, as well as our forebears in this country, in order to break the iron grip of autocratic government.

Let me remind you of a letter that was sent by the Synod of New York and Philadelphia in the year 1775. This letter was written a month after the Battle of Lexington and Concord and about a year before the Declaration of Independence was signed. With great dignity and feeling the leaders of the Presbyterian Church laid before the people of America the reasons for the Revolution. Our church was one of the earliest to be founded in this country and fortunately had a good deal to do with the early development of America. (In England, where they didn't like the Revolution, of course, they spoke of it as the Presbyterian Rebellion in America.) With great dignity and feeling the American churchmen stressed the reasons for the American Revolution. They sought to guide the people in the ways of Christian conduct during this kind of crisis: "The reason for the revolt," they said, "is not lawlessness. We are not urging you to be lawless people, but it is for the preservation of the rights of free men." These were the sentiments, not of firebrands but of our most responsible Christian leaders. Listen to what they said: "Be careful to maintain the Union which at present subsists through all the Colonies. The Continental Congress now sitting in Philadelphia consists of delegates chosen in the most free and unbiased manner by the body of the people. Let them not only be treated with respect but encouraged in their difficult service." That is what we are trying to do here this morning for the representatives in public office. We are trying to encourage you in your difficult service. So, quoting from this letter of many years ago—1775, "Let them not only be treated with respect but encouraged in their difficult service. Not only let your prayers be offered up to God but adhere firmly to their resolutions. Let it be seen that they are able to bring out the whole strength of this vast country to carry them into execution. The Synod cannot help but think that this is a proper time for pressing all of every rank seriously to consider what belongs to their eternal peace." In other words, they are now saying that if you want these things preserved in our country, you had better look after your own soul's salvation, "Suffer them now to lay hold upon your present temper of mind. And exhort especially the young and the vigorous by assuring them that there is no soldier so undaunted as the pious man, no army so formidable as those who are superior to the fear of death. We think it is of importance at this time to recommend to all of every rank, but especially to those who may be called to action, a spirit of humanity and mercy. That man will fight most bravely who never fights until it is absolutely necessary and who ceases to fight as soon as the necessity is over." Thank God that has represented the American spirit in every war in which we have been engaged and in every conflict. I hope it always will.

It seems to be a law of nature that liberty and freedom are possible only to a people when they are strong and self-reliant. In the past, with all our faults, our forebears were that kind of people, thank God! The question is, are we today? Or have we gone soft and flabby? Will we be tomorrow? Who can say? One of the things that has encouraged me is what I have detected in the last six months or year, an uprising of the younger people of our community in behalf of these great ideals about which we are talking this morning. I say this is an encouraging thing. Let their breed and their number increase, because this is the only way that we are going to preserve this country. So far as I am concerned, we have no battle to give except to try to help our country, our Church, and our communities be what they ought to be, let the chips fall where they may! These things only matter. As John Knox said: "I stand in the position where conscience bids me SPEAK THE TRUTH, impugn it he who lists."

III. Bread and Circuses

This is not the first time in history when the multitude have cried out, "Give us bread and circuses." We say it differently, however, for we say, "Let the government do these things for us." Those who speak thus forget of course that all the government does for us comes out of taxes, which we ourselves have to pay, ultimately. Some people vote only for those things which seem to promise them great benefits individually in their own pocketbooks. Not like someone said the other day: "You know it would be such an easy thing to let the government provide for all the problems concerning medical care, hospitalization, etc." We said: "Yes, it would be a very easy thing to do. You think you don't have to pay for it, but you ultimately will. Furthermore, you will lose one of your great freedoms when that comes to pass." This is not the first time that the people have asked their government to give them bread and circuses. They did so in the time of Rome and Athens. That kind of appetite destroyed the liberty and freedom for them, and it will do so for us. When the people begin to ask, "What can I get from the government? What will it pay me?" or "The government owes me a living," the time is at hand to call a halt, for we are then already well on the way to collapse. So this is not the kind of thing that is the anatomy of freedom. It is the very opposite. If we are to preserve liberty and freedom we must keep ourselves worthy of it, and I fear today that many Americans are not worthy of it.

This brings us again to the observation, that the real danger to American freedom is within ourselves. Our problem is not our enemy. Our problem is threefold: ignorance, apathy, and a desire to get something for nothing. These are the three foes by all odds the most menacing, not the foes from the outside.

> Ill fares the land to hastening ills aprey,
> Where wealth accumulates, and men decay.

When the people cried, "Give us bread and circuses" someone should have reminded them of the words of Jesus, who said: "Man does not live by bread alone but by every word that proceedeth out of the mouth of God." Those foes within us are stealthy and are very insidious. Their invasion is gradual, they steal away our liberties and our freedom while we sleep. We are not even aware that some of these things are happening until they have happened, and that is why we have to be eternally vigilant. The cry of the hour is for God to give us men.

Last year we read a letter that we had received from an Assemblyman in this State, and I'm repeating it this morning because I think it is pertinent. It shows some of the problems which the public official faces. I withhold the name of the Assemblyman. He said: "If we expect to have men to match our mountains we will have to pay our Assemblyman more than four hundred dollars a month, to guide the destinies of this great State." He went on to say: "The expenses of a man in public office are large and they are continuous. The salary is not adequate to carry such responsibility unless it is supplemented by money from the lobbyists. If we want our legislators to be free from outside temptation, then we must pay them enough to support themselves and their families adequately." To this plea I most heartily agree. There is much to be said for his point of view. If our leaders are to be men of courageous action they must be free from outside temptation. All of us must be ready to sacrifice for the good of the land. Ease and comfort meant very little to our founding fathers. Ease, comfort, and convenience meant very little to our Lord, when compared with the print of the nails that appeared in his hands. "God give us men," men of courageous action, yes! Remember that a pebble has the force of a bullet if there is a David behind it.

God give us men! A time like this demands
Strong minds, great hearts, true faith and ready hands:
Men whom the lust of office does not kill;
Men whom the spoils of office cannot buy;
Men who possess opinions and a will;
Men who have honor; men who will not lie;
Men who can stand before a demagogue
And damn his treacherous flatteries without winking!
Tall men, sun-crowned, who live above the fog
In public duty, and in private thinking;
For while the rabble, with their thumb-worn creeds
Their large professions and their little deeds,
Mingle in selfish strife, lo! Freedom weeps,
Wrong rules the land and waiting justice sleeps.

We must always remember that the good people of the world who have determined the outcome of great movements for good have usually been in the minority. One with God is always a majority, even if there are only three, or one. Those who work for constructive good will probably always be in a minority, but the price of leadership is that you are willing to stand up for right regardless of whether the majority votes with you or not. This has always been so and it always will be. That is what leadership consists of. Remember the story we spoke about here a few weeks ago, Shadrach, Meshach and Abednego, who wouldn't knuckle down to the powers of a foreign government when they were held as prisoners of war. They were cast into the fiery furnace but were all miraculously saved. They were in the minority. Yes! Indeed they were in the minority, but their memory is honored.

Education can't save us, even though as a country we have gone far over in that direction. We are in favor of schools and colleges, do not misunderstand. The Presbyterian Church owns and operates forty-six colleges across the United States, of which our own Occidental is one, and nine Theological Seminaries, of which San Francisco Seminary is one. We believe in education but we do not believe in an over-balance of education and a neglect of religion. Education alone cannot save us, for if it could, Athens would never have collapsed. While our ancestors were still living in caves and trees and eating raw meat, the people of Athens were debating philosophies. The great philosophic systems of Greek thought were then being discussed. If education could save the world it would have done so a long time ago. Only men under the inspiration of God's Holy Spirit are equal to the hour, for "where there is no vision the people perish, but he that keepeth the law, happy is he."

IV. Pagan or Christian?

So this morning, as we come to the conclusion of our thought about *The Anatomy of Freedom,* I would like to remind you that it leads us to a choice that is basic to all these other questions: there is a rising secularism and materialism in our country that gives us great concern. The question is, do you wish America to be pagan, or do you wish it to be Christian? Do you wish society to be God-oriented, or do you wish it to be man-centered? In every country where the socialist super-state prevails, religion and belief in God have deteriorated. I have visited many of these countries in Europe. This is exactly what has happened. Or to speak conversely, it is where religion and belief in God have deteriorated, that the socialist super-state, the paternalistic welfare society, has taken over. I, for one, do not want to see that happen in the United States of America. Paternalism weakens responsibility, weakens self-reliance, weakens the spirit of enterprise by which the people have to live. It has forces working today which, if unchecked, will most certainly undermine the principles for which we stand.

There is a college in which ninety-five percent of the students were Gentile Christians and five percent of the students were Jewish. Some of those on the campus whose sentimentality was greater than their conviction came to the President and said: "It must be very offensive to these Jewish students, five percent of them here, to have to listen to preaching about Jesus Christ in our chapel, and we think that we should keep our religion quiet and so not offend by speaking publicly about it." The President was a very wise man and he replied to the students: "If the Jewish students wish to come here they are welcome, but this is a Christian college, and was built by money given by Christian people. If those outside our faith wish to enroll here, they may, but then they should not object to hearing about our faith, as it is presented in the college chapel." There are many who would bow religion out the back door, because of their worship of tolerance. Soon by that method we would have breadth, but no depth. We would stand for everything, but believe in nothing particularly. "In this college if they wish to stay here, they will attend the chapel service, and will hear some Christianity. Some of them will become Christians." Thus spoke the College President.

When the charter of the United Nations was discussed in November of 1945, a delegation from Panama proposed that the name of God (a simple phrase concerning Him) be inserted in the preamble of the charter. It was overwhelmingly voted down, with our country voting against it, and the only country that joined Panama was Colombia. One of the most vigorous opponents of this movement was the head of the American delegation, Librarian of Congress, and for a time Assistant Secretary of State. We tell you this incident to let you know, if you don't remember. This was almost two decades ago. It shows what some of our public leaders have been doing in dragging our own name down to the level of secularism among the nations of the world. We like to think back to John Harvard, who came to this country and who lived between the years of 1607 and 1638. He left his library so that the college bearing his name might be established, and also left half his estate to the college. This is what he said: "Every student in this college shall be plainly instructed and earnestly pressed to consider the main ends of life and to know God and Jesus Christ, whom to know is eternal life." On that basis Harvard University was founded. Until 1934 the Latin motto "Christo et ecclesiae" which means "For Christ and the Church" appeared on every title page of Harvard University's official documents. Since 1934 it has been omitted from the official documents, and the man who gave the explanation said: "The college must not be accused, you know, of being narrow."

Our country was established by men and women who believed in God. They knew it was belief in God that sets men free and keeps them free. When a man believes in God no one thereafter can ever permanently enslave him. Erase that belief in God and anything can happen. I love my country. I believe most of you gathered here this morning do so as well. We call upon you to come back to Him and His Church and His Book. Help our country regain its greatness, which cannot be measured by the size of its budget, nor by the size of its national debt, which is a disgrace, nor by the number of its bureaus, which are increasing on every hand. The greatness of our country can only be measured by the greatness and the dignity of its people. Let us remember that this is one of the missions we have to perform in the world, as Americans. This is a mission which our country has to perform. God intended, I believe, that we were to be a "chosen generation" a sort of a "royal priesthood" among the nations, a "holy nation, a people for God's own possession" in order that we might "show forth the excellencies of him who called us out of darkness into his marvelous light." In the light of this truth, in the light of these ideas, consider these things that are thrust at us—the Supreme Court decision about prayers in public schools (which action I abhor), the action concerning medical care of the aged, etc. We are in favor of medical care for the aged, but let it be done through regular channels and not by the Federal Government. Federal aid to education, and all these things are under this same bracket. Think of it! In the light of our mission as a Christian country among the nations of the world, God grant us wisdom and help to stand for what we believe!

Sermon Twenty-seven

THE PRINCE OF PEACE SPEAKS TO US ABOUT PEACE MAKING

REVEREND ROBERT W. MOON, D.D., MINISTER
First Methodist Church, Fresno, California

Robert Moon, a native Californian, is an economist turned clergyman and a crusader for honesty in government and peace in our modern world.

In his sermon "The Prince of Peace Speaks to Us about Peace Making" he speaks out about the causes of war and the need of peace; he points to Russian and American errors, shows how the present world tensions and armaments could explode into World War III at any time. His discussion of our use of the atomic bomb will annoy some, will disturb others, will make still more think.[1]

Dr. Moon was a leader in a critical Church and State controversy in California several years ago when the church he served was a successful litigant in the case where the U. S. Supreme Court declared the California law requiring a non-disloyalty declaration from all churches to be unconstitutional. In another civil liberties matter he was an articulate exposer of the errors and injustice in the movie, "Operation Abolition," a picture showing scenes from the House Un-American Activities Committee Hearings in San Francisco. In this instance university students protested the fascistic tendencies of the committee and the distortions in the scenes shown in the film.

Born and educated in Bakersfield, California, he graduated from the University of California in 1937 with a major in economics, then became an accountant and auditor for General Electric in Schenectady, N. Y., and Ashland, Massachusetts. Feeling the call of the Christian ministry, he entered Boston University School of Theology in 1943 and took his STB there in 1945. Pacific School of Religion recently conferred the honorary doctorate on him. He has been pastor of Park-

---

[1] See also the sermon, *Hiroshima: Our Guilt and Our Atonement,* by Reverend Arthur Mielke of Park Central Presbyterian Church, Syracuse, New York, in Volume VII of *Best Sermons,* 1959-60 Protestant Edition.

Presidio United Church in San Francisco, First Methodist Church, San Leandro, and has been at First Church, Fresno, since 1960.

In 1948 he traveled through thirteen countries of Europe, including two Iron Curtain countries; in 1958 he spent two months in a rural Japanese village. He is chairman of the Methodist Church Board of Christian Social Concerns, Vice-Chairman of the Division of Peace and World Order, a member of the National Council of the Fellowship of Reconciliation and of the Advisory Board of the American Civil Liberties Union of Northern California.

THE PRINCE OF PEACE SPEAKS TO US ABOUT PEACE MAKING

If I were making a list of the sins of our enemy, Russia, the list would include at least the following:

Russia is an atheistic dictatorship aggressively trying to destroy faith in God.

The Russians are willing to lie and deceive and break treaties whenever it suits their purposes.

The Russians interfere in the internal affairs of other nations.

The Russians call their form of government a peoples' democracy, but it is a totalitarian government that despotically manipulates the individual for the good of the state.

I believe that these are true and honest indictments which I can prove with evidence that seems conclusive to me. But even if we all agreed that these are true, and if we devoted our resources to spreading this truth, it would not prevent the war that can destroy our civilization.

Suppose we were to add to that list another which many believe to be true:

Russia is responsible for most of the tension in the world; and if there is war, Russia will be responsible for starting it.

Even if we could prove that, it would not prevent the war. It would not stop the bombs that can destroy all of us.

It is right here that Jesus has something to say to us. Whenever we start listing someone else's sins—not our own, but someone else's—we ought to remember Jesus' advice to those who went around condemning others: "Why do you see the speck that is in your brother's eye, but do not notice the log that is in your own eye? . . . You hypocrite, first take the log out of your own eye, and then you will see clearly to take the speck out of your brother's eye." (Matthew 7:3-5)

Are there logs in our eyes so that we cannot see clearly?

We are arrogant, and our arrogance keeps us from knowing the truth about ourselves. This is not a pleasant thing to hear. It is so unpleasant that society has a habit of crucifying those who speak frankly about society's sins. We don't like to be told that we have lied, but there is the U-2 incident and there is Cuba. We don't like to be told that we are treaty breakers, but what about the treaties we have broken with France and Spain and the Indians. We don't like to be reminded that a short time ago we were begging Russia to break a treaty she had just signed with Japan. We don't like to be told that we have interferred in the internal affairs of other nations, yet there are Mexico and Guatemala and Cuba and Vietnam. We don't like to be reminded of the alliances we have made with cruel dictators, but there is one who has been using our planes and ammunition to wipe out whole communities of people in a gross example of genocide.

We are more comfortable telling ourselves how good and generous we are.

There's a passage in the New Testament that reads something like this: "Jesus told this parable to some who trusted in themselves that they were righteous and despised others: Two nations went up into the temple to pray. One stood and prayed thus with himself, 'God, we thank thee that we are not like other nations, liars, treaty-breakers, greedy, despotic interferers with other nations' affairs. We fast and give tithes of all we get.' The other nation stood far off and said, 'God, be merciful to us sinners.' I tell you," said Jesus, "any nation which can pray like this nation will be honored by God, but the nation which exalts itself will be humbled."

If Jesus were here today he might say to us that false pride is our nation's greatest sin. He would tell us again the parable of the Pharisee and the tax collector. He would tell us that it is a dangerous illusion to believe that the evil and the error are always out there in someone else and never in ourselves.

To be sure, all of the arrogance is not on our side. Remember the mirror image. The present conflict has been described as a conflict between "two organized systems of self-righteousness." But no man and no nation may repent for another's sins. We must repent of our own.

Is there any cure for arrogance? A history professor said recently, "If we can get rid of arrogance, we can get rid of war."[2] Curing us of our arrogance is fundamental to our peacemaking efforts. How do we take the log from out of our own eyes so that we can see things as they are? A man has a wife to keep him humble, but a nation has to find some other way. Let me make a few suggestions:

Increased contacts at every level with people from other nations may help us to see ourselves as others see us. The writer of a recent book raised a relevant question: "The fall of Athens need not have been inevitable. It could have been saved at almost any point—if only the people could have seen themselves as history later saw them—How do you fashion a full-length mirror for a nation?" One of the ways is to study and travel and talk with people of other lands. Richard Nixon came back from one of his trips around the world to report that most of the people of the world believe that if there is a third world war, it will be started by the United States. We, of course, believe these people are wrong; but to know that they think this of us ought to make us do some serious self-examination. As another has put it, "Perhaps the best thing we can do for the Voice of America is to develop an Ear of America." We need to see ourselves as others see us.

Let's stop describing the difference between the United States and Russia as white and black, good and evil. This has the appeal of simplicity, and it appeals to our pride and that's part of the trouble. It leads to moralistic attitudes, then to the claiming of divine sanction for everything we do; soon we begin to convert the cold war into a holy crusade. Most of the differences between the United States and Russia are not black and white. The judgment of the historians will undoubtedly be that they are gray and grey.

We must stop judging other nations by their actions and ourselves by our own ideals. Read the Universal Declaration of Human Rights and then reflect on how far below this ideal the United States is in some areas. Read the Constitution of the United States and then think of those places where we have not yet established justice, insured domestic tranquility, promoted the general welfare, nor secured the blessings of liberty to ourselves and our posterity. If we would look at what we do, and not at what we say, we would discover that we are not so moral or truthful or generous as we claim. That's why a speaker recently revised the Golden Rule: "Do unto others twenty percent more than you would have them do unto you—to compensate for subjective error."

[2] Quoted from a Lecture by Edwin P. Booth at Boston University.

Let's be quick to see and admit where other nations outdistance us. We have prided ourselves on our nation's hospitality to refugees; but with all of our vast medical resources we refuse to accept those with physical handicaps or a history of T.B., while Sweden welcomes them. We boast about our financial support for the U.N., but several smaller and poorer nations give more per capita than we do. We boast of our concern for freedom; but civil liberties in Great Britain are more firmly rooted and widespread than here, and the health of the democratic spirit there demonstrates it. If we can learn to appreciate the greatness in other nations, it will help to temper the arrogance in us.

Let's stop taking credit for something for which we are not responsible. I am thinking, for example, of our boastfulness about our standard of living and the productiveness of our economy. Some of this is the result of our ingenuity and industriousness. But some of it is the result of accidents of history and geography that have spared us the destruction of war and the impoverishment of overpopulation and have blessed us with an abundance of natural resources. It is out of place and irrelevant to brag about our bathtubs, telephones, cars and television sets. People of other lands resent it, and the arrogance of it poisons us.

We ought to have our history books edited by an international committee of historians. There is a desperate need for honesty and impartiality in the telling of world history.

We ought to pray the prayer of the tax collector in Jesus' parable every day. "God be merciful to me a sinner." If there is one message clearly taught by the New Testament, it is that all of us are called to repentance. We are not to point at someone else's sins. We are to repent of our own.

"If we can get rid of arrogance, we can get rid of war," our historian said. If Christians are to make a creative contribution to the peace of the world, the one indispensable quality we must have is humility. And we must so live that we make it possible for others to be humble too. Until we have this quality, we are not worthy to be trusted with great power.

II

We are seeking to know what Jesus has to say to peacemakers today.

In the Sermon on the Mount, Jesus rejected some of the old laws and customs that had guided his people, the laws that said you shall not kill, nor commit adultery, that you shall take an eye for an eye, and hate those who hate you. Jesus rejected them because they were dead-end streets. He knew how futile it was to hope that laws against murder would touch its source—hate, that laws against adultery would put an end to lust, and an eye for an eye put an end to the enemy, or hatred put an end to hate. In another place he pointed to the futility of trying to guard a palace with armed men (Luke 11:21 f).

If Jesus were here today he would see the futility and the immorality of our seeking security with bombs and bigger bombs. This is not going to be pleasant to hear. But it wasn't pleasant when Jesus spoke about the sin of his day. There will be some here who wish that the church wouldn't mention such things. But if the Church of Jesus Christ won't speak out today, who will?

Let's look first of all at the weapons we hold in our hands. One of them is an atomic bomb.

On the 6th of August 1945 an A-bomb was dropped on Hiroshima. The decision to drop it was made in spite of the pleas of scientists who worked on the bomb to have it dropped as a demonstration on some uninhabited spot and in spite of the knowledge that the Japanese were at that very moment trying to arrange a surrender. Three days later a similar bomb was dropped on Nagasaki. The second bombing had some of the characteristics of an experiment about it. It was exploded at a different altitude from the first. Later a U. S. officer remarked: "We were afraid the Japs would surrender before we had a chance to try out the Nagasaki bomb." [3]

I have stood on the hill beside the Atomic Bomb Casualty Commission office in Hiroshima and seen the damage that first bomb did. It destroyed a city three times the size of Fresno. One hundred and eighty thousand people were killed on that day by that one explosion. Sixty thousand more died in the next three months from injuries they received. Some are still dying from the radiation received that day.

Russia has tested a bomb that approached 100 megatons in size. We too can build and deliver a 100-megaton bomb. The explosive power of such a bomb is equal to the explosive power of a Hiroshima-size bomb dropped on a different city every day for thirteen years. If it were exploded at a certain altitude over the western part of the United States it would set everything on fire in the six western states. These fires could suck the oxygen out of most of the bomb shelters in our cities so that we would die of suffocation. Others are prepared to do this to us, and we are prepared to do this to them.

---

[3] See Earle Reynolds, *Forbidden Voyage* (New York: David McKay, 1961), p. 7.

We have other weapons. We have put our scientists to work breeding disease germs and developing poison gasses. We are prepared to infect people with "Q" fever: one ounce of these micro-organisms is enough to kill eleven times the population of the entire world. We have a nerve gas called G.B. It is lethal in seconds. As a liquid, one drop the size of a period will penetrate the skin and kill within fifteen minutes. We have one weapon the military calls "The most humane weapon of all," because it kills only humans. It leaves buildings and crops undamaged. We can infect—with radioactivity or poison or disease germs—the air people breathe, the food they eat, the water they drink, the clothes they wear.

The amount of money that both the United States and the Soviet Union are spending in preparation for this kind of war is equal to all the money spent by all of the other nations of the world for all government activity. We are spending this money in preparation for a war that could kill us all. It is no wonder that President Kennedy said, "Let us call a truce to terror."

Does anyone doubt that Jesus would condemn this? He would condemn it for its immorality and its futility. Let's be realistic and apply the pragmatic test. Power like this is a dead-end street. It cannot take us to where we want to go.

The vast power that we have cannot solve any of the major problems our world faces. It cannot protect us from destruction by the enemy; we can destroy each other but not save ourselves from destruction. It cannot prevent the spread of communism; communism has an appeal to oppressed and hungry people that crosses barbed wires and crawls under missiles. It cannot feed the hungry nor heal the sick; money spent for bombs cannot be used for bread; money spent for missiles cannot be used for medicine. It cannot produce greater understanding and good will among the peoples of the world; it increases suspicion, fear and tension. It cannot help us regain the moral leadership of the world; the power we have is a symbol of madness but not of wisdom or integrity. It cannot solve any of the problems our world faces. It can destroy the very values we seek to serve.

Anyone who wants to be known as a realist must face the fact that one unanswerable argument about our trust in weapons of violence is its futility. It does not achieve its purpose. If we cannot achieve what we want to we are impotent. It's a dead-end street. Death is at the end of it. The futility of it was decisively stated by the Master: "They who take the sword will perish by the sword."

Let's look at the way we try to justify our vast stock-pile of weapons:

We claim that our weapons deter the enemy. This kind of deterrence is itself immoral; but even aside from that, it doesn't work. Russia is winning victories today without firing a shot. One of our nation's leading experts on armaments referred recently to "the waning power of nuclear weapons to deter Soviet and Chinese aggression." [4]

We say that our alliances require us to be armed, that we have a responsibility to protect smaller and weaker nations. This becomes a moral smoke screen for moral atrocities. Alliances are not so cohesive as they once were. Since Korea and Hungary those under the protection of either the United States or the Soviet Union have feared that their protectors would come to deliver them. There is a restlessness in every Russian satellite, and the nations where we have SAC and missile bases are uncomfortable, and some are asking us to leave.

We say that we need these weapons for self-defense. Take another look. They are offensive weapons. If we are not going to use them aggressively, then their only use is for an act of retaliation and revenge. And retaliation and revenge are sterile of any peacemaking power.

We say that force is the only language the enemy understands. But the Communists have demonstrated that our displays of military strength have not persuaded them to re-think their political philosophy nor deterred them from expanding their influence in other lands. They understand and use other weapons very effectively—diplomacy, economic aid, cultural exchange programs, printed and broadcast materials. Sometimes it seems that force is the only language *we* understand. Suppose it were true that force is the only language the enemy understands. If, in order to conquer him, we become like him, then he is the victor. He has dragged us down to his level.

There is no realistic way to justify our nation's obsession with the military approach to the world's problems. Let's not forget that Jesus rebuked his disciples when they wanted to call down fire from heaven to consume their enemies. In *The Last Temptation* Jesus said to Peter: "Put your knife in its sheath. If we meet the knife with the knife, when will the world be free of stabbings?" [5] Jesus knew that the way of violence is a dead-end street.

There's a moral issue that is more fundamental than the futility of putting our trust in weapons of violence: It is wrong to kill. It is immoral

---

[4] F. A. Lindsay, "Where We Stand in National Defense," p. 31.

[5] Nicos Kazantzakis, *The Last Temptation of Christ* (New York: Simon & Schuster, 1960), p. 433.

to wage war. It is immoral to make weapons and prepare for war. It is immoral to think of others of God's children as potential victims of our bombs. If war is not a betrayal of the teachings of Jesus, if war is not contrary to the will of God, then nothing is. If you can justify war morally, then you can justify any crime and any sin; and nothing in Christianity is relevant to our way of living. But I believe that Christianity is relevant and that war and preparation for war are immoral and a betrayal of the teachings of Jesus.

There is hope in the revulsion that soldiers feel at killing. A study conducted by our military authorities indicates that less than twenty-five percent of our riflemen fired at the enemy when they got the chance. General Marshall, in his book, *Men Against Fire*, says that "fear of killing, rather than fear of being killed," was the most common cause of battle failure in the individual.[6] Captain Butcher in his book, *My Three Years with Eisenhower*, tells of the day in 1944 when Eisenhower came back to headquarters greatly distressed. He had just visited a hospital where there were 1,100 soldiers with self-inflicted wounds.[7] Perhaps, as General Marshall said, they were more from fear of killing than from fear of being killed.

Americans are not the only ones who rebel at killing. Recently I read through some of the documents connected with the Hungarian revolution. Again and again there are accounts of Russian soldiers who refused to fire at the Hungarians. Some of them fired into the air. Some of them threw down their guns and walked away. Something that God put within man revolts at the taking of the life of another of God's creatures.

There is hope in the moral revulsion we feel at taking human life.

Dear friends, every attempt to justify war, and preparation for war, fails. It cannot solve any of the pressing problems of our world. It cannot be defended as necessary or realistic. And it is immoral. It's a dead-end street. It cannot take us where we want to go.

III

The alternatives put before us today to justify our vast military establishment are "prepare to kill or be killed."

The government has had to persuade us to swallow two large, irregular-

[6] S. L. S. Marshall, *Men Against Fire* (New York: William Morrow & Co., 1947), pp. 54 and 78 ff.

[7] Harry Butcher, *My Three Years with Eisenhower* (New York: Simon & Schuster, 1946), p. 645.

shaped pills: (1) the draft. The best young men that our society produces are taken from home and school and job at a critical time in their lives and trained to be obedient servants of the war machine. (2) Steep income taxes. For a succession of decades most of our federal budget has been spent for military items. Both the draft and taxes are unpopular. We would take them more willingly if we could feel they were essential. So the government has had to provoke our insecurity and our hatred of an enemy and then to persuade us that the alternatives are to be prepared to kill or to be killed. We are so heavily armed, and the octopus of military influence so pervades every phase of our culture, that ours has been called "the warfare state."

No one really sees any great hope for peace in the course our nation has followed. Our military personnel are reluctant soldiers from the generals on down. If you talk with them about this or read books they have written, you discover they are uncomfortable and wistful. They wish they knew a better way to make peace. They don't have great enthusiasm for fighting. They don't have great confidence that a victory over Russia would establish peace. And it won't. As Norman Cousins said in a recent editorial: "Peace cannot be found if we look for it in the wrong place."

There is a growing conviction in our land that the war against war is the only war worth waging. But our entire society is oriented to the war psychology. We are obsessed with the military approach to diplomacy. Our economy is dependent on it. Some congressmen owe their tenure in office to their ability to keep military expenditures high in their districts. College faculties and research departments are subsidized by military grants. Manufacturers run tax-deductible advertisements in magazines glorifying their participation in the war preparations. Radio and TV shows, paid for with tax money, exalt the armed services. So serious is this matter that Eisenhower, in his farewell address, warned us that, "We must guard against the acquisition of unwarranted influence . . . by the military-industrial complex."

It is going to take a radical idea to root this obsession with the military approach to peace out of our culture. A book-reviewer in a current magazine [8] says that "in our time the folly of men is so menacing, so criminal, that nothing can displace it short of the foolishness of God which is wiser than men."

Let me suggest an idea which may be radical enough and Godly enough to serve us in this hour: We should wage massive reconciliation

[8] *Fellowship*, Nov. 1, 1961, p. 33.

with the enemy. We are prepared now for massive retaliation. We have nuclear armed missiles in the ground and on submarines, we have nuclear bombs in the air twenty-four hours a day, and we have a Pandora's box of chemical and bacteriological weapons read to be opened. These are all ready to be used in a massive retaliatory attack. Is this the only way for civilized men to meet frustrating situations? Is it kill or be killed?

Gandhi once said that if he were ever given the choice of kill or be killed, he expected he would choose to kill. He then said that our choices are not that limited. There is a third alternative, the way of aggressive goodwill. Do you know where he learned that? In the Christian's Bible. He found it in the Sermon on the Mount. It is the ethic of the second mile that Jesus talked about and his first followers honored. Let's see if we can express it in specific proposals for our day:

First of all, it will require us to disarm. We need to disarm ourselves of many things: hatred, arrogance, ignorance, provincialism, and suspicion. Most of all we must disarm ourselves of our trust in weapons that cannot be justified, either morally or practically. President Kennedy said that "Men no longer pretend that the quest for disarmament is a sign of weakness." Any program for achieving world peace that does not include the destruction of our ability to wage war does not meet the crying need of this hour. We ought to do this multilaterally if possible—by agreement with other nations. Whether other nations join with us or not, our nation ought to disarm. It could turn out to be not only the most Christian and the most noble, but also the safest and wisest course to follow.

Secondly we should rearm ourselves with generosity. Toynbee, the historian, has expressed the hope that our age may "be remembered chiefly neither for its horrifying crimes nor for its astonishing inventions, but for its having been the first age . . . in which people dared to think it practicable to make the benefits of civilization available for the whole human race."

Most of us are probably under the impression that our nation has been generous in our foreign aid. The truth is that we have given very little to other nations, and over ninety percent of what we have given to other nations has been for military purposes. This has led one person to observe that if Jesus stands among the generals, he has been well provided for. If he stands among the hungry of the world, he has been very poorly treated.

We need to multiply the amount of money we are giving to Christian missions. Pilots flying over India say they can tell which villages have Christian missions—their fields are richer and greener. We need to multiply our support for some of the specialized agencies of the UN—for example, the World Health Organization and the Food and Agriculture Organization. We need to share our surplus foods. Our government today is storing enough surplus wheat to provide twenty-five loaves of bread for every man, woman and child in the entire world,[9] most of whom are hungry. We need to give substantial sums of money and food and medicine to the UN to be distributed without any political strings attached, purely on the basis of need, to friend and enemy alike.

Mr. Eisenhower said, on one occasion, "Every gun that is made, every warship launched, every rocket fired signifies in the final sense, a theft from those who hunger and are not fed, those who are cold and are not clothed." He said, "The peace we seek . . . can be fortified, not by weapons of war, but by wheat and by cotton, by milk and by wool, by meat and by timber and rice." These are words that translate into every language of peace. We need to speak it.

Thirdly, we must do many more of those things that can help to change the atmosphere of our world. Increased trade and cultural exchange programs with every nation are essential. We must learn to speak the words that will heal and conciliate instead of words that poison and provoke tension. And we must demonstrate our readiness to negotiate any differences with others.

I do not believe in disarmament. Let no one go forth this day saying the minister said we must lay down our arms. I do believe that if we will disarm ourselves of hatred and arrogance and ignorance and provincialism and suspicion and our weapons, and if we will rearm ourselves with the generosity and the commitment to be reconcilers that can give substance to our good will, then we could create the kind of atmosphere that could make wars unnecessary.

But someone asks, "Can we trust the Russians?" If we disarm, won't Russia then be able to get everything she wants?

We can't really expect a day to come, as Walter Lippman suggested, when every Russian baby will be born with wings and singing, "God Bless America." But it is reasonable to expect that Russia's behavior would have been substantially different if we had not isolated her from the counsels of the nations after 1917 and had not ringed her with nearly a thousand armed bases after 1945.

---

[9] *The Reporter,* Sept. 17, 1959, p. 27.

Sociologists are familiar with the mechanism of the self-fulfilling prophecy. An anxious student *prematurely* convinced that he is going to fail an examination does more worrying than studying, and he does fail the examination. A *false* rumor of a bank's insolvency in 1932 started a run of depositors until the bank was insolvent. The *mistaken* assumption that certain kinds of mental patients are violent and unmanageable led to strong-arm methods; and, sure enough, they were violent and unmanageable. The lesson to be learned here is that often what we expect from a situation determines what we will get. If we act as if war were inevitable, it will be. If we act as if the Russians can't be trusted, they can't be. This is the mechanism of the self-fulfilling prophecy.

Will you listen now to Secretary Harry Stimson, the man who served in the cabinets of four presidents, both Republican and Democratic. He once wrote to the President: "The chief lesson I have learned in a long life is that the only way to make a man trustworthy is to trust him . . ." Winston Churchill, who's a realist on these matters, has said that he believes we can trust the Russians to keep agreements if we are able to negotiate agreements that are to our mutual interest.

What is it that we are trusting when we trust the Russians? We are trusting that together we can discover that we have common interests, that we have a common and precious stake in avoiding war, that there are some universal standards of truth and rightness that are communicated to all the children of God, that as together we become more aware of the right answers to problems we will move toward them together, and that Russia will respond to our integrity and trust in positive and trustful ways.

To be sure, there is risk in trusting Russia, but the risk is not nearly so great as the risk we are taking with our present program where we are bomb-to-bomb with the enemy and ready to fight.

What we are really asking for is trust in God.

Our moral sense has been so subordinated to nationalism and to expediency that we have tolerated the military approach to peace. We have allowed this to insulate us from what Jesus said about peacemaking. It may be that we don't really believe that love can conquer hate and that good can overcome evil and that truth can out-weary falsehood, and that belief in God makes a difference. If we don't, then we are morally bankrupt, and it doesn't really matter whether Russia or the United States survives.

I cherish the hope that we will find the moral and spiritual strength to decide to trust God. Either the United States or the Soviet Union must do this or we are doomed. Surely none of us expects the Soviet Union to have more moral and spiritual resources than we.

I also hope that the next generation will not be able to rebuke us for failing to speak out against the barbarity and the immorality of the war, World War III, we are preparing to fight now. I hope that they will not be able to say that we were too busy to care and to study, too untrustful to do what God expects us to do, too selfish to give our resources for peace.

If we are to achieve peace in our time, some of us are going to have to give the cause a top priority on our resources of energy, and decide to work at it as if we believed what Jesus said.

Sermon Twenty-eight

PRAYER AND A POULTICE

Reverend William M. Elliott, Jr., Ph.D., D.D., L.H.D., Litt.D.

Minister, Highland Park Presbyterian Church, Dallas, Texas

Prayer and a Poultice represents Dr. Elliott's practical, pragmatic, and spiritual approach to religion and the problems men and women face in daily life today.

He is the author of: *Coming to Terms with Life, For the Living of These Days, Lift High That Banner, Two Sons.* He has preached on the radio for the National Council of Churches and *The Presbyterian Hour* and has been special preacher at conferences at Montreat, N. C., Massannata Springs, Virginia, and at Chautauqua, New York. He is popular as a speaker at the University of Georgia, Washington and Lee, Duke, Agnes Scott College, Vanderbilt, Southern Methodist University, Texas A. and M. and other colleges and seminaries. He has made two trips to the Far East for the Board of World Missions of the Presbyterian Church and in 1946-47 spent four and a half months surveying mission work in China, Japan, Korea. In 1957 he made a second trip to the Far East to attend conferences in Japan, Korea, Taiwan. He was Moderator of the General Assembly of the Presbyterian Church, U. S., 1957-1958, and is chairman of the Board of World Missions of the Presbyterian Church.

Born in Charlestown, Indiana, Dr. Elliott is the son of a Presbyterian minister. He attended high school in Clovis, New Mexico. He graduated from Park College, received his B.D. from Louisville Presbyterian Theological Seminary and a Ph.D. from the University of Edinburgh in 1938. Davidson College conferred the honorary D.D. and Park College the honorary L.H.D. upon him. He was ordained a Presbyterian minister in 1930, was instructor in Homiletics and Church History at Louisville Presbyterian Seminary in 1929-1930. He became pastor of Fifth Avenue Presbyterian Church in Knoxville, 1930-1935; pastor of Druid Hills Presbyterian Church, Atlanta, 1935-1944, and has been pastor of Highland Park Presbyterian Church, Dallas, since 1944. Austin College conferred the honorary Litt.D. in 1963 in recognition of his work.

PRAYER AND A POULTICE

> Hezekiah turned his face to the wall and prayed to the Eternal . . . Isaiah ordered a poultice of figs to be applied to the eruption that he might recover.
>
> 2 Kings 20:2, 7 (Moffatt's translation)

Hezekiah, king of Judah, was a mighty sick man. His condition, in fact, was critical. An infection of some sort had gotten out of control and he was "at the point of death."

It fell to his spiritual counselor, a prophet named Isaiah, to inform the king of his real condition. It was an unpleasant duty, to be sure, but his sovereign must know the truth. Standing beside Hezekiah's royal couch, Isaiah spoke these dark and solemn words: "Put your affairs in order, for you are to die, not to recover."

The announcement came like a bolt out of the blue. In desperation Hezekiah turned his tearful face to the wall and poured out his heart to God in a torrent of earnest and beseeching prayer. He pled with his Maker to reward his faithfulness and to spare his life. Hezekiah put everything he had into that prayer and God responded with an affirmative answer, something which He does not invariably do. Before Isaiah had left the courtyard of the palace, God sent him back with another and more cheerful message: "I have heard your prayers, I have seen your tears, and now I heal you; the day after tomorrow you will be able to go up to the temple of the Eternal. I will add fifteen years to your life." And then follows this interesting statement: "Isaiah ordered a poultice of figs to be applied to the eruption, that he might recover."

Two things then were responsible for Hezekiah's rapid recovery: prayer and a poultice, faith and works. A practical man of the world used prayer and a practical man of God used a poultice. If the king was to recover his health, both of these remedies were needed and it is not possible to say which was the more important or efficacious. Without either of them Hezekiah would have perished in the prime of life and at a time when his country most needed his services.

I

One lesson which lies on the surface of this story is that while prayer is essential it must never be made a substitute for human effort. Isaiah was a man of strong faith and piety but he was a sensible man and he did not neglect the poultice.

Prayer should be used as a prelude to human ingenuity and as an accompaniment of human effort but never as a substitute for either one of them. "Faith without works is dead" (James 2:20). We must pray as if everything depended upon God and then work as if everything depended upon us. That is the formula for real achievement in any realm. Said Nehemiah, the Hebrew patriot, as he set out to rebuild the shattered walls of Jerusalem, "We made our prayer unto God, and set a watch against (our enemies) day and night" (Nehemiah 4:9).

George Washington Carver, the famous Negro scientist, left this testimony: "I took a peanut and I put it out in my hand and said, 'Mr. Creator, what's in that peanut?' And the Creator said to me, 'You've got brains; you go and find out.' " And that is what he did. The remarkable discoveries of this great man were the result of a happy alliance of prayer and a poultice. Dr. Carver was a devout man—a man of childlike faith who believed that every discovery was a revelation, which it is, but he was also a man of action who toiled unceasingly in his laboratory. It was this combination of faith and works which made him such a blessing to mankind. "Here," wrote George Muller of England, "is the great secret of success: work with all your might but trust not in your own power to achieve. Pray with all your might for God's guidance and blessing. Pray then work; work and pray; and again pray and work."

II

Prayer and a poultice! What a fruitful and healing partnership! How many of life's failures might be averted if there were a more faithful use of both of these essential components.

But some people make the mistake of choosing between them. They have the idea that one must choose, for example, between faith and medicine—between prayer as a means of healing, and science. There are those who, under the mesmerism of a strange piety, scorn the marvels of medical science. Witness the healing cults with their fantastic reasoning. As if God were not the Fount of all knowledge and the Giver of every good and perfect gift! And there are those who, in defence of human pride, disdain the power of believing and importunate prayer in a healing ministry. Witness the practical paganism of some of our men of science.

Why such a choice between faith and medicine is necessary is difficult to see, since each is so obviously a gift of God and each has power. A new day for the healing of men's minds and bodies will speedily dawn when the representatives of medicine, psychiatry and religion pool their resources and work together as a team in mutual confidence and practical helpfulness.

I am glad to say that some significant progress is being made along this line. More and more responsible doctors and ministers are recognizing their interdependence and are establishing a real partnership. In an address before the Annual Meeting of the American Psychiatric Association in April 1956, Dr. F. Finley Gayle, Jr., said this regarding the relationship between psychiatrists and clergymen: "By and large . . . the present status of our relationship seems to be most adequately described as one of 'peaceful co-existence.' This is largely an attitude of 'we won't bother you if you don't bother us' . . . What I want to do now is to express my conviction that we are ready to move gradually from a status of peaceful co-existence to one of active cooperation." [1] Such words are most heartening, but we have a long way to go in bringing into a proper relationship prayer and a poultice.

We must remember that the human self is never at any time wholly body, or mind, or emotions, or spirit; he is all four at the same time, so that there is a very definite and vital connection between the state of one's mind and spirit and the state of his physical health. One of the leaders of American medical science has said this: "It is not an overstatement to say that fully 50 percent of the problems of the acute stages of illness, and 75 percent of the difficulties of convalescence have their primary origin not in the body, but in the mind of the patient." [2] The ill person needs more than drugs or surgery, as wonderful and essential as these are; he needs hope, reassurance, inner peace and nearness to God. It is a fact that simple faith and believing prayer can sometimes tap healing forces which medical science is powerless to release.

We clergymen certainly need the dedicated and skillful physician, but the physician also needs us. In the contest against disease we play different positions, but we are on the same team. Dr. Ruget, the late president of the National Urological Society and a splendid churchman, said some time ago that "in the pursuit of scientific wizardry we (doctors) may have lost some of the heart and soul of our profession. Men of science are unbelievably intolerant and narrow when they fail to recognize that it is God's creative power, working through us, that brings success to our ef-

---

[1] This address printed and issued by the National Academy of Religion and Mental Health, 2 E. 103 St., New York 29, N. Y.

[2] Edward A. Strecker, "Mental Hygiene," *Nelson New Looseleaf Medicine,* VII (1927), p. 413.

forts; that the healing resources of this universe were not invented by us. Whether or not we admit it, we are always dependent upon that Power which is greater than ourselves."[3] Those are wise words.

Yes, prayer and a poultice belong together and it is both stupid and sinful to neglect the benefits of either. Faith and medicine are both agents of a compassionate God and they must learn to cooperate ever more closely if the highest well-being of the ill person is to be secured. One finds an acknowledgment of this truth in these words of Galen, a Greek physician of the second century: "I dressed the wound and God healed it."

Part of our trouble is that we are victimized by the philosophy of *either-or*; either faith *or* medicine, either prayer *or* a poultice. What is needed is a fresh baptism of the philosophy of *both-and*.

This either-or philosophy has gotten us into trouble in other realms. It has, for example, militated against a full and balanced expression of the Christian faith. One weakness of the Christian movement is the way in which the followers of Christ are forever dividing into groups for the propagation of a single feature of Christianity to the practical exclusion of all others.

Such groupings might well prove a blessing if they were content simply to give emphasis to some truth of our faith, but so often the emphasis becomes a religion in itself and other vital aspects of the Christian message are obscured if not repudiated. The emphasis becomes the whole truth and the only truth, dividing Christians into competing camps. It is a great pity.

The scandal of Christianity, as I see it, is not that we have so many divisions but that these various divisions are forever claiming or implying that the particular thing they emphasize is the whole truth about Christianity and that the stressing of that particular thing is "the sole responsibility of the Church." If Christianity is to make its full impact upon the life and conscience of our modern world, we must have more churches and more preachers who are faithfully declaring what the apostle Paul called "the whole counsel of God" (Acts 20:27), and not some partial or mutilated thing.

I was interested in this statement by Dr. Walter Horton: "In our country, generally, the liberals do not have the vivid faith in the Bible and the Christian tradition that the conservatives have, and the conservatives usually do not believe in a determined program of Christian social

[3] As quoted by Louis H. Evans in *Make Your Faith Work* (Westwood, N. J.: Revell, 1957), pp. 139-140.

action." That, it seems to me, is a good description of our plight. Again I ask, Why not have both? Why must we choose between them? I have read that a famous pianist once rebuked a favorite pupil of his who had performed brilliantly as a concert piece one movement of a concerto. "If you ever again," he cried, "perform one movement without giving all the movements, I shall disown you!" [4] Something like that needs to be said to some of our Christian leaders. When we witness to the Christian faith, why not play the entire concerto as it is contained in the New Testament?

We hear a good deal these days about the "individual gospel" and the "social gospel," as if there were two gospels and a person must choose between them. I for one refuse to be impaled on the horns of such a dilemma. I stubbornly refuse to choose between doctrine and ethics, between Christianity as a creed and Christianity as a life; between the inner life of the soul and the outer life of conduct; between individual salvation and social action. I want both! And why not? They are both in the New Testament and there they are not divided. "What therefore God hath joined together, let not man put asunder" (Mark 10:9).

He is no friend of Christianity who sets the individual gospel over against the social gospel. God meant them for a holy alliance and to neglect either is to lose both. These two parts of the faith are vascular; part them and each will bleed to death. "By logical necessity the individual gospel involves the social gospel." It is a fallacy to think that a choice must be made between personal salvation and social crusading. Whenever either of these emphases is forgotten or neglected Christianity loses its dynamic thrust and becomes an insipid thing. "The full truth," writes Dr. Fosdick, "flies like a bird with two wings, and maimed in either by our partial thinking it flutters a crippled creature on the ground." [5]

What is needed in the Christian Church today is a combination of personal regeneration and social concern. There must be no feud between private faith and public morals, between a personal experience of the redeeming grace of God and the fearless application of Christian ethical standards to living situations. Walter Rauschenbusch, the father of the social gospel movement in this country, believed strongly in both. "Go at both simultaneously," he pleaded; "neither is possible without the other."

Let the partisans of the "individual gospel" remember that a faith

---

[4] Halford E. Luccock, *In the Minister's Workshop*, Nashville: Abingdon-Cokesbury, 1944, p. 233.

[5] H. E. Fosdick, *The Meaning of Service*, New York: Association Press, 1937, p. 33.

which does not issue in Christlike acts and attitudes—which does not work for social justice and civic righteousness—is a counterfeit faith. A religion which does not make a person care about "man's inhumanity to man" is a false religion. Every true Christian is duty bound to apply Christ's spirit and principles in all areas of man's existence. Any Christian who is not deeply and sensitively interested in "conditions that war on human joy" [6] has never really met the Man of Nazareth as He stands revealed in the gospels.

And let the partisans of the "social gospel" remember that apart from changed men and women—"new creatures in Christ Jesus"—the victories they yearn for in society are impossible because there will be lacking the mind that sees the right, the heart that loves the right and the will that works for the right. As Elizabeth Barrett Browning reminds us,

> It takes a soul
> To move a body: it takes a high-souled man
> To move the masses, even to a cleaner stye;
> It takes the ideal to blow a hair's breadth off
> The dust of the actual. Ah, your Fouriers failed
> Because not poet enough to understand
> That life develops from within.[7]

I plead for a full-orbed presentation of the Christian gospel. Each phase of the divine revelation is important because God-given and is entitled to its proper attention and emphasis. Let there be in our teaching and preaching, and in our living, a more perfect blending of the various aspects of God's saving truth.

---

[6] The phrase is from G. A. Buttrick, *Preaching in These Times*, New York: Scribner, 1940, p. 9.

[7] From the poem, "Aurora Leigh."

Sermon Twenty-nine

THE TOUGH-MINDED OPTIMIST

REVEREND NORMAN VINCENT PEALE, D.D., L.H.D., LL.D., TH.D.

Minister, Marble Collegiate Church (Dutch Reformed), New York, New York

Norman Vincent Peale has had a very special ministry to thousands of people many churches forget—those who have personal, religious, psychological, or psychiatric problems. In his preaching he has made a special study of the needs of the discouraged, he has sought ways to open doors for the ambitious, the frustrated, those mentally oppressed. He has tried to find ways to show businessmen how to combine faith and business, he has tried to lighten the loads of the older men and women who need a light to guide them.

Born in Bowersville, Ohio, on May 31, 1898, Dr. Peale studied at Ohio Wesleyan University and Boston University School of Theology, and began his ministry in the Methodist Church at Berkeley, Rhode Island, serving from 1922 to 1924. He then went to Kings Highway Methodist Episcopal Church in Brooklyn, where from 1924 to 1927 he attracted much attention by his preaching and made his church grow rapidly. He moved to Syracuse, New York, in 1927, remaining there until he was called in 1932 to Marble Collegiate Church, where he has been ever since.

He has recorded much of his philosophy in his books, which include *A Guide to Confident Living, The Power of Positive Thinking, Stay Alive All Your Life, The Art of Living, The Tough-Minded Optimist,* and *Adventures in the Holy Land.*

With all his great following, Dr. Peale keeps his sermons simple, his delivery direct. He stands at his pulpit without notes and talks with his congregation as though all were his personal friends in the privacy of his home. He steps beyond technique to reach the human heart. He has been criticized for over-simplification and popularization, but those who follow him find his philosophy helpful.

He has been honored with the doctorate by Syracuse, Ohio Wesleyan, and

Duke Universities, and by Lafayette and William Jewell Colleges. Milliken University conferred the Doctor of Sacred Theology and Iowa Wesleyan the Doctor of Letters. He is President of the American Foundation of Religion and Psychiatry, which conducts clinical counseling without regard to race, creed or color. A motion picture, *One Man's Way*, based upon his life and work, was produced by United Artists in 1963.

THE TOUGH-MINDED OPTIMIST

A psychiatrist is reported to have said, "The chief duty of a human being is to endure life." At first such a remark is impressive and of course not without truth. Life with all its pain and sorrow must indeed be endured. Anyone who has lived for very long is well aware of that hard fact.

But this is not the whole story by any means. And the rest of the story highlights one difference at least between Christianity and psychiatry. For whereas psychiatry says the chief duty of a human being is to endure life, Christianity teaches that a man's chief duty is to master life. And furthermore Christianity tells how this mastery is accomplished. The formula is stated in I John 5:4, "For whatsoever is born of God overcometh the world: and this is the victory that overcometh the world, even our faith."

The kind of person who is able to implement such a faith I like to describe as a "Tough-Minded Optimist." This phrase is one that I came upon as a result of my reading practice which includes, among others, two books: the Bible and the dictionary. The former I read for the Word, in capital letters. The latter to better understand words, those dynamic tools of communication.

It so happened that I had written a book for which a title has not yet been selected. I knew what I wanted the title to say but had not evolved a satisfactory combination of words to express the content of the book.

One day in reading the dictionary I happened to notice the word "Tough." This word like some others has been loaded with meanings that give it a rather unattractive connotation.

Another word that has fallen into disrepute is the word "Love," originally a strong concept meaning esteem and respect, but which under the touch of Hollywood has assumed sticky, sentimental, softish or sexy overtones.

Well, "Tough," does not mean hardboiled, sneering or gangsterish; but is described by Webster as follows:

"*Tough:* Having the quality of being strong or firm in texture, but flexible and not brittle; yielding to force without breaking; capable of resisting great strain without coming apart."

To live in this world on a higher level than mere endurance of life one's personality will need to develop a texture of such strength that it can bear pressure without breaking apart. It must, in the sense that Webster uses the word, become tough.

I then looked for a word descriptive of a certain personality trait that might be joined with the word "tough" to produce a life-mastery combination. I found it in the word "optimist" which again is an expression that is often used wrongly in general usage. It does not, as generally supposed, refer to a super-bright and cheery, fortuitous attitude—one that is blithe and ultra-chipper. The dictionary describes optimism as:

> The doctrine that the goods of life overbalance the pain and evil of it, that life is preponderantly good. The inclination to put the most favorable construction upon actions and happenings, minimize adverse aspects, conditions and possibilities, or anticipate the best possible outcome; a cheerful and hopeful temperament.

An optimist may be characterized as an extraordinarily well-balanced individual who sees the facts, all the facts—bad as well as good—without blinders; and who is entirely and realistically conversant with all the difficulties involved. But these difficulties and problems, however complicated and even hopeless, do not in any sense abash or overwhelm him. Certainly they do not discourage him for always behind difficulties and beyond problems he sees possibilities and potentials for good outcomes. He is so well versed in the nature of men and circumstances that he is aware that good is always inherent in the difficult—that in the long run the universe is loaded in favor, not of the bad, but of the good.

So taking my two reconstructed word concepts I put them into combination to denote a type of person who with the help and assistance of God has what it takes to move up from a supine endurance of life to a creative mastery of life. The Tough-Minded Optimist is the sort of person who derives his victory potential from the spiritual process outlined in our text: "For whatsoever is born of God overcometh the world: and this is the victory that overcometh the world, even our faith."

One result of such rebirth and application of Christian faith to life situations is the development of a dynamic philosophy about problems.

The average person's reaction to problems is negative, even one of dull defeatism. Since I have presumed to publish several books dealing with techniques for meeting common difficulties I receive quite a large volume of mail from persons who outline their own problems. After reading a huge number of such letters I concluded that generally speaking, most people seem to regard a problem as a bad thing—something unpleasant with which you have to deal. But is this appraisal a correct one? Is a problem of good or bad valuation in the life pattern?

Let us illustrate the answer to this question from a sidewalk conversation. I was walking along Fifth Avenue in New York when I met a friend named George. It was evident from his depressed demeanor and dispirited countenance that he was not what you might describe as effervescently happy. In fact he was a picture of disconsolate woebegoneness. This excited my natural sympathies and I asked, "How are you, George?" When you get right down to it this was a rather routine inquiry. But George took it seriously and for fifteen minutes meticulously enlightened me on how badly he felt.

"What seems to be the matter, George?" I asked.

"It's these problems," he barked. "Nothing but problems and more problems! I'm fed up with problems."

"Well," said I, "I would surely like to help you."

"I wish you would," he replied. "In fact I will give you one thousand dollars if you will get me relief and release from this mass of problems."

Not being one to turn down such an offer, I said, "Well, George, perhaps I can offer a thought that may be helpful, though hardly one you might like. I was recently in a place where there were over one hundred thousand people and not a single person had a problem."

"Where is this place? That's for me!" George responded with the first show of enthusiasm.

"This place," I told him, "is Woodlawn Cemetery in the Bronx. . . . No one in Woodlawn has a problem. They all rest from their labors. Nothing at all concerns them; they are dead."

It would seem logical then that the possession of problems is a sign of life. Perhaps the person who has, let us say, ten problems may be considered but half as alive as the one who has twenty problems. The more problems one has the more trustworthy he might consider that God regards him. And if by chance you have no problems at all you had better go to your knees and pray earnestly to the Lord saying, "Lord, don't you trust me any more? Give me some problems."

Actually there are few experiences in life quite as exciting as taking hold of a hard, knotty problem, tearing it apart and putting it together again properly. The late Charles Kettering, at one time the research genius of a very large industrial corporation, used to say to his aides: "Do not bring me your successes for they weaken me. Bring me your problems; they strengthen me."

The Tough-Minded Optimist, being born of God, is open to God's guidance, his mind experiencing the creative effect of God's mind working within him. Forces operate upon his life that enable him to claim the promise of the text, namely, "the victory which conquers the world, even our faith." He develops the spiritual power to solve life's problems according to the will and direction of God. It has been to me a source of amazement to note the mental penetration and insight into problems given to people whose academic training was inadequate but who compensated for this lack by spiritual depth.

In one of my early churches there was a wholesale grocer, Harlowe B. Andrews, whose formal schooling had been limited to three years, but the quality of his mind was such that he rose to a position of eminence in business and was a leader in his city. He has been credited among other achievements with the earliest invention of the electric dishwasher, and he operated the first supermarket in the United States and brought perishable foods from California into Syracuse by fast express train, long before air freight came into being. In a university community and church he easily took his place among scholarly men, who respected his mind and spirit.

He always said that he "went to school to the Bible." Indeed in all my experience I never knew a man whose knowledge of the Holy Book was at once so detailed and exact and at the same time so urbane and truly spiritual as "Brother Andrews." In fact, the Bible was so much a part of him, of his whole life of thought and action, that it became through him a living, vital reality. It never once occurred to me as strange to receive a telephone call from him, as I often did, and to hear him say, "I was just speaking with God and He said to me . . ." Judging from the subtlety and exactitude of his insights I had no recourse other than to believe in the validity of his communication with his Lord.

This life-long education in the things of God gave to Brother Andrews a tough-minded optimistic quality in problem solving that made a profound impression upon me. It taught me that it is actually given to men to have a profound victory capacity over problems if they truly are born of God as was this red-blooded saint, this rare character at whose feet I had the privilege to sit.

Once I had a most difficult problem which seemed to defy solution and I decided to go to Brother Andrews, so respectful was I of his understanding and insight. He listened intently then went at the problem in his characteristic manner. "Now, son," he said, "let's just lay this problem out on the table so we can walk around it." He proceeded to do just that. He walked around the table poking my invisible problem with a long knotty forefinger. This finger had arthritic knobs so that the end made a crook but he could point straighter with that crooked finger than most people with a straight one.

"One thing you must realize is that every problem has a soft spot and when you find it you can get inside the problem and break it apart. Now let's ask God to show us," he said as he continued poking with that crooked finger. Then he chuckled with glee. "Here's that soft spot, son!" and he pushed into my problem with incisive analysis and amazing insight so much so that a sudden clarity came and with it the beginnings of a solution. "Always remember," Brother Andrews admonished me, "there is no problem that God and you together can't solve." He never heard the term, but this spiritually-conditioned scholar was a Tough-Minded Optimist.

A second result of being born of God into a victory status in life is to become a believer in depth. By this we mean of course a quality of belief that goes far beyond intellectual acceptance of the truth of the Gospel. Conceivably one can believe mentally with little or no obscuring doubt and yet not know in the central control of his life any access of power. Belief in depth means of course to move out confidently in the sure knowledge that the promised power will sustain. The Bible itself seems to predicate spiritual-power results upon the penetration or depth of one's faith. "According to your faith be it unto you." Perhaps the question is not how much faith you have but how real is what you do possess. A little faith could mean little results but a big faith can result in big accomplishments through God. We limit, or expand, our victory over life in proportion to the depth quality of our belief. "If ye have faith as a grain of mustard seed . . . nothing shall be impossible unto you." (A mustard seed is very tiny.) But if that small growth in faith is the real thing, bona fide, pure and unadulterated, it brings the impossibles into the area of the amazingly possible.

Belief! What a tremendous force. It even hurls mountainous defeats and doubts from our path and casts them into the sea, which is another way of saying that they are gone, out of sight, to blacken our lives no more.

The longer I work with the Gospel of Christ the more I have become convinced that while most of us believe in it we do not believe deeply enough to activate its potential power in our lives. If it continues forever only an article of intellectual, even worshipful faith, its enormous force remaining inert, then no matter how devout we may be, we fall short of experiencing the most dynamic power in life. The Gospel is power—the power of God. "But ye shall receive power, after that the Holy Ghost is come upon you . . ." "For I am not ashamed of the gospel of Christ: for it is the power of God unto salvation to every one that believeth . . ." And again the text of this sermon: "For whatsoever is born of God overcometh the world: and this is the victory that overcometh the world, even our faith."

And how is this deeper release of power effected in human beings? Simply by the act of surrender; but it must be a thoroughgoing, utterly desirous surrender to Jesus Christ. Then He the Savior by an act of Divine Grace gives the power in response to the faith thus humbly and longingly offered.

One brief instance will illustrate the process. It is that of a man who in June of 1954 was told that he had an "incurable" disease with a life expectancy of only a few months. In telling me about it, six years later, he said, "Dr. Peale, I had been a very bad boy." And he proceeded to confess his sinfulness. "When I was told that I was going to die my first thought was to get right with God; otherwise I knew I would go to hell. And that is exactly what I deserved."

He told how he went to his room and fell to his knees imploring God earnestly to forgive his sins and give him salvation. He did not pray to live, but to be changed.

His prayer was answered by a "great peace coming into my heart and I knew that Christ had received me, a truly black sheep." So great was his joy that now he wanted to live and work for God. His spiritual experience was so real, so very profound that his faith was now of an in-depth quality. Humbly he asked the Lord to take his life and use it.

I saw a letter written on the stationery of a famous cancer clinic signed by the head physician stating that on a day five years later there was no evidence of the disease. A miracle? Perhaps. But what is a miracle but a demonstration of power beyond the usual? There was a miracle but it was the miracle of grace, the miracle of God's power in human life, a miracle of overcoming the world through faith-in-depth. So great is the power of God that no matter what difficulties may confront us, victory can be ours if we approach our problems as Tough-Minded Optimists.

Sermon Thirty

WITH ALL THY MIND

REVEREND LISTON POPE, PH.D., D.D., S.T.D., L.H.D.

A Minister of the Congregational Church, Gilbert L. Stark Professor of Social Ethics, and Fellow of Saybrook College in Yale University, New Haven, Connecticut

Dr. Pope was ordained a Congregational minister in 1935 and held two pastorates before joining the distinguished Yale University Divinity School faculty. He served as associate pastor of Wesley Memorial Church, High Point, North Carolina, 1932-35, and was pastor of Humphrey Street Congregational Church, New Haven, 1935-38. In 1938 he became a member of the faculty of Yale Divinity School, and is presently Gilbert L. Stark Professor of Social Ethics and a Fellow of Saybrook College. From 1949 to 1962 he was dean of Yale Divinity School.

A native of North Carolina, he has been a resident of New Haven since 1935. He studied at Duke University, took his Ph.D. at Yale. Boston University, Duke Bucknell, Bradley, Rollins, Grinnell, Geneva University and Coe college each conferred the honorary doctorate upon him in recognition of his outstanding work in the field of religion and education.

He is the author of *Millhands and Preachers, The Kingdom Beyond Caste,* editor of *Labor's Relation to the Church and Community,* and former editor of *Social Action Magazine* (1944-48). He was a trustee of Vassar College and of the Phelps-Stokes Fund. In 1949 he was a Rosenwald Fellow and Phelps-Stokes Visitor to Africa. He was chairman of the pace-setting Congregational Council for Social Action, 1950-52. He asks disturbing questions in this sermon on education and the human mind.

WITH ALL THY MIND

Doubtless each of us has been asked, on one occasion or another, one of the most appropriate questions that can be addressed to a human being —namely, why don't you use your head? That question is generally a reproof or a warning; a reprimand for some foolish thing we have done or a warning against some stupid thing we are preparing to do now. In effect the question means, why don't you grow up and learn to think calmly, rather than blow up emotionally? Why not act like an intelligent human being instead of one of the lower animals?

Surely the human intelligence is one of man's most distinctive characteristics. And one is to use one's head, not lose it.

And one of the most important questions to use your head about is this: What is the human mind to be used for? Put another way, why have you been here in school trying to improve your mind?

Various answers have been given, some of them trivial. When asked why she had come to college, a coed is reported to have replied: "I came here to be went with." If that was the only motive she had, I hope that she had happy hunting and was soon gone from. More serious answers have been proposed.

One theory holds that the object of the mind is to promote the self-preservation of the individual and the survival of the race. About one hundred years ago a group of scientists and philosophers, inspired largely by Charles Darwin, developed the idea that the human mind is a kind of cunning developed in the struggle for survival, a variety of instinct comparable to the wisdom by which squirrels store nuts, and birds migrate. Man has survived, they taught, because he is a *thinking* animal; by the cunning of intelligence he has learned to outwit other animals and to make himself more or less secure against the perils of nature. The intellect figures out how to build a shelter against the Sun and the cold and to plant seeds against hunger and to use weapons against marauding beasts. When it helps the individual and the race to survive and prosper, the mind has performed its full duty.

This is doubtless an accurate description of most of the uses to which human beings put their minds. This theory is still supported very widely and not least of all in educational circles.

For the most part, it exalts technical and vocational education, and the best school is one in which students are taught to use their heads to get ahead in the world, or to make a practical contribution to the world's work, as nurses, fashion designers, social workers, engineers, farmers, machinists, and printers. So-called practical research becomes more important than pure research; to train people to win better control over their environment is more appropriate than to train them to enjoy Beethoven.

If this theory of the mind is adequate one of the greatest of seers was that prehistoric cousin of ours celebrated in a limerick of prehistoric vintage:

> Said a monkey as she swung by her tail
> To her offspring, female and male,
> Keep evolving, my dears
> And in ten million years
> You may be a professor at Yale.

Those of us who are Yale professors doubtless would agree in our darkest moments, which generally come between Easter and Commencement, that this arboreal forecast was entirely plausible and that very little evolution has been required.

With its great emphasis on technology, this naturalistic theory of the mind leads toward a culture of which Times Square has become in large measure a symbol. Gilbert Chesterton's comment on first seeing it points to the essential fault in that brilliant spectacle: "What a beautiful sight," said Chesterton, "if only a man could not read." Here is one of history's most remarkable displays of technical ingenuity, but it is devoted to the advertisement of commodities fundamentally cheap and transitory.

According to this theory, then, the mind is primarily a tool for promoting the survival and security of life. The mind is a superior monkey wrench; learn to twist things with it.

This theory of the mind is quickly enlarged by persons who have learned to ask more basic questions: why survive? Why get ahead? Why plant corn or build a bridge or make a hydrogen bomb or become skilled in a trade or craft? Generally these questions are answered by pointing to something more fundamental in life, the ability to appreciate and to enjoy certain things for their own sake and not because they are means to some other end. Of all pleasures, it is said, the most satisfying are those of the mind, and it is the primary purpose of education to prepare the mind for intellectual pleasures. What is the use of taking a monkey wrench to a Bach concert? The mind has a nobler function than that of designing and twisting gadgets. As a practical matter, education designed only for practical purposes is likely to leave its possessor bereft when his working days are over.

For advocates of this second theory of the mind the most appropriate education is a liberal arts education, one that introduces the mind to the culture and the arts of all ages and sets it free, liberates it, from provincialism and animal levels of enjoyment. Sir Edward Dyer defined a truly educated man:

My mind to me a kingdom is,
Such present joys therein I find
That it excels all other bliss
That earth affords or grows by kind. . . .
Some have too much, yet still do crave;
I little have, and seek no more.
They are but poor, though much they have,
And I am rich with little store.
They poor, I rich; they beg, I give;
They lack, I leave; they pine, I live.

The purpose of the mind, in this view, is to cultivate itself, to steep itself in great books, great music, great literature, great ideas—not because these great things will improve one's health or house or pocketbook, but because they are intrinsically good. The mind is not a monkey wrench; it is a greenhouse, whose purpose is that of creating and preserving lovely things within itself no matter how violent the storms or bleak the winter outside.

Once a simple German peasant discovered the treasures of the mind. Over his doorway he wrote, "Dante, Moliere and Shakespeare live here." He lived in a crude house, but remarkable guests came there to abide.

A third theory of the mind arises from a still more fundamental question: what will satisfy the mind? Bach can transport it for an evening into a gentler, lovelier world, but Bach morning, noon and night would begin to pall. Shakespeare can be read throughout life, but not steadily; in any case, he often provokes the mind to restlessness rather than soothes it to repose, so that it leaps out beyond his pages to explore new countries of its own. Any doctrine that makes the intellect its own reason for being does not recognize properly its quest for something beyond itself—for new knowledge and for truth, if you please. The person who strives to cultivate his mind for its own sake only soon becomes a dilettante unless he has extraordinary discipline; he flits from one art to another, like a bee seeking fresh nectar. Or he becomes an intellectual recluse, shutting himself off in a ready-made world of his own.

The mind, according to this third view, is neither a monkey wrench nor a greenhouse; it is a telescope, probing for knowledge about the unknown, always discontent with its existing horizons. It is the function of the mind to know, not merely to do or to enjoy. Truth alone can satisfy it. Knowledge for its own sake is the goal; whether the knowledge proves useful or brings pleasure is purely secondary.

Many of the remarkable achievements of the human mind have resulted from the passion simply to know. Socrates standing all day and all night in a trance of thought; Darwin watching lowly earthworms; Einstein writing formulae so complex that they were virtually incommunicable—these activities seemed of little use at the time and pleasure in them was incidental. But in all these pursuits, it is said, the mind was being true to itself; it was enlarging the boundaries of knowledge and exploring far countries of truth.

These three are the principal theories of the mind in our contemporary education. One or another, or some combination of them, underlies our vocational and professional schools, our preparatory schools, our liberal arts programs, our graduate schools of arts and sciences. Each has some merit; the mind is to be used in all these ways.

The Old Testament law and Jesus offered a fourth possibility in the great commandment: "Thou shalt love the Lord thy God . . . with all thy mind."

Insistence on any such purpose for the mind would arouse great hostility in many educational circles. Historians can remind us of the bondage imposed on the intellect in times past when religious dogma was all-powerful in the educational realm. They can recall many instances of the opposition of devout people to creative arts and to new truth—was not Galileo forced to recant? Is there not to this day an index of prohibited books for the members of one great religious body? Do not clergymen still cast a skeptical eye, and generally a disapproving one, on the theatre and on naturalistic art? Are religious leaders not often anti-intellectual? A pious Christian member of the Georgian legislature some years ago advised: "Read the Bible. It teaches you how to act. Read the hymn book. It contains the finest poetry ever written. Read the almanac. It shows you how to figure out what the weather will be. There isn't another book that is necessary for anyone to read, and therefore I am opposed to all libraries." [1]

Education in this country began largely under religious auspices. There were many abuses—emphasis on dogma, resistance to lively arts and to new truth. Perhaps the most striking feature of American education during the last hundred years has been its increasing secularization. Most institutions have emancipated themselves from ecclesiastical control, and

---

[1] Quoted by Virginius Dabney, *Liberalism in the South,* p. 289.

not a few have deserted their religious background. Public schools and state universities have become predominant, and, under the conditions of American life, have become almost entirely secular, though not necessarily anti-religious.

Emancipation of the schools from ecclesiastical control has had much to recommend it. The outreach of education has increased enormously in the history of America; many of our institutions were founded largely in order to supply an educated ministry, but now a rudimentary education is compulsory for all children, and millions of persons in all walks of life are college-trained. Education has moved out of the church into the school, and even into the factory and market place. And surely this is a laudable advance.

But in the process of becoming independent and dispersed, education has also become disorganized and diffuse. A Roman Catholic observer recently defined a State University as "a City of God that is all suburbs," and his definition might be applied to many of our schools and colleges. Now a college or university is likely to be composed of a congeries of departments or faculties whose members can hardly communicate with each other across their lines of specialization. At most faculty meetings it is almost dangerous even to pass a comment on the weather. There is likely to be a meteorologist who can tell you more about the weather than you really wanted to know. Professional specialization has proceeded so far as almost to justify a libelous limerick about the profession:

> I once had a classmate named Guesser
> Whose knowledge got lesser and lesser;
> It at last grew so small
> He knew nothing at all—
> And now he's a college professor.

So far as instruction is concerned, the organizing center of education has disappeared, leaving only a void that each department would like to fill with its own enthusiasms. Such values as we profess in common have been taught us largely by our common American culture, not by our educational institutions.

And so it is today—in nearly every realm of life—that we know a great deal about a prevailing situation and very little about values by which to live in the situation. On this particular day of the year for example, it behooves us to remember that we know far more than the last generation did—at least we think we do. About the dynamics of family life; the mechanisms of psychological attractions; about sex, about inter-personal adjustment; about patterns of child development and the rearing of children. We know so much about Mother love as to be suspicious of it; so much about Mother fixation as to discredit it. We know nearly everything about family life except how to preserve it; and nearly everything about children except how to keep them from becoming juvenile delinquents. Of what use is all our bright new information; our bright new ideas if there are no common values of love and loyalty, of patience and sacrifice, of shared loyalty and suffering; values by which our knowledge may be brought to focus and our families be preserved. And knowledge of divorce statistics is of little use without a fresh perspective by which our parents and grand-parents lived out their lives in devotion and faithfulness. Knowledge for a happy family comes from mutual respect in reverence, not only for each other, but for a power under which all human life is sacred and forgiveness a divine attribute; from values seldom taught as a central purpose in our specialized curricular of higher education as once they were.

We are not likely to find again an educational philosophy adequate to integrate our lives and our society until we reckon seriously with the Great Commandment, "Thou shalt love the Lord thy God . . . with all thy mind." Note that we are not commanded to love a particular religious denomination or to accept a particular creed—though these loyalties have much to commend them. Above all lesser loyalties, the mind is intended to adore, to stand in reverence before Him who is the Truth, the Light, the Creator of our lives and the object of our deepest longing. Our minds are restless unless they explore, but each fresh vista should bring them to worship anew Him beyond whom there are no farther horizons. Fallible and presumptuous religious groups have sometimes put the mind in chains; the love of God is the truth that sets it free. Contemporary education divides the mind into compartments; the love of God can make it whole again.

The mind is not merely a tool, or a plaything, or a puzzle solver. It is a spark from an eternal fire, and after flitting through the dark it must come again home, or die. It is capable of great ingenuity, productive of exquisite pleasure, competent for magnificent excursions. But it finds fulfillment only when it bows before Him whom to know is to adore and to love with all one's mind.

Sermon Thirty-one

LIFE'S SECOND BEST

REVEREND LOWELL M. ATKINSON, PH.D.

Minister, First Methodist Church, Montclair, New Jersey

Lowell Atkinson is one of the younger men of "intellectual distinction and spiritual vigor" in the pulpit of our time.

Born in Collingswood, New Jersey, he is the son of a Methodist preacher and likes to think of himself as essentially just that—a Methodist preacher. He received his divinity degree and his Ph.D. from Drew University. He was awarded the Ezra Squirer Tipple Fellowship in Preaching and in 1949 occupied the fellowship at Oxford University. While at Oxford he served as pastor of the Marston Road Congregational Church. He also studied at the University of Birmingham Summer School in Shakespeare at Stratford-upon-Avon.

Filled with enthusiasm by his experience of England, Dr. Atkinson wrote an article *On Visiting England* which was immediately published in *The English-Speaking World*, used by the Methodist Board of Missions as counsel for exchange preachers going to England, and reprinted in the American magazine *Freedom and Union*. He attended the last three Methodist Ecumenical Conferences at Oxford, 1951, Lake Junaluska, 1956, and Oslo, 1961.

He has served Methodist pastorates in Roselle, New Jersey, Vienna-Oakton, Virginia, East Harford, Maryland, and Hackensack, Elizabeth, and Englewood, New Jersey. In 1963 he became pastor of First Methodist Church, Montclair.

His published articles include "Plutarch" in *Religion in Life*, "The Achievement of Arminius" in *Religion in Life*, "They Lived Happily Ever Afterwards" in *The Christian Advocate*, "The Wonder of the Presence of God" in *Christian World Pulpit*. He has traveled in Europe, Africa, the Middle East, and South America. He has been sent on preaching missions for the Methodist Church to various countries, was Protestant Chaplain on the *Rotterdam* and exchange preacher in Bermuda in 1963.

LIFE'S SECOND BEST

> So Shishak king of Egypt came up against Jerusalem and took away the treasures of the house of the Lord . . . He carried away also the shields of gold which Solomon had made. Instead of which King Rehoboam made shields of brass . . .
>
> II Chronicles 12:9-10

I

How can we make the best of life? Is not this the central concern of all serious-minded persons? Given the materials of our mortal life—our personal abilities and inabilities, our inheritance of character from ancestors, our environment with its strange power to influence our life, the circumstance that finds us in history at a certain time and place and seemingly shapes fate and fortune—given these materials, what shall we do with them? And if life's materials seem imperfect, what then?

Dr. Harry N. Holmes used to say that life is one-tenth what you make it and nine-tenths how you take it. Certainly we seldom have our best wish come true, if ever, and we must learn to live with life's second best. John Henry Newman stated it more strongly when he wrote, "in a particular instance it might easily happen that what is only second best is best practically, because what is actually best is out of the question." When we learn to accept our world for what it is—no Utopia fashioned of dreams and heart's desire but a gloriously hazardous testing-ground where the worth of a man is proved and the soul can wake and grow, then we shall "welcome each rebuff that turns earth's smoothness rough," and content to know that it is God who guides us, we shall face life unafraid, strong to do and endure.

II

These thoughts on victorious living have been stimulated by the Bible story of the courage of Rehoboam. Known primarily for his folly, this son of King Solomon may seem a most unlikely source of inspiration, for it was he who caused the division of the Hebrew kingdom. Yet he had one splendid hour. When a foreign foe took away the shields of gold that Solomon had made, Rehoboam made shields of brass. When life's best was taken from him, bravely he hung up shields of brass—life's second best, but a tribute to the indomitable spirit of man.

How heartening to read this story of a man who took hold of life and won victory when his world had crumbled and he had to accept life's second best! For the life of Rehoboam is a story of almost unrelieved failure apart from this one shining hour. He inherited from his brilliant father King Solomon all of his bad traits, and they were many. Solomon had made his way to the throne through a bath of blood, murder following murder. He had abandoned the simplicity of the children of Israel and emulated the external magnificence of the heathen world until he became world famous for his golden magnificence. Not only did he gather vast numbers of wives and concubines from many lands, but he also recognized their various religions by building for their worship, heathen temples. Solomon had so oppressed his people with heavy taxation to support this magnificence that by the time of his decease the people were ripe for revolt.

Then Rehoboam came to the throne. What kind of king would he be? Another Solomon in the wisdom that had made the Hebrew Kingdom renowned? Or another Solomon in the tyrannies that threatened the future of the land? The answer was not long in forthcoming. Rehoboam was petitioned for justice by the people, and his reply was ominous. "My father chastised you with whips," he said, "but I will chastise you with scorpions." It was hardly an auspicious beginning for a new king's reign!

Popular discontent found a powerful leader in Jeroboam. The ten northern tribes rallied to his cry, "To your tents, O Israel." Rehoboam was bereft of most of his realm at one stroke, and only two of the twelve tribes remained under his control. To the watchful eyes of Shishak, King of Egypt, here was opportunity to attack the weakened land of Palestine. He swept into Judea, conquered Jerusalem, ransacked the city. In this conquest, Shishak took away the golden shields Solomon had used in religious processions. It had been Solomon's custom to worship in glittering splendor. The procession to the Temple was an event of breath-taking magnificence, as the Queen of Sheba discovered when she paid a visit.

Now the shields of gold were gone. What would Rehoboam do? To our astonishment this weak and wretched king rises to the challenge of the hour with a great deed of heroic defiance. When the shields of gold were gone, Rehoboam made shields of brass!

Some time ago I rode the train along the valley of the Nile from

Cairo southward to Luxor and the magnificent Temple of Karnak. On this ancient Egyptian temple I saw the wall-carvings showing Egyptians leading Israelites into captivity. They commemorated this very event when Shishak, King of Egypt, went against Jerusalem, and took away the shields of gold. I thought of the brave deed of Rehoboam. Weak as he was, unfortunate in character, heredity, and circumstance, yet in one shining hour he was every inch a king. When the shields of gold were gone, dauntlessly he hung up shields of brass—life's second best, yet a symbol of the dignity of man.

III

Like Rehoboam, most of us must live with life's second best. Nor is it easy. We are ambitious for the best. Our Lord commands us, "Be ye perfect." John Wesley stressed Jesus' teaching of complete love toward God and toward our fellow man and gave such love the name of Christian perfection. We need the lifting power of the ideal and rightly we fear such phrases as "the art of the possible," so much abused by politicians whose strategy is to work from one expediency to the next.

Nevertheless, the question persists. When the shields of gold are gone, can we resolutely hang up shields of brass? Let us take a humble example. A Christian is asked to do a job in the church. He refuses, saying, "I'm not sure I could do it well, and if I can't do the job well, I don't want to do it at all." With all due respect for honest humility, this is an attitude that if universal, would cripple the work of Christ's Kingdom. We are not creatures of perfection; we are creatures of earth, limited by heredity, environment and circumstance, yet free to give faith, devotion and effort to a job worth doing. Of course we will not only want to do our best, but also to make our best ever better. Then let us not fear life's second best, but dedicate it to God, and trust Him to make good use of it! James Russell Lowell once said of Abraham Lincoln, "He was the greatest kind of statesman because if he could not have what he wanted most, he would take the next best thing, if he could get even that!" John Milton wrote his greatest poems after he had been afflicted with blindness.

> Yet I argue not,
> Gainst Heaven's hand or will
> Nor bate a jot of heart or hope
> But still bear up and steer right onwards.

So Milton boldly hung up his shields of brass when the shields of gold were taken from him. So proudly we hail those who, when life's best is denied them, hold their heads high and willingly accept life's second best.

IV

Who can say what is life's best? Is it not true that to make something out of life, not given the best material is the challenge to most of the people who live on the earth? Should we expect perfection in this life, or accepting something less, should we not learn to live bravely with life's second best, forging greatness out of the inferior? Occasionally a married couple will seek to impress me by saying, "We have been married thirty years and have never had a quarrel." I always say a silent prayer that God will somehow save that marriage! It seems more dead than alive! No, it is for us to face problems with intelligence, with spirit, with understanding, and making the best of it, build creative vitality into the life of the home. Not the absence of the unpleasant, but the power to live well in the terms that are given us is the important matter.

Doubtless if God had wanted us to live as perfect automatons, He would have created us that way. A race of puppets in a flawless Utopia would have been possible, but it would also have been meaningless. So God created men free to choose between alternatives in the light of truth. The hazards of freedom are great, so great that man has stumbled and fallen from the beginning of the race to the present moment. Yet, somehow in the midst of man's struggle with his wrong choices, God continues to challenge and inspire with the vision of the right. He calls us to make the best out of what we are and what we have and gives us through His grace the power of going on.

St. Paul said, "I know how to be abased and how to abound." Most of us do not know either. When we are abased, we plunge into unnecessary despair; and when we abound, we have unwarranted elation. We are to learn to live steadily through life's ups and downs, through abounding and abasement, through the shattering of our cherished hopes and be able to cling to life's second best and thank God for it.

Only God knows what is best! We think we know what we want in life, but it is so easy to be deceived! A famous legend of India tells of a wise man who promises three pilgrims their greatest desire. Each one eagerly names what he thinks is life's best. One wants long life. Another wants wealth. The third asks for great strength. Their wishes are granted, but the result is not happiness, but terrible tragedy. The man of long life suffers through the years a terrible disease. The man of wealth finds himself the center of jealousy, bickering and murder. The man of great strength is subjected to horrible tortures which are prolonged indefinitely because of his great strength.

Who knows what is best? Only God, and our best wisdom is to trust Him and learn His will. To be able to pray, "Thy Kingdom come. Thy will be done," is to know how to live. As we learn in the university of life the deeper lessons often taught in pain, we come to understand that apparent ruin may bring good things with it, that disaster is by no means the worst thing that can happen to a man. Our Saviour prayed in agony on the eve of Calvary and His final victory of faith points us the way. Did it seem to Him that the shields of gold were taken from Him in that dark hour in Gethsemane? Then He would bravely hang up shields of brass, "Not my will, but Thine be done!" The touch of God upon our prayer of faith transfigures life's second best with the shining splendor of God's purpose.

Even from disaster a man may rise ennobled! All honor to the brave, who unceasingly give praise to God that life's troubles but link us more closely to Him!

Sermon Thirty-two

CIVIL RIGHTS AND CHRISTIAN DUTIES

REVEREND ROBERT JAMES MCCRACKEN, D.D., S.T.D., L.H.D.

Minister, The Riverside Church, New York, New York

Always known for his courage and leadership, Dr. McCracken here preaches one of the outstanding sermons of his distinguished career, showing the close affinity of racial problems and the Christian religion. This problem, one of the major ones of our time in our country, is a serious threat to our national life and one which needs solution on a fair, just and Christian basis with the recognition of the responsibilities of all men of all races and creeds. Dr. McCracken points out many facets of the problem.

Born in Motherwell, Scotland, Robert McCracken grew up in a Scottish Presbyterian home, went to the local school, and became a member of the Baptist Church in Motherwell. He graduated from Glasgow University and became minister of Marshall Street Baptist Church in Edinburgh. In 1933, he became minister of Dennistoun Baptist, Glasgow, and lecturer in Systematic Theology at the Baptist Theological College of Scotland. Thus he became both preacher and teacher. In 1937, he was called to teach theology and the philosophy of religion at McMaster University in Hamilton, Ontario, Canada.

During 1937 and 1938 he took a special year of study at Cambridge University to prepare himself for his work at McMaster, then assumed his chair in 1938. In 1945 and 1946 he was president of the Baptist Convention of Ontario and Quebec. In 1946 he was called to the Riverside Church to succeed Dr. Harry Emerson Fosdick when he retired. In 1955 he became a naturalized citizen of the United States.

In this new post he again became both pastor-preacher and teacher, for he was appointed Lecturer in Practical Theology at Union Theological Seminary, New York and is now Associate Professor of Practical Theology there. He has lectured at Andover, Yale, Union (Richmond), Princeton Seminary, Southern Baptist Seminary, McMaster, Pacific School of Religion, and Auburn Seminary. He preaches on the National Radio Pulpit every year.

Dr. McCracken's books include *Questions People Ask, The Making of the Sermon,* and *Putting Faith to Work.*

In 1957, he traveled to Japan at the invitation of the Japan Committee for Intellectual Interchange. While in the Far East, he visited Hong Kong, the Philippines, Thailand, Burma, India, and Pakistan. He saw the U.N. at work and visited missionaries, State Department officials, and leaders in education and religion.

The importance of his work has been recognized by the conferring of honorary doctorates by thirteen universities or colleges: the S.T.D. by Columbia University; the D.H.L. by Bates College, Shurtleff College, Pratt Institute; the D.D. by McMaster, Bucknell, Glasgow, Colgate, Denison, Princeton, Vermont, Wake Forest, and Colby.

CIVIL RIGHTS AND CHRISTIAN DUTIES

> Have we not all one father? Has not one God created us? Why then are we faithless to one another, profaning the covenant of our fathers?
> Malachi 2:10

We are hearing a great deal these days about civil rights. The subject is headline news in the press, is prominently featured on television and radio, is without a doubt *the* national issue facing Congress. While a political issue, it is prior to that a moral and spiritual issue. A preacher would be guilty of dereliction of duty if he said nothing about it.

Americans have affirmed repeatedly their belief in human equality. The belief has often been called the American Creed. It is written into the Declaration of Independence and the Bill of Rights. It is reflected in the claims made for the United States—"the land of the free," "the land of opportunity," "the cradle of liberty," "the home of democracy." If I had a black skin and had to go through an experience like that of James Meredith I am sure I should find it hard not to be cynical about those slogans.

In the matter of civil rights the churches are inescapably involved. There is no social issue on which their charter is clearer. The belief in human equality has biblical origins. The biblical principle is unambiguous and emphatic. Underlying race, class, color there is a fundamental fact which is universal and everywhere the same. God is the creator of all mankind. In His sight we are all equal. He cares for us equally and it is His will that we should live in community with one another and love our neighbors as ourselves. The explicit teaching of the Bible is that there are no inferior races, no second-class citizens, that God has no favorites, that Christ died for all and in Him there is neither Jew nor Greek, neither bond nor free, neither male nor female; all are one in Him. Racism is an affront to the native dignity of man and an insult to God. The Church of Christ will forfeit its leadership unless it stands unequivocally by its God-given gospel that we are all made "in the image and likeness of God" and that in consequence every human being is endowed with inalienable rights.

There was a day when Jesus rose in a synagogue, opened the Scriptures, and read: "The Spirit of the Lord is upon me, because he has anointed me to preach good news to the poor. He has sent me to proclaim release to the captives and recovering of sight to the blind, to set at liberty those who are oppressed, to proclaim the acceptable year of the Lord." The Church came out of that. The Church must keep going back to that as a mandate and directive. What concerned Jesus must concern it. He was concerned for all that affected the well being of men and women, and we must be no less concerned.

Where my brother man has a right I have a duty. Every civil right carries with it a civil obligation, a Christian obligation. Rights are not merely privileges, prerogatives, ends in themselves; they are opportunities, instruments, trusts. The value of any human right lies in the use to which it is put. Freedom does not consist in having rights but in fulfilling them. Mazzini, when people were insisting on the Rights of Man, came forward with a list of the Duties of Man to balance the account. This is where we have been at fault. We have made more of rights than of duties. A distaste for the very idea of responsibility is widespread. It is part and parcel of the weakness of democracy and of our moral confusion and futility. We complain loudly enough that things are not what they should be, but we are not morally sensitive about them to the extent that we feel an obligation to do something personally and specifically about putting them right.

There are Negro leaders who are saying to the churches, "You have stopped justifying racial wrongs but have you begun to rectify them?" It must be acknowledged that we have been tardy in rectifying them. We have been tardy even in recognizing them. An adult class in a church school was studying the booklet, "Jesus Christ the Light of the World" in anticipation of the Third Assembly of the World Council of Churches. One of the discussion questions asked, "What, in your own life and your local community, are the forms of opposition to Christ?" When the teacher raised the question the members of the class sat racking their brains, trying to think of one genuine foe to the

Gospel. Finally, someone said, "I read in a recent issue of the *Saturday Evening Post* about Bishop Pike. He thinks the story of the Virgin Birth is a myth." That was as big an enemy as anyone in the class could come up with.

The extension of full and equal rights to all citizens goes on under the direction of government, under the pressure of the courts, under the determined prodding of minority groups (with churchmen often in their leadership), but the big religious bodies in America have been slow in getting into concerted action. So much so that Martin Luther King was constrained to write a letter from a jail in Birmingham to clergymen who protested that the Birmingham crusade was ill-timed: "I must confess," he wrote, "that over the past two years I have been gravely disappointed with the white moderate. I have almost reached the regrettable conclusion that the Negro's great stumbling block in his stride toward freedom is not the White Citizen's Councilor or the Ku Klux Klanner but the white moderate who is more devoted to 'order' than to justice; who prefers a negative peace which is the absence of tension to a positive peace which is the presence of justice; who constantly says, 'I agree with you in the goal you seek, but I cannot agree with your methods'; who paternalistically believes he can set the timetable for another man's freedom . . . and who constantly advises the Negro to wait for 'a more convenient season.' Shallow understanding from people of goodwill is more frustrating than absolute misunderstanding from people of ill will. Lukewarm acceptance is much more bewildering than outright rejection."

A conscience-probing statement! One sentence in it puts a finger on a common attitude: "I agree with you in the goal you seek, but I cannot agree with your methods." The methods—the sit-ins, the freedom marches, the prayer vigils, the non-violent protests—merit more consideration, as to their nature and purpose, than some of us are giving them. Leaders of the Negro churches see their Christian duty in regard to civil rights in the light of the teaching of the Sermon on the Mount. They have forsworn violence as immoral, as profaning the sanctity of the human spirit and outraging the innate dignity of man. They have reiterated as a cardinal principle of the non-violent movement any blood shed should be Negro blood. In classes for the training and discipline of volunteers they stress such rules as these: "Walk and talk in the manner of love, for God is love." "Refrain from the violence of fist, tongue or heart." "If you are arrested, go to prison quietly; if assaulted, bear it cheerfully; if shot, die peacefully."

Recall the injunction of Jesus: "You have heard that it was said 'You shall love your neighbor and hate your enemy.' But I say to you, Love your enemies and pray for those who persecute you, so that you may be sons of your Father who is in heaven." This is the spirit in which Martin Luther King makes his stand for civil rights. Governor Barnett on Friday denounced him and resorted to the old McCarthy tactic—the Communist smear. It is extraordinary how so much that is essentially Christian is condemned as Communist. Bearing in mind the injunction of Jesus, listen to the words of Dr. King! "To our most bitter opponents we say: 'We shall match your capacity to inflict suffering by our capacity to endure suffering. We shall meet your physical force with soul force . . . We cannot in all good conscience obey your unjust laws, because non-cooperation with evil is as much a moral obligation as is cooperation with good. Throw us in jail and we shall love you. Bomb our homes and churches and threaten our children, and we shall still love you . . . But be assured that we will wear you down by our capacity to suffer. One day we shall win freedom, but not only for ourselves. We shall so appeal to your heart and conscience that we shall win *you* in the process, and our victory will be a double victory.' "[1] Does that strike you as Communist teaching?

The man who makes a stand like that never stands alone. Ministers, teachers, students, teenagers have rallied in support. Many of them have been arrested and lodged in jail—William Sloane Coffin, Chaplain at Yale, Robert McAfee Brown, Professor of Theology at Stanford, Eugene Carson Blake, executive officer of the United Presbyterian Church who will preach here in September. The consensus is growing in the churches that the Negro must not be left to bear the whole brunt of the struggle. The Secretary of State has said that if he were a Negro he would demonstrate. He has put the weight of his office behind the demonstrations. If I were a Negro I would want to say to the White: "Don't leave us to demonstrate alone. Take your stand alongside of us." Pledged to non-violence he is attempting to further the cause of human rights peaceably. It would be an evil day for this country if instead there should be an eruption of raw force. There are ominous signs that patience is growing thin and that leadership could pass into other and belligerent hands. One wonders whether white people who criticize the strategy of non-violence realize what the alternatives are. The American Negro is determined to gain his rights by *some method.*

---

[1] Martin Luther King, *The Strength to Love,* New York: Harper & Row, 1963.

Either the struggle for justice will proceed peaceably or it will break out in violence. Those are the alternatives and there are no others.

In these turbulent days, days of peril, days of opportunity, what should be the role of the churches? They must get out from behind closed doors. They must be social action institutions. They must move from the rear to the forefront of the crusade *for* civil rights legislation, *against* segregated schools, segregated housing, discrimination in employment. They must take a strong stand against the indignities and injustice imposed on minorities. They must follow the lead taken last month by the General Board of the National Council of Churches and support negotiations and demonstrations and direct action in areas of particular crisis.

The call is to members of local congregations and not only to denominational executives and ministers. About the remedying of some social evils you may feel well-nigh helpless. They are so vast and complex; you do not know where to take a hold; there seems so little that one individual can do. The encouraging factor in regard to civil rights is that it is an issue about which every Christian can do something. He can begin where he lives, where he works, where he worships. Committing himself to belief in an unsegregated church and an unsegregated society, he can conform his personal, family, church, business, and social life to his beliefs. He can cultivate contacts and friendships with members of minority groups. He can invite them to his home and visit theirs. We reject the myth of racial supremacy. We believe in integration. Are we putting our belief into practice in everyday relationships? Christian race relations begin with these immediate person-to-person contacts.

But that is only to make a start. These are days that demand more than fraternization. Members of a church like this, living in a city like this, ought to identify themselves with school problems, community problems, recreation, the enactment and enforcement of fair employment practices, the right of every citizen to acquire housing on the basis of personal preference and financial capacity without regard to race, religion, or national origin. It is not enough for the minister to preach about such matters or a social study committee to survey them. The whole church should face them. City concerns ought to be church concerns, and not abstractly but specifically, situations known at first hand, people involved in the situations known by name. Here the vital consideration is not program promotion so much as it is personal identification and involvement.

Last Sunday I preached on personal religion and social concern. On Monday I received a letter from a member of the congregation. He is white, married and the father of one child. He expressed regret that in what I said I had not struck closer home to Riverside Church members. He shared with me his conviction about the challenges confronting church members in the present crisis. Here, as he sees them, are the challenges: (1) To welcome Negroes and Puerto Ricans into our social and civic clubs; (2) To hire and advance minority group members in business firms; (3) To welcome Negroes and Puerto Ricans into our residential areas and stay there ourselves so that the areas may not be re-segregated; (4) To keep our own children in public schools with minority children. Those are some of the specific challenges confronting us as church members. Where our brother man has a right we have a duty. That needs to be sharpened, made specific. Where a Negro or Puerto Rican has a right we have a duty. Every civil right carries with it a civil obligation, a *Christian* obligation. We take pride in our rights. What do we intend to do about our duties?

God is known in many ways, in churches and out of them, and especially "where cross the crowded ways of life, where sound the cries of race and clan." [2] Religion has well been defined as Ultimate Concern. Mahatma Gandhi, with all his emphasis on private prayer, stated in his autobiography that God was never so real to him as when he was actively identified with the struggles of the poor farmers in the north of India. Social concern is not only the inevitable consequence of personal religion; it validates and deepens and enriches personal religion.

---

[2] Pilgrim Hymnal, hymn #423.

Sermon Thirty-three

THE GOD OF OUTER SPACE

REVEREND WALKER N. STOCKBURGER, TH.D.

Minister of Trinity Baptist Church, Norfolk, Virginia

This sermon by Dr. Stockburger is filled with ideas that should help many doubting people, especially young people troubled by questions concerning science and religious faith. It relates Biblical truth to our modern scientific age.

Born in Chattanooga, Tennessee, Dr. Stockburger attended Carson-Newman College, was ordained in 1939 at Northside Baptist Church, Chattanooga, then took his theological training at Southern Baptist Theological Seminary, Louisville, Kentucky, where he received his Th.D. in 1951. He has held pastorates at Stevenson Baptist Church, Stevenson, Alabama, 1939-1941, Indian Fork Baptist Church, Bagdad, Kentucky, 1941-1944, and Union Baptist Church, Cynthiana, Kentucky, 1948-1952. He has been pastor of Trinity Baptist Church, Norfolk, Virginia, since 1952.

He has taught school, was an army chaplain in the European and Pacific theaters, 1945-47, returned to Louisville for his doctoral work in 1948. He has been President of the Norfolk Baptist Pastors' Conference (Southern Baptist), President of the Norfolk Ministers Association (Interdenominational), Moderator of the Norfolk Baptist Association; Chairman of the Pastor-Church Relations Committee of the Baptist General Association of Virginia; he is a Member of the Mayor's Youth Commission of Norfolk.

THE GOD OF OUTER SPACE

> When I consider thy heavens, the work of thy fingers, the moon and the stars, which thou hast ordained; what is man, that thou art mindful of him? and the son of man, that thou visitest him?
> Psalm 8:3-4

The whole world has been amazed at recent events that have taken place. A few years ago most of us read only in scientific fiction concerning space travel. We considered such stories entertaining and exciting, but not to be taken too seriously. But now man has been able to circle the earth in satellites and return to tell of his exploits. It still seems almost beyond our imagination.

We live in a very exciting age, in spite of much suffering and anxiety that fill it. What is to be our attitude toward these things that are happening around us? Are we to bury our heads in the sand and let the world go by? Are we to say that men are just doing things they have no business doing, that they are tampering with God's created work, and, as a result, will bring terrible punishment upon themselves? Are these the proper attitudes for Christians to take? Certainly there are many thinking Christians who could never adopt such a position. They are interested in this magnificent universe and seek to find out everything they can about it.

In light of more and more scientific knowledge, and in view of man's increasing realization of the magnitude of the universe, certain questions are inevitable. Can God be a personal God? Can He be concerned about life on this tiny planet? Are there people living on other planets? If so, how will they know about God's love? Is God really the God of outer space?

We have a good precedent for such honest inquiries. The ancient psalmist raised some of these questions: "When I consider thy heavens, the work of thy fingers, the moon and the stars, which thou hast ordained; what is man, that thou art mindful of him? and the son of man, that thou visitest him?" (Psalm 8:3,4). We can approach such questions without fear of finding some truth that is going to destroy our faith. God is the source of all truth.

I. The Scientific Hypothesis and the Bible

It would be well for us to see briefly the general scientific explanation of our universe. We have to face it; we cannot hide. Most of the scientists of the world today, if I understand their position correctly, believe that this tremendous indescribable universe has been developed over a period of billions and billions of years. The scientists believe that the universe has developed in orderly processes according to universal laws throughout an incalculable period of time. They have seen through their telescopes and spectroscopes many things that have been happening in our universe. They have discovered and analyzed tremendous explosions of stars that have scattered particles through the heavens. One was so far away that it took 4,000 years for the light of that explosion to reach the lens of the telescopes on earth. It seems that scientists with ever-accumulating evidence have presented a logical case for the development of the universe over an immeasurable period of time. This includes not only the physical universe, but all forms of life. The scientists would explain the development of life as coming from the very simplest forms, even chemical reactions, until, eventually, organic life came into being. The principle of evolution indicates that all life has come through innumerable steps to reach the present forms we see today.

What are we to do with this explanation of life and reality in our universe? Can we just laugh at it and push it aside? Or, should we honestly try to understand it and see how God fits into such a picture? We ought to be exceedingly slow as Christians to push aside all of the scientific evidence that has accumulated for centuries and say that we do not believe it.

It would be far more sensible to realize that the scientists are trying to explain the process through which this universe has been and is being developed, and not its ultimate origin. In fact, most scientists are quick to admit that they make no attempt whatever to explain the ultimate origin of the universe. They say that such a question lies in the realm of metaphysics, which is beyond their scope of study. There is no scientific evidence whatever that disproves the fact that God is the source of this universe. The manner of development and the length of time involved are nothing like as important as the fact that it is all the work of God. I assume the existence of God, as did the Biblical writers. Although it cannot be proved or disproved scientifically, it is the most logical assumption I know anything about. I cannot conceive of any other logical explanation for the reality and meaning of our universe.

In light of the scientific evidence presented by geologists, paleontologists, biologists, astronomers and other scientists, how are we to interpret the Biblical account of creation? In order to interpret intelligently the book of Genesis or the Bible as a whole, we must recognize that it is a book of religion and not a book of science. The Bible was not written to explain various scientific theories about any subject, including the creation of the world. The Bible as a book of religion describes in many places in child-like language the fact that God is behind this universe, that He is the source of all life, and that out of His majesty and might this universe has come into existence.

The creation stories in Genesis can be interpreted as the attempt of ancient Biblical writers to explain the universe in which they lived. Their simple, yet majestic, description stands in happy contrast to the artificial and sometimes fantastic creation stories from other sources. The Biblical account of creation, in my opinion, is not intended to be a literal account or a scientific description of the creation of the universe. It is presented in the language and thought patterns of that day, not in the scientific terms of this day.

However, the most important fact in the whole account is that this universe, including all forms of life, is a result of God's creative process. This fact stands out so clearly that no one can miss it. The length of time involved in this process, and the infinite number of stages through which life has been developed are almost incidental when compared to the main truth that God has done it. The fact that God has extended his creative process over an unimaginable period of time makes it even more miraculous. Rather than minimizing God, it magnifies Him. Such an interpretation of Genesis, rather than destroying the Bible, gives it real meaning and validity even in our own scientific age.

II. The Magnitude of the Universe

One cannot seriously consider the scientific hypothesis described above without being made aware of the magnitude of the universe. A preacher recently said that he had preached for twenty years assuming that God was merely the God of this earth of ours. Finally, it dawned on him that he had been making God a mighty small God. He had not thought of God's relation to this limitless universe. We need to realize that this earth is just a tiny speck of dust in the universe. Our sun, with a mass 332,000 times that of the earth, is just one star in one galaxy, which we call the Milky Way. And this one galaxy is made up of about

100 billion other stars, many of them far bigger than the sun. Our solar system is revolving around the center of this galaxy at the speed of 175 miles per second, which is not exactly crawling along. Yet, it takes 200 million years for our solar system to go around the center of our galaxy one time. But we cannot stop there, because ours is just one galaxy among the billions and billions of galaxies in the universe. When we begin to think in these terms, even though man has accomplished fantastic things, they appear to be rather insignificant in comparison with the whole universe. If man in his blindness and selfishness succeeds in destroying this earth on which we live, we have to remind ourselves that it would be just a local disturbance.

Intriguing questions come to our minds with regard to the other stars and planets throughout the universe. Has it been God's plan to develop life over a period of billions of years on the other planets, scattered throughout space? We should be slow to answer with a dogmatic negative. It would be rather presumptuous to think that in this vast universe God is concerned with life only on this tiny planet we call the earth. That would be good for our ego, but it would be hard to substantiate with logic. Why would God have created such an infinite universe if He were going to have life on only one small planet?

Scientists are raising these questions today, and we have to raise them. We have to be honest about it, unless we want boys and girls to grow up in our church with such a narrow concept of God and the Bible that when they get to college and learn some scientific facts their whole religion is knocked from under them. They will throw it out the window as an old fairy story, saying that they have outgrown such childish teachings. We need to investigate seriously the questions they raise. Our young people have a great advantage over us. They talk in terms of space and rocket travel just as naturally as they do about playing cowboys and Indians. It is hard for adults to do that. We get set in our pattern of thinking, and find it hard to change.

Suppose for our own imagination that we consider the possibility of life on other planets. Harlow Shapley, an eminent astronomer, has speculated about it in the following manner.[1] Let us say that only one in a hundred is a single star, and of them only one in a hundred has a system of planets, and of them only one in a hundred has an earth-like planet, and of them only one in a hundred has its earth in that interval of dis-

---

[1] Harlow Shapley, editor, *Science Ponders Religion* (New York: Appleton-Century-Crofts, Inc., 1960), p. 8.

tance from the star that we call the liquid-water-belt (neither too cold nor too hot), and of them only one in a hundred has the proper chemical resources similar to ours—suppose all those chances were approximately true, then by the most conservative estimate there would be ten billion planets suitable for organic life something like that on the earth.

This raises many questions for us, many of which may never be answered. Will it be possible to communicate with other planets? After the recent accomplishments of science, all of us will be rather slow to say what is impossible. But, even if we develop communication and travel between the planets of our own solar system, which would be a gigantic achievement, we need not get too excited about our accomplishments. For scientists tell us that in our galaxy, which is a very tiny part of the universe, the nearest star to our sun is some 4¼ light years away, something like 25,000 billion miles. Scientists estimate the nearest suitable planetary station to be at least ten light years away. We think that we are traveling pretty fast in rockets at a speed of 25,000 miles an hour, but light travels at 186,000 miles a second. This means that it would take ten years to get a signal of light from this earth to the nearest possible planetary station, and ten more years to get the answer back. Thus far no one is seriously considering traveling at a greater speed than that of light. We appear to be isolated from other life-bearing planets.

III. The Validity of the Christian Revelation

What does this mean for us? Are we no more than mechanical toys? Must we jump to the same conclusion that some scientists have reached that God is no more than an impersonal force which lies behind the universe? Even granted that God is personal, could He possibly be concerned about life on this little earth surrounded by innumerable planets and stars?

The Biblical writers believed in a personal God who was greatly concerned about life on the earth. Not only did they see the stars as the handiwork of God, but they believed that this same God knew His people by name and loved them. This fact, which God revealed through the Old Testament writers, came to its highest expression in the New Testament. God has broken into human history through His Son, Jesus Christ. The incarnation staggers our imagination. It cannot be explained; nor can it be explained away. The life, death, and resurrection of Jesus Christ are historical facts which must be interpreted in some way. The Christian interpretation of these facts cannot be proved scientifically; nor can anyone disprove this interpretation. In the last analysis, whatever interpretation you reach, the final step is one of faith. For some it is a faith that there is no God; the universe is meaningless. For others it is a faith that nothing more than an impersonal Power is behind the universe. For millions of us, however, it is a faith in the living personal God, whose love we have seen shining through the face of Jesus Christ (II Corinthians 4:6). This kind of faith has brought multitudes to a relationship of such integrity and vitality that it cannot be dismissed casually.

Apparently, as far as we can determine, God's greatest creation thus far has been the development of persons who are able to respond to His love. If He has developed persons on billions of other planets, from our experience with God on this planet we know that He would love other persons just as much as He does us. In spite of the difficulties involved, which are beyond our comprehension, we know that God would reveal His love to those persons in some way. If God has developed life throughout the other planets, He has a purpose in it. And, as we know that purpose, it will involve relationships of love and understanding as far as God is concerned.

How God will reveal Himself to life on other planets, if there is life, is really a matter of speculation. We will never know in this life. The important thing is that we know that He is the God of inner space, the God who lives in our hearts, which is much more important as far as our daily lives are concerned than to know that He is the God of outer space.

In view of this, I challenge you to face with an open mind any truth that you can find. God is behind it all; He is the source of all truth. We do not need an apologetic scared Christianity that frantically tries to keep God in a tiny mold of our own shaping. We need to expand our minds and our concept of God, realizing that after we have learned all that we are capable of learning through a lifetime of investigation, we will have only a smattering of knowledge concerning God's great creation. Thanks be unto God that He has revealed Himself to us through Jesus Christ, His Son, or we never could have known Him as we do.

Sermon Thirty-four

SPIRITUAL PRESENCE

REVEREND PAUL TILLICH, PH.D., TH.D., D.D.

A Minister of the Evangelical and Reformed Church and Professor of Theology at Harvard Divinity School, Cambridge, Massachusetts

Dr. Paul Tillich is one of the leading theologians of the Protestant faith today and has exercised a profound and far-reaching influence upon contemporary religious thought in Europe and America.

Born in Starzeddel, Kreis Guben, Prussia, in 1886, he is the son of Johannes Tillich, a Protestant minister, and Mathilde (Dürselen) Tillich. He studied at several German universities: Berlin, Tübingen, and Halle. He received his Ph.D. from the University of Breslau in 1911. Since that time, he has received honorary degrees from the University of Halle (Th.D., 1926), Yale (D.D., 1940), the University of Glasgow (1951), Princeton University (1953), Clark University and Harvard University (1954).

A member of the Evangelical and Reformed Church, he was ordained in August, 1912, in Berlin. He served as an army chaplain in the German army during World War I, 1914-18, then began his teaching career as Professor at the Universities of Berlin, Marburg, and Leipzig, at the Technical Academy in Dresden, and as professor of philosophy at the University of Frankfurt-am-Main, 1929-1933. He came to the United States in 1933 and was naturalized in 1940.

He was Professor of Theology at Union Theological Seminary, New York, 1933-55. In 1955 he was invited to become Professor of Theology at Harvard University Divinity School. In 1962 he became John Nuveen Professor of Theology at the University of Chicago.

Dr. Tillich is the author of *The Religious Situation*, *The Interpretation of History*, *The Protestant Era* (1948), *The Shaking of the Foundations* (1948), *Systematic Theology I* (1951), *Systematic Theology II* (1957), *Systematic Theology III* (1963), *The Courage to Be* (1952), *Love, Power and Justice* (1954), *Dynamics of Faith*, and *Theology of Culture*. He wrote several volumes in Germany on the philosophy of religion.

The theology of Paul Tillich is his greatest contribution to the contemporary religious world. In recent years he has been honored by Germany with the Goethe Plakette Award, 1956; the Grosse Verdienstkreuz of the West German Republic, 1956; the Goethe Prize, 1958. He gave the Bampton Lectures at Columbia University in 1961, and has given many other famous lectureships.

This distinguished sermon will also be included in Dr. Tillich's new book, soon to be published by Scribner's.

SPIRITUAL PRESENCE

> Not that we are sufficient of ourselves to claim anything as coming from us; our efficiency is from God who has qualified us to be ministers of a new covenant, not in written code but in Spirit; for the written code kills, but the Spirit gives life.
>
> II Corinthians 3:5-6

I

"Not that we are sufficient"—writes Paul. Who are the "we"? Obviously, the apostle himself and those who work with him. This includes all those who are qualified to serve the "New Covenant," as he calls it, namely the new relationship between God and man, and through it the "New Creation," the new state of things in man and his world, of which Paul is a messenger. And qualified to serve is everyone who himself participates in it, however fragmentarily. But if we ask, who *does* participate in the new creation, then we soon find this to be a question without answer. For nobody can look into the innermost center of any other being, not even fully into his own heart. Therefore, nobody can say with certainty that anyone else shares in the new state of things, he can scarcely say it of himself. Even less can he say of another one, however distorted this man's life may be, that he does not participate at all in the new reality, and that he is not qualified at all to serve its cause. And, certainly, nobody can say this of himself.

Perhaps it is more important in our time to emphasize the latter, namely the qualification of ourselves and those around us to serve the New Creation, our ability to be priests in mutual help towards achieving it. Not long ago many people, especially members of the churches, felt qualified to judge others and to tell them what to believe and how to act. Today we feel deeply the arrogance of this attitude. Instead of that a general awareness of our lack of qualification is everywhere manifest, especially in the middle-aged and younger generations. We are inclind to disqualify ourselves and to withdraw from the service of the New Creation. We feel that we don't participate in it and that we cannot bring others into such participation. We decline the honor and the burden of mutual priesthood. Often this is caused by unconcern for our highest human vocation; but equally it is caused by despair about ourselves, by doubt, guilt and emptiness. We feel infinitely removed from a new state of things and totally unable to help others towards it.

But then the other words of our text must become effective, that our qualification is from God and not from ourselves; and the all-consoling word that God is greater than our heart. If we look beyond ourselves at that which is greater than we, then we can feel called to help others just in a moment in which we ourselves need help most urgently—and astonishingly, we *can* help. A power works through us which is not from us. Perhaps we remember a situation in which words came out of the depth of our being, maybe in a state of our own great anxiety, which hit another one in the depth of *his* being and *his* state of great anxiety so strongly that they helped him to a new state of things. Perhaps we remember another situation in which an action of a person whose disrupted life we knew had a priestly, awakening, healing effect upon us. It came not from him, but it was in him, as on the other occasion it came not from us, but was in us. Let us not assume the task of being mediators of the New Creation to others arrogantly, be it in personal or in ecclesiastical arrogance. Yet, let us not reject the task of being priest for each other because of desperation about ourselves or in unconcern about what should be our highest concern. Against both arrogance and despair stands the word that our qualification does not come from us, nor from any man or any institution, not even from a church, but from God. And if it comes from God it is his Spiritual Presence in our spirit.

II

When we now hear the word Spirit, we are somehow prepared for it: the power in us, but not from us, qualifying us for the service of a new state of things, that is what Spirit means. This may sound strange to the many inside and outside the churches for whom the term Holy Spirit is the strangest of the strange terms which appear in the world of Christian symbols. Rarely a subject of preaching, it is also neglected in religious teaching. Its festival, Pentecost, has almost disappeared in the popular consciousness of this country. Some groups which claim Spiritual experiences of a particular character are considered unhealthy—and rightly so. Liturgically, the use of the term "Holy Ghost" produces an impression of great remoteness from our way of speaking and thinking. But Spiritual experience is a reality in everyone, as solid as the experience of being loved or the experience of the air one breathes. Therefore, we should not shy away from the word Spirit. We should become fully aware of the Spiritual Presence, around us and in us, even if we realize how limited may be our experience of "God present to our spirit." For this is what Divine Spirit means: God present to our spirit. Spirit is not a mysterious substance, it is not a part of God; it is God himself; but not God as the Creative ground of all things and not God as directing history and manifesting himself in its central event, but God as present in communities and personalities, grasping them, inspiring them, transforming them.

For Spirit is first of all power, the power which drives the human spirit above itself towards what it cannot attain by itself: the love which is greater than all other gifts, the truth in which the depth of being opens itself to us, the holy which is the manifestation of the presence of the ultimate.

You may say again: "I do not know this power, I never had such an experience. I am not religious or, at least, not a Christian and certainly not a bearer of the Spirit. What I heard from you sounded like ecstasy; and I want to stay sober; it sounded like mystery, and I try to illuminate what is dark; it sounded like self-sacrifice and I want to fulfill my human possibilities." To this I answer: Certainly, the Spiritual Power can drive some people into an ecstasy which most of us have never experienced, it can drive some towards a kind of self-sacrifice of which most of us are not capable, it can drive some to insights into the depth of being which remain unapproachable to most of us. But this does not justify our denial that the Spirit is also working in us. Without doubt, wherever it works, there is an element, possibly very small, of self-surrender, and an element, however weak, of ecstasy, and an element, perhaps fleeting, of awareness of the mystery of existence. Yet these small effects of the Spiritual power are enough to prove its presence.

But there are other conscious and noticeable manifestations of the Spiritual Presence. Let me enumerate some of them, while you may ask yourselves whether and to what degree they are your own experiences. The Spirit can work in you with a soft but insistent voice, telling you that your life is empty and meaningless, but that there are chances of a new life waiting before the door of your inner self to fill its void and to conquer its dullness. The Spirit can work in you, awakening the desire to strive towards the sublime over against the profanity of the average day. The Spirit can give you the courage which says "yes" to life in spite of the destructiveness you have experienced around you and within you. The Spirit can reveal to you that you have hurt somebody deeply, but it also can give you the right word which reunites him with you. The Spirit can make you love with the divine love, someone you profoundly dislike or hate or who has no interest for you. The Spirit can conquer the laziness towards what you know is the aim of your life, and it can change your bad, aggressive and depressed mood into stability and serenity.

The Spirit can liberate you from hidden enmity against those whom you love and from open revengefulness against those by whom you feel violated. The spirit can give you the strength to throw away false anxieties and to take upon yourself the anxiety which belongs to life itself. The Spirit can awaken you to sudden insight into the way you must take, and it can open your eyes to a view of your world which makes everything new. The Spirit can give you joy in the midst of the ordinary routine as well as in the depth of sorrow.

The Spirit can create warmth in the coldness you feel within you and around you, and it can give you wisdom and strength where your human love towards a loved one has failed. The Spirit can throw you into the hell of despair about yourself and then give you the certainty that life has accepted you just when you felt totally rejected, and when you rejected yourself totally. The Spirit can give you the power of prayer, which nobody has except through the Spiritual Presence. For every prayer—be it with or without words—that reaches its aim, namely the reunion with the divine Ground of our being, is a work of the Spirit speaking in us and through us. Prayer is a Spiritual sighing and longing of a finite being to return to its origin.

These are works of the Spirit, signs of the Spiritual Presence with us and in us. In view of these manifestations, who can assert that he is without Spirit? Who can say that he is in no way a bearer of the Spirit? He may be it in a small way; but is there anybody amongst us who could say more than that about himself?

One can compare the Spiritual Presence with the air we breathe, which surrounds us, is nearest to us, and works life within us. This comparison has a deep justification: In most languages, the word spirit means breath or wind. Sometimes the wind becomes storm, grand and devastating;

but mostly it is moving air, always present, not always noticed. In the same way the Spirit is always present, a moving power, sometimes in stormy ecstasies of individuals and groups, mostly quietly entering our human spirit and keeping it alive; sometimes manifest in great moments of history or of a personal life, mostly working hiddenly through the media of our daily encounters with men and world; sometimes using its creation, the religious communities and their Spiritual means, often making itself felt in spheres far removed from what is usually called religious. Like the wind the Spirit blows where it wills! It is not subject to a rule or limited by a method. Its ways with men are not dependent on what men are and do. You cannot force the Spirit upon you, upon an individual, upon a group, not even upon a Christian church. Although he who is the foundation of the churches was himself by the Spirit and although the Spirit as it was present in him is the greatest manifestation of Spiritual Presence—the Spirit is not bound to the Christian churches or any one of them. The Spirit is free to work in the spirits of men in every human situation, and it urges man to let him do so: God as Spirit is always present to the spirit of man.

But why does the psalmist pray: "Take not thy Spirit from me!" And why do we speak today of the "absent God," a term which plays a role in literature and art, and most of all in the personal experience of innumerable people? How can we unite the message of the Spiritual Presence with the experience of the absent God? Let me say something of the "absent God," asking, what is the cause of his absence? We may answer: our resistance, our indifference, our lack of seriousness, our honest or dishonest questioning, our genuine or cynical doubt! All these answers have some truth; but they had not the last truth. The final answer to the question who makes God absent, is God himself!

It is the work of the Spirit that removes God from our sight, not only for some men, but sometimes for many in a particular period. We live in an era in which the God we know is the absent God. But in knowing God as the absent God, we *know* of him; we feel his absence as the empty space which is left by something or someone which belonged to us and has vanished from our view. God is always infinitely near and infinitely far. We are fully aware of him only if we experience both. But sometimes, when our awareness of him has become shallow, habitual, not warm and not cold, when he has become too familiar to be exciting, too near to be felt in his infinite distance—then he becomes the absent God. The Spirit has not ceased to be present. The Spiritual Presence can never end. But the Spirit of God hides God to our sight. No resistance against the

Spirit, no indifference, no doubt can drive the Spirit away. But the Spirit which always remains present to us can hide itself and that means it can hide God. Then the Spirit shows us nothing except the absent God and the empty space within us which is *his* space. The Spirit has shown to our time and to innumerable people in our time the absent God and the empty space which cries in us to be filled by him. And then the absent one may return and take the space which belongs to him, and the Spiritual Presence may break again into our consciousness, awakening us to recognize what we are, shaking and transforming us. This may happen like the coming of a storm, the storm of the Spirit, stirring up the stagnant air of our Spiritual life. The storm will recede, a new stagnancy may take place, and the awareness of the present God may be replaced by the awareness of its empty space in us. Life in the Spirit is this up-and-down. And this means: Whether we experience the present or the absent God: It is a work of the Spirit.

III

And now let me describe a symptom of the Spiritual Presence in us, the greatest of all, powerfully expressed in Paul's words: "Not in written code, but in Spirit; for the written code kills, but the Spirit gives life." This means that the work of the Spiritual Presence in a man reaches its height when it liberates from the yoke of the commandments to the freedom of the Spirit. This is like releasing from the sentence of death to a new life. A tremendous experience lies behind these words, an experience in which we all can share, although it is rare in its full depth and is then a revolutionary power which through men like Paul and Augustine and Luther has changed the Spiritual world and through it the history of mankind. Can we, you and I, share in this experience?

First, have we felt the deadening power of the written code, written not only in the ten commandments and their many interpretations in Bible and history, but also written with the pen of the authority of parents and society into the unconscious depths of our being, recognized by our conscience, judging us in what we do and, above all, in what we are. Nobody can flee from the voice of this written code, written internally as well as externally. And if we try to silence it, to close our ears against it, the Spirit itself frustrates these attempts, opening our ears towards the cries of our true being of that which we are and ought to be in the sight of eternity. We cannot escape this judgment against us. The Spirit itself, using the written code, makes this impossible. For the Spirit does not give life without having led us through the experience of death. And certainly the written code in its threatening majesty has the power to kill. It kills the joy of fulfilling our being by imposing upon us something we feel as hostile. It kills the freedom of answering creatively to what we encounter in things and men by making us look at a table of laws. It kills the ability to listen to the calling of the moment, to the voiceless voice of the others, and to the here and now. It kills the courage to act by the scruples of an anxiety-driven conscience. And in those who take it most seriously, it kills faith and hope and throws them into self-condemnation and despair.

There is no way out under the written code. The Spirit itself prevents us from becoming compromisers, half fulfilling, half defying the commandments. The Spirit itself calls us back if we want to escape into indifference or lawlessness or the most usual escape: average self-righteousness. But when the Spirit calls us back from all this, it does so not in order to *keep* us under the written code, but in order to give us life.

How can we describe the life which the Spirit gives us? I could use many words, well known to everybody, spoken by Paul himself and after him by the great preachers and teachers of the Church. I could say that the work of the Spirit, liberating us from the law, is freedom. Or I could say that its work is faith, or that its work is hope; and above all, I could say that the Spirit creates love, the love in which all laws are confirmed and fulfilled and at the same time overcome. But if I used such words, the shadow of the absent God would appear and make you and me aware, that we cannot speak like this today. If we did, freedom would be distorted into willfulness, faith would be distorted into belief in the absurd, hope would be distorted into unreal expectations, and love—the word I would like most to use for the creation of the Spirit—would be distorted into sentimental feelings. The Spirit must give us new words or revitalize the old words to express true life. We must wait for them, we must pray for them, we cannot force them. But we know, in some moments of our lives, what life is. We know that it is great and holy, deep and abundant, ecstatic and sober, limited and distorted by time, fulfilled by eternity. And if the words are failing us in the absence of God, we may look without words at the image of him in whom the Spirit and the Life were manifest without limits.

Sermon Thirty-five

"THE SAME: YESTERDAY, AND TODAY, AND FOREVER"

REVEREND HENRY PITNEY VAN DUSEN, PH.D., S.T.D., D.D., L.H.D., LITT.D.

A Minister of the Presbyterian Church U.S.A. and President Emeritus of Union Theological Seminary and of Auburn Theological Seminary, New York, New York

Dr. Van Dusen has had a part in the training of many of the leading ministers of the United States during nearly forty years at Union Theological Seminary, first as an instructor, later as professor and in recent years as President. His emphasis is always upon sound scholarship, research, and personal faith so that the men trained under the faculty at Union will go out well equipped to preach and to administer the Christian church they are called to serve.

Born in Philadelphia in 1897, he studied at Princeton University, Union Theological Seminary, and at Edinburgh University, where he received his Ph.D. in 1932. He became associate executive secretary of the Student Division of the YMCA, 1927-28, then began his career as an educator at Union Theological Seminary, where he was instructor in systematic theology and philosophy of religion, 1926-28; assistant professor, 1928-31; associate professor, 1931-36, dean of students, 1931-39. In 1936 he was made Roosevelt Professor of Systematic Theology and President of the Faculty in 1945. This same year he was also made President of Auburn Theological Seminary.

Dr. Van Dusen's training, friendship, and guidance have helped hundreds of men to find themselves in the Christian ministry; his knowledge of world religions, the New Testament, the Old Testament, of philosophy, of theology have given him a world view of religion which he imparts in his sermons, teaching and lectures. He has participated in so many important church conferences that the list alone would fill pages; some of the more significant have been: Delegate to the Oxford Conference on Church, Community and State, 1937; Madras World Missionary Conference, 1938; Whitby Enlarged Meeting of International Missionary Council Committee, 1947; First Assembly, World Council of Churches, Amsterdam, 1948; Chairman, Study Program; Member, Provisional Committee, World Council of Churches, and of its Administrative Committee, 1939-48. Chairman, Study Committee, World Council of Churches, 1939 to 1954. He was an important member of the now famous New Delhi Assembly of the World Council of Churches in 1962.

He is a Fellow of the National Council of Religion in Higher Education; former President, American Theological Society; President, American Association of Theological Schools, 1942-44; chairman, Inter-Seminary Movement, 1940-48; president, Union Settlement Association; member, Foreign Missions Board, Presbyterian Church U.S.A.; President, United Board for Christian Higher Education in Asia and Fund for Theological Education in Southeast Asia; member, Board of Trustees, Princeton University, Smith College, the Rockefeller Foundation, and of the General Education Board. He holds sixteen honorary doctorates in recognition of his important contributions to religion and education.

Among his more than twenty books are: *In Quest of Life's Meaning, The Plain Man Seeks for God, For the Healing of the Nations, Methodism's World Mission, What IS the Church Doing?, World Christianity: Yesterday, Today and Tomorrow, Het Christendom in de Wereld, God in Education, Spirit, Son and Father, One Great Ground of Hope, The Spiritual Legacy of John Foster Dulles.* He is Editor of *Ventures in Belief, The Church Through Half a Century, Church and State in the Modern World;* contributor to *Dynamic Faith, The Vitality of the Christian Tradition, Religion and World Order, Education for Professional Responsibility.* This is the fifth volume of *Best Sermons* to which Dr. Van Dusen has contributed a distinguished sermon.

Dr. Van Dusen has traveled around the world three times, has visited South America, Asia, Africa, Europe. His world view is reflected in the sermon included below.

"THE SAME: YESTERDAY, AND TODAY, AND FOREVER"

> Grace to you and peace from Him who is and who was and who is to come.
>
> Revelation 1:4
>
> Jesus Christ is the same yesterday and today and forever.
>
> Hebrews 13:8

Christianity was born into a world electric with fervent expectation, expectation of an early end of the present evil age. Among devout Jews, that false hope took the form of mistaken conceptions of the Messiah—as a conquering warrior or a supernatural vicegerent—conceptions which Jesus was compelled to disavow throughout His life.

The first Christians were children of their times. Many were infected by the powerful appeal of that misguided anticipation. Almost without exception, they lived from day to day, went about their tasks in the world, and preached the "good news" of Christ in confident certainty that Jesus, who had lived among them, and had suffered a shameful death upon the Cross, and had risen from the grave in defiance of death, would shortly reappear—almost surely during their lifetimes—to terminate the tragic times in which they dwelt and bring in His Kingdom with power by a mighty miracle.

With all the variations in details, the early followers of Christ proclaimed a single message to those who would listen. This was it: "Jesus of Nazareth, consecrated by God with the Holy Spirit, went about among you, doing good, healing the demon-possessed and revealing His divine commission by mighty acts; He was put to death by the Romans at the instigation of the Jewish rulers; God has raised Him from death, and made Him Lord of all; to those who believe, He sends at once His Holy Spirit. He will soon return in glory to usher in the New Age."

While the concluding prediction was most vigorously declared by Jesus' own companions in Acts and by the author of Revelation, it was shared by Paul, especially in his early ministry, and by most of the others. If the early imminent expectation of Christ's soon return was not the heart of their faith, it was the consummation toward which everything pointed.

But year followed year . . . The years lengthened into decades . . . The first followers of Jesus, who had been so sure that they would outlive the world and welcome their Lord reappearing on clouds of glory, aged and died. Christ did *not* come. The very foundations of their faith seemed threatened. The Christian Church confronted its first—and perhaps its most threatening—crisis.

I

As we look back upon those critical days, we can see that there were three alternative ways in which these first Christians might have met this staggering disappointment—Christ's failure to fulfill their confident hope. And that, in fact, some among them, had recourse to *each* of the three ways:

First, many focussed their imaginations even more doggedly upon the future, with even more feverish and extravagant forecast. It is the Book of Revelation which voices that expectation, concluding with an assertion and plea for His immediate advent: "He that testifieth these things saith, 'Surely, I come quickly.' . . . Even so, come, Lord Jesus." This way led nowhere. As Professor C. H. Dodd has said: "This line of development led into a blind alley. In the second century its stream of thought ran out into the barren sand of millenarianism, which in the end was disavowed by the Church."

But we do well to remind ourselves that God's refutation of this hope, through the failure of history to fulfill it, did not succeed in silencing it. In every Christian century, it has captured some minds. And not merely the feeblest or least well-balanced. To mention but two of the most powerful: Augustine and Luther. Each, at some point in his career, was firmly convinced that the evil age in which he dwelt could not outlast his lifetime; Christ would surely return to terminate history. It is in that historic perspective that we should view the resurgence of this outlook in our own day.

Second, others were moved to turn their thoughts back from the uncertain future, and even the disappointing present, toward the past. They fed their spirits upon recollections of what Jesus had said and done and been while He had accompanied them in the flesh. Possibly, it is to this mood that we owe, in no small measure, our Gospel records of Jesus' life. They are reminiscences of Jesus by those who awaited His return; or, perhaps, *had* expected His return, and were disillusioned in their anticipation.

But, there was a third response to disappointed hope. Paul is its principal spokesman. Whether his final message was direct reaction, conscious or unconscious, to the disproof of his confidence in Christ's soon-return which loomed so prominently in his earlier letters, or whether it was, rather, the inevitable bodying-forth of the present experience which possessed him with ever-deepening meaning, we cannot be sure. We do know: in his later letters, mention of Christ's return fades into relative insignificance. Its place, at the heart of his faith, is taken by glad assertion of the living presence of Christ, as the surest reality of his existence, here and now. "To me to live is Christ!"

Yes; and he urged that that same possession of (or, better, by) the living present Christ was the indispensable mark of the true Christian: "That Christ may dwell in your hearts by faith." He further insisted that the gift of the Holy Spirit, in which his fellow-Christians gloried and which set them aflame with missionary zeal, was authentic only as it did not direct their excited expectations toward a Christ-who-would-return, but, as it was, unmistakably, the Spirit of Christ livingly present in their lives now, and producing now the manifest fruits of His Spirit:

> The LORD is that Spirit . . . If any man have not the Spirit of Christ, he is none of His.

II

Thus, we see that the faith of the Early Christians spoke of Christ's coming among them in three tenses—*past*, *future*, and *present*. Each had its inadequacies and its dangers:

The *first* alone—concentration upon recollections of Jesus' earthly life —tended to clothe Christian experience with the fading glow of reminiscence, without present vitality and kindling fire. It might beget inertia and inactivity.

The *second* alone—focussing hope wholly upon some future miracle—tended to consume its holders in ecstatic and futile expectation, drawing their attention from immediate realities of faith and urgent responsibilities of life. It issued in disillusion; or even more frantic prediction.

The *third* alone—enjoyment of the immediate presence of Christ—might encourage excited and shallow enthusiasm, lacking historic roots or enduring effectiveness.

It was left to the brooding minds of the writers of the Gospel of John and the Letter to the Hebrews to rise to the larger vision and comprehension, to unite all three tenses of Christian experience and to affirm "One who was, and is, and is to be": "Jesus Christ—the same—yesterday, and today, and forever."

III

The relevance of all this for the life of the Christian Churches in our day is obvious. We see our current situation in perspective only as we recognize its historic antecedents among the First Christians, and also recall that all three moods have persisted through the whole of Christian history into our own day. Always, and still, Christians tend to speak of the presence of Christ, and of His power upon them, in one of three tenses—past, future or present. Always, the testimony of the individual Christian tends to be one-sided and incomplete. Each of the three emphases is partially authentic and brings its priceless gifts to full-orbed Christian experience. Each of the three alone is not only gravely inadequate. It fosters aberrations: false views of Christ and His Father, God.

IV

For many, Christian faith is mainly a *Religion of Recollection.* This is especially prevalent among Christians of middle life and beyond. Their religion tends to be a reverie of recollection, a pensive glance toward a dimly fading sunset. Their memories turn back over and over again to some event or events now long gone: a childhood simplicity and certainty of faith; a vivid and compelling conversion in adolescent years; an enlistment in Christ's service in the daring days of youth; the remembrance of a first fine careless rapture. "Those were the times of my truest Christian experience," they insist. "*Then,* God was real to me. *Then,* prayer meant everything to me. *Then,* I knew Christ as Companion and Saviour." But no more. The effort of faith, now, is to recall and reclaim realities of experience out of an ever-receding past.

In our moments of truer apprehension, we know well this should not be. God is not the God of the dead, but of the living. It is of the very essence of faith that He Who came to us, Who spoke to us, Who dwelt with us, so vividly, so surely in those bygone days, is no less alive and at work in this living present, ever eager to open to our spirits—today, and tomorrow, and beyond tomorrow's tomorrow—pathways of spiritual discovery heretofore untrodden, riches of Christian experience beyond anything we have ever previously known or dreamed. Less than that assurance is, in all truth, atheism—denial of the Living God whom our Faith affirms.

Yes; and this correction should yield more than a truer conviction. It should bring to each life new and deeper and richer discoveries of God and of His good gifts for us with every passing year.

But this is a practical atheism, the *Religion of Recollection,* of which not only individual Christians are all too often guilty. It is the supreme apostasy of the Christian Church. In every age, and in our own also, there are always those who fix their eyes longingly upon First Century Christianity. Their ideal and hope for the contemporary church is that it rediscover and recapture the temper and vitality of the Early Christians. "Back to First Century Christianity" is their cry.

That, too, is a form of atheism. More particularly, it is a denial of the Holy Spirit, the living, potent Spirit of Christ, who accompanies His Church through all the ages of its pilgrimage, ever ready to lead it into new and fuller Truth. The God of Christian Faith is a Living God. He intends for Christ's Church in the twentieth century other and different gifts, at least in part, than for the Earliest Church. He holds for it other plans. Yes; and He expects from it new and even greater achievements, appropriate to the days in which He has placed it.

V

For others, again, in every age, Christianity is a *Religion of Anticipation.* It speaks not primarily of what God has done, certainly not of what He is doing or is prepared to do, but of what He *will* do in some undated future. It knows the Christ who was and is to come again, but *not* the Christ who is. If one were seeking a single phrase to characterize the type of Christian attitude which has been widely prevalent in the modern period, the attitude from which we are in such sharp reaction just now, it might well be the Religion of Anticipation.

Almost its most characteristic word has been "quest." It has invited men to a common search for truth, for God. It has hovered forever on the brink of new things, great discoveries. It was always just on the point of developing a new synthesis in theology, a thought-transforming, epoch-making synthesis. It stood always on the very door-sill of a new social order; it was just about to perfect the building of the Kingdom of God. Its fingers were perennially just about to lay hold of some new spiritual discovery which, like the pocket-book small boys lay on the pavement on April Fool's Day, forever eluded its grasp. It was always "not quite" but "just about to be" something. Indeed, its adherents were always just about to be saved.

Now practical minds grow weary, if not distrustful of year-by-year prophecies, however sincere, of what is going to happen, but is never quite realized. This is a voice with a strangely familiar accent. In life, we are constantly meeting those who are always just about to make a fortune, just about to perfect a wonderful new invention, just about to recover their financial feet. One learns to be a trifle sceptical. A kindly world calls them chronic business failures. Society classifies them as incurable mendicants. Well, there is a touch of incurable mendicancy about the Religion of Anticipation.

But the more serious charge is: this whole outlook is far from Christian. Think how the Gospels would require to be revised to bring them into conformity with this attitude. For the point of Jesus' story of the diligent woman was not merely that she persisted in her search, but that she actually found the lost coin. And of that other woman, a widow, not merely that she beat her knuckles raw on the unyielding door, but that she actually aroused the judge and obtained justice. The Religion of Anticipation would need to revise the stories to picture the tireless women, sweeping, sweeping, sweeping, knocking, knocking, knocking, through the timeless aeons of eternity. While the revised version of the famous pearl-merchant would portray him, somewhat like an inexperienced tourist, moving from market to market, forever pursuing with undiscouraged hopefulness the ever-illusive pearl-of-great-price.

We have been delivered from the worst aberrations of that type of interpretation. But not from its underlying falsity. The Christian message of today which stands in sharpest contrast, which is most violent in condemnation, which bids fair to replace it, is infected with the very disease it professes to cure. The tense of its proclamation is, likewise, future, not present. Not, perhaps, tomorrow, or the day after tomorrow, but at some undated "end of history" is the fulfillment of Christian hope promised. The mood of its proclamation is conditional, not declaratory; what God may do for us rather than what He has done and is doing. About it there is a strained, hectic note, of expectation, not certainty. Faith is the "substance of things hoped for" but never the "certainty of things not seen." Above all, it seems to speak from a little outside Christian assurance, longingly looking in, rather than from the very heart of a secure Christian certitude. Its most confident word is "I believe; help Thou mine unbelief," not "I know in whom I have believed."

VI

No; the authentic note of living Christian faith is neither recollection nor anticipation. It is—*affirmation.* It speaks, most naturally, not in the past tense, not in the future, but in the present. Its most characteristic word is not, "I seek"; but "I have found"; not, "I hope"; but "I know."

So, likewise, with respect to Christ's meaning for men. He is not simply one who lived a life of matchless faith nineteen hundred years ago. He is certainly not mainly One who will return in some distant future. Rather, He is, above all, a living Presence among us and within us here and now. Let two very modern contemporaries voice that affirmation: One, a woman, a writer of distinction, Winifred Kirkland:

> I did not choose this Presence in my life. In many ways, existence would be easier without it. If it were not for that incessant, ironic comment in my ear, it would be a simple matter to accept herd opinion, either religious or secular. Does that Presence make for quiet in the soul or disquiet? One thing only I know, Jesus is for me an unavoidable and constant challenge.

The other—a man and a physician—one of the most revered servants of mankind in this century, Sir Wilfred Grenfell:

Faith came to me with the vision of Christ still alive in this world today. Christ means to me a living personality today who moves about in this world, and who gives us strength and power as we endure by seeing Him who is invisible only to our fallible and finite human eyes, just as any other good comrade helps one to be brave and do the right thing.

An unusually sensitive Christian, commenting upon the testimony of young men and women who had lately come into a vital experience of Christ through one of the well known movements of today, said that what struck him most was that these young folk were recounting not what had happened on a hill outside Jerusalem nineteen hundred years ago, but what had occurred on a hill outside their own home-town day-before-yesterday.

VII

And yet, even that is not quite all that needs to be said. Even Christian *affirmation* is not wholly complete or without dangers. For, the religious soul, even the most earnest and sincere, is notoriously subject to self-deception. That danger is especially acute when it is under sway of an intense experience and immediate inspiration. How shall we be sure that the vision which captures its allegiance with such glowing splendor is not the figment of its own imagining rather than a divine illumination? How shall we know that the ardor which directs its endeavors so confidently is really the power of God, and not rather the overflowing energies of ambition and self-expression? How shall we be certain that the Voice which speaks so definitely to its inmost certainty is truly the Word of God?

To these queries and misgivings, Christian faith has a clear and sure reply: The *Vision* with which God illumines our imaginations now is unmistakably of-a-piece—not identical, but of-a-piece—with the picture of the Kingdom of God, unforgettably set before men with matchless imagery of parable and vivid saying by Jesus in Galilee long ago.

The authentic *energies of God* flow through human lives in our day in fashions which remind us unfailingly of their action in One who healed and taught and inspired and died in utter fidelity on a Cross outside Jerusalem in the reign of Pontius Pilate, not the same, but in like fashion.

The *Voice of God* speaks in the souls of men today in accents which echo—new words directing new duties on new occasions but in similar accents—quite beyond question the Voice which spoke of the deepest truths of God and man in tales of a Dissolute Son and a Compassionate Traveller and a Sermon on a hillside—and which declared sharp doom upon hypocrites and sure mercy for penitents.

All that is truly God, and of God, is unmistakably continuous with that Life and His Faith.

So, likewise, when we turn our thoughts toward the future and seek to penetrate its unfathomable uncertainties, especially in these dark days of hazardous and foreboding prospects, Christians do look toward the future with high and confident expectation. But only because they have already discovered the priceless pearl, because they already possess here and now the true secret of tomorrow's promise: "I know whom I have trusted; therefore, I am persuaded that He is able to keep that which I have entrusted to Him against that day."

The authentic Christian expectation is not one which seeks to reach out far, far ahead—overleaping the intervening years or centuries or millennia—to lay secure hands upon some "far-off Divine Event"; but one which moves forward, fearlessly, confidently, out into an immediate future, awaiting the ever-ready return of the ever-adequate Christ. With Newman, it declares: "I do not ask to see the distant scene; one step enough!" It looks, at once, ahead and up; onward and upward; knowing that "tomorrow and tomorrow and tomorrow" God promises to those who trust Him all that they have a right to desire, far more than they are entitled to expect, such good things as pass man's comprehension; the gift, in this immediate tomorrow, of the Living, potent Christ.

Finally, if Christ should come again in one specific event of history, it is altogether improbable that His coming would be along the lines of a supernatural intervention, a fulfillment of the expectation which He so decisively rejected at His first coming in Jesus of Nazareth. On the contrary, Christians may expect that He would come again, as He came in the days of His flesh, in the power of humility and utter fidelity, as He has continued to come to those who so looked for Him through all the centuries, as He is now—the most certain reality in this world of shadows and shams—"Jesus Christ: The Same." Studdert Kennedy is probably right:

Then will He come—with meekness for His glory,
God in a workman's jacket as before,
Living again the Eternal Gospel Story,
Sweeping the shavings from His workshop floor.

In *that* perspective, we can join our voices with that of the writer of Revelation: "Even so, come, Lord Jesus."

And so, the fullest Christian certitude, true Christian Faith, dwells neither in memory, nor in expectation, nor in immediate experience alone, but in all three. It speaks in three tenses, and in all three at once, of "Him who was, and is, and shall be." This is its word—"Christ lived: Christ lives: Christ shall live forever more."

From the disclosure of Himself in the man, Christ Jesus, and especially from Jesus' clear faith in Him, we possess, in final clarity, the lineaments of the character of the God who was and is and is to come. In the vivid life-transforming power of His impact upon our life today, we are certain of His ever-living Presence. In the light of that faith which comes to us from His faithful Son in the past, and our assurance of His powerful Presence now, we know that He shall continue to sustain all those who Trust in Him through undisclosed aeons of the future—until the end, and in the End. The Ruler of History, and the Saviour of Today, and the Determiner of the Future *is*—the God and Father of the Lord, Jesus Christ: "the same: yesterday and today and forever."

INDEX

This index has been prepared for clergy and laity alike, but particularly with the needs of the busy pastor-preacher in mind, to be suggestive, helpful, convenient, for the man in search of sermon ideas and illustrations. The reader is advised to add other words and pages as he finds them useful for his own reference. All entries under the heading of God, Christ, Salvation and similar subjects are not listed in this Index because they are the basic subjects of all sermons in the book.

BEST SERMONS INVITATION

In order to make BEST SERMONS more representative of all denominations and to afford every clergyman anywhere an opportunity to have a sermon considered for inclusion in these volumes, this invitation is issued to ALL CLERGYMEN EVERYWHERE to submit a sermon to the editor.

Laymen are also invited to send sermons by their pastors or to send the names of ministers they would like to nominate as worthy of being considered for inclusion in BEST SERMONS.

Please observe the following simple rules:

1. Sermons may be on any topic suitable to the Christian church.
2. Not more than one serman should be submitted. Please send your BEST SERMON.
3. Length does not matter. But please send each sermon double-spaced and typewritten. Keep a copy for your files as no sermons can be returned.
4. Differences in theology are welcome, but denominational bickering will not be considered.
5. Please be patient and do not ask for an immediate answer; it requires from three to twelve months to read and consider the mass of sermons received. MINISTERS WHOSE SERMONS ARE SELECTED FOR INCLUSION WILL BE NOTIFIED.
6. Please send a one-page biographical sketch or outline with each sermon.
7. No honorarium is offered as all available funds are put into printing, postage and stenographic work to search for sermons by new men who have not been discovered in print as yet.

Sermon Submission Blank

Date____________________

Please read and consider the attached sermon for the next volume of BEST SERMONS. The sermon is my own original work; all quotations included will be cleared with publishers by securing permission if the sermon is accepted for inclusion.

Name____________________ Church____________________

Address____________________ City____________________

Denomination____________________ Phone____________________